Modernization in Romania Since World War II

Trond Gilberg

The Praeger Special Studies program—utilizing the most modern and efficient book production techniques and a selective worldwide distribution network—makes available to the academic, government, and business communities significant, timely research in U.S. and international economic, social, and political development.

Modernization in Romania Since World War II

PRAEGER SPECIAL STUDIES IN INTERNATIONAL ECONOMICS AND DEVELOPMENT

Praeger Publishers New York Washington London

Library of Congress Cataloging in Publication Data

Gilberg, Trond, 1940-
Modernization in Romania since World War II.

(Praeger special studies in international economics and development)
Bibliography: p.
Includes index.
1. Romania--Economic conditions—1945- 2. Romania—Social conditions. 3. Romania—Politics and government—1945- 4. Partidul Comunist Roman. I. Title.
HC407.R8G55 1975 309.1'498'03 73-15187
ISBN 0-275-28783-1

PRAEGER PUBLISHERS
111 Fourth Avenue, New York, N.Y. 10003, U.S.A.
5, Cromwell Place, London SW7 2JL, England

Published in the United States of America in 1975
by Praeger Publishers, Inc.

Printed in the United States of America

PREFACE

This book is a case study of socioeconomic and political modernization in Romania. Since the approaches of the Romanian modernizers are based on elements common to all socialist states, a more general knowledge and understanding of modernization in Communist systems can be gained from it.

A study of this kind must of necessity rely rather heavily on official Communist sources. This is particularly true of Part II of the book in which official statistics are used to illustrate the modernization process in the fields of education, industrialization, agriculture, transportation, and health and social services. There are many problems associated with the use of such statistics, ranging from possible falsification to biases due to different classifications and categories. Most of these problems have been discussed in great detail and with brilliant insight by John Michael Montias and others; the general conclusion of these scholars is that while there are biases in Communist statistics in general and Romanian statistics in particular (most in favor of the regime's goals and claims) there are no blatant attempts to systematically falsify such figures. I see no reason to question such expert evaluation, and I have therefore made use of a fair amount of such statistics. It is my considered opinion that the figures presented do represent a generally correct picture of the modernization process in Romania. Given the possibility of some bias due to classification systems, however, the reader should be cautioned that the exact figures may give an impression of precise measurement that is somewhat overstated.

Confronted with a mass of data from statistical yearbooks and censuses, the analyst must of necessity select the figures to be included and the form in which they are to be presented. One way is to analyze statistics without actually presenting them; another is to produce reams of tables that are available in the original sources themselves. I have chosen a compromise: presentation in full of a few tables that I considered crucial but footnoted commentary on others. In this way relative completeness and economy can be preserved, and the reader can engage in his own form of instant analysis of the complete table if he should choose to do so.

Many persons have been instrumental in providing criticism and insightful comments on the concept of modernization and on the manuscript itself as it progressed through various stages. I owe special gratitude to Robert R. King, who commented on a detailed outline of the manuscript, and to Vernon V. Aspaturian for the many inspiring discussions on the major subject of this book and many other topics. A special note of thanks also is due Karen Sweeney and Jean Cutler, who typed the manuscript from my many erratic drafts. The evaluations and conclusions are, of course, my own.

CONTENTS

Chapter | Page

Chapter Page

LIST OF TABLES

Table		Page

Table		Page

PART I

MODERNIZATION, AGENTS, AND IDEOLOGY

CHAPTER 1

INTRODUCTION: THE CONCEPTS OF "MODERNIZATION" AND "MULTILATERAL DEVELOPMENT"

MODERNIZATION

"Modernization" is a much-touted concept in the contemporary world. Practically all political elites, whether in the industrialized countries or in the "developing" states, express their commitment to modernization and development and a wide variety of practical policies are launched under the auspices of this concept. In contemporary political science the study of modernization is very much in vogue. Scholarly concern with the concept seems to focus on a number of major questions: What is the proper, scientific definition of modernization, and how can the definition be operationalized?[1] What are the major approaches (in practical terms) to modernization in various areas of the world and in various political systems?[2] How effective have political elites been in their attempts at producing "modern" societies?[3] What is the relationship between political power and modernization?[4] What will be the effect of achieved modernization on the political system functioning within a society at the modernized level?[5]

Definitions

Although numerous conceptual schemes have been devised, there seems to be relatively broad agreement that the concept modernization includes two major subcategories, a socioeconomic and a political form. Karl W. Deutsch in his famous article on social mobilization outlined the following processes as being fundamental in socioeconomic modernization: urbanization, industrialization, increased literacy, increased wealth (in total terms and per capita), and growth of communication, especially through the mass media. The social component of modernization would include improved social services, more doctors, nurses, and other medical personnel per capita, and better hospital facilities, with the resulting increase in life expectancy and decrease in infant mortality. The cultural effects of socioeconomic modernization as defined would be to break up traditional mores and behavior patterns, secularization, emancipation of women, and a general "nationalization" of life which would tend to reduce regionalism and promote equalization in life styles and standard of living between the city and the countryside. Upward social and economic mobility is based on achievement rather than ascription.[6]

Political modernization, as envisioned by Deutsch and others, would entail increased mass knowledge about the political system; increased political participation in various forms; disappearance of old, regional, and tribal allegiances and the development of a national political focus; and gradual political integration of ethnic minorities (although in differing degrees, depending upon the status of each nationality in premodern society).[7]

Other students of modernization have tended to accept many of Deutsch's categories, but with significant additions. Samuel P. Huntington, for example, emphasizes that political modernization is primarily a question of institutionalization: a premodern political system, with its diffuse patterns of political participation, can only become modern through institutionalization, specialization of function (but also some institutional-functional overlapping), and the development of professional political cadres, whose task it is to moderate political articulation from emerging socioeconomic groups, thus making political compromise necessary and possible. On this basis, Huntington strongly emphasizes the development of the party system as a necessary condition of political modernization.[8]

According to Huntington, not only will the processes outlined above be crucial to the success or failure of political modernization in a system but of fundamental importance is the speed with which this transformation takes place. Premodern societies and fully modernized systems tend to be stable; it is the modernizing society, moving from one stage to the other, that will experience social, economic, cultural, and political dislocation. In many cases socioeconomic modernization requires political centralization, perhaps even dictatorship; political modernization must follow the socioeconomic trends by providing the requisite institutionalization, especially toward the end of the socioeconomic modernization process. A modern political system is almost always a politically centralized one, albeit with functional differentiation at the center. Huntington sees the U.S. political system, with its balance of power, as a curiously atrophied polity in a modern socioeconomic environment; other modernized systems tend to produce the centralization in the political realm so characteristic of Western democracies and Communist systems alike.[9]

The Huntington analysis, together with the pioneering work of Karl W. Deutsch, offers a meaningful framework for my own research effort. This does not mean that the two approaches mentioned will be treated as ironclad models for this book but simply that they will offer some parameters, some ways of organizing the present research and analysis. The Romanian case will most likely offer additional insights that can perhaps be included in a revised framework at a later stage.

Strategies

The contemporary world scene can provide a variegated mix of strategies for modernization. While most modernizing elites tend to accept urbanization, industrialization, literacy, and education as goals of their modernizing efforts, there is great variation in the ways chosen to achieve these goals. In some countries the military, especially the middle echelons, provides the political leadership and a dose of coercion often needed for development toward perceived goals. In other systems an urban middle class, at times in collaboration with some rural elites, will provide the mechanism. In yet other cases a small band of Western-educated intellectuals, with support from existing socioeconomic elites, will attempt to propel their traditional societies into modernity through oligarchic authoritarianism or individual dictatorship. Finally, in the Soviet Union, Eastern Europe, and China, monopolistic political parties have launched some of the most ambitious modernization schemes on record.[10]

Just as the modernizing elites differ throughout the world their strategies for modernization show great variety. In some cases, a "measured" approach is taken, in which the modernizing elite attacks the problems of development semi-incrementally by focusing on a few areas at a time. One may choose to slow the population increase and produce widespread literacy before undertaking massive industrial development; perhaps an infrastructure of communication networks will be built before construction of factories; intensive development of agriculture may be tried before industrialization so that the profits of the former may be used for the development of the latter. Then there is the political problem of how to deal with traditional elites. Perhaps some of these can be coopted into the new order; alliances may be established, paving the way for ruthless destruction of those left out. There is also the possibility of a wholesale attack on existing elites, a clean sweep that will destroy the potential of any structure interfering or hampering the program of the modernizers.[11]

The Communist strategy for modernization, as practiced in the Soviet Union and Eastern Europe, has represented a fairly distinct brand. The Communist parties of the area launched massive and concerted simultaneous attacks on the modernization problem. Industrialization was undertaken while the Communists, through ruthless use of terror and coercion, were in the process of eliminating the remnants of "bourgeois" elites; collectivization of agriculture proceeded simultaneously (in most cases) with industrialization, and urbanization was helped along by the establishment through political fiat of brand new cities on the steppes and tundras of the Soviet Union or in remote rural areas of Eastern Europe. At the same time the Communist regimes in this area launched a massive attack on the low literacy levels, and in a relatively short time both universal literacy and the creation of highly skilled cadres were achieved.[12]

The Communist model of modernization, it should be noted, differs from the Deutsch scheme in important ways. While Deutsch to some extent posits a unilinear development (industrialization leads to urbanization, better education is developed to meet the needs of industry, and national consciousness follows socioeconomic development, and so on), the Communist parties of the Soviet Union and Eastern Europe frontally and simultaneously attack all of the perceived important aspects of modernization. While Deutsch and others, on the basis of gross achievement measures, postulate that some countries are modern while others are not, the modernizing Communist elites have grasped the fundamental truth that it is people who are modernized or traditional, not countries; on this basis, the Communist modernizers have made education and development of skills a cornerstone of their efforts.

Modernization in Romania follows the Communist pattern in all essential features.

The Relationship Between Political Power and Modernization

To some extent, the relationship between political power and modernization is fairly clearcut: it takes political power to launch a modernization drive and to sustain it. This is nevertheless a somewhat simplified perception of the different amounts of power employed in the modernization process. Some scholars have shown that a number of premodern societies had developed to a stage where socioeconomic and political modernization became a necessity and the political power required to get the process underway was relatively modest.[13] In other societies modernization came about as a result of a conscious desire for development in the minds of a political elite at a time when social, economic, and cultural conditions were far from ripe.

The latter must certainly be considered true of several of the countries of Eastern Europe, where predominantly agrarian societies with high incidences of illiteracy, only minor industrial bases, and typically traditional social structures were rudely subjected to political revolution, destruction of old elites and the imposition of a new Communist party elite, and forced industrialization and reorganization of the rural economy. In these states modernization came about because someone willed it and took the steps necessary to carry out the policies required. The vehicles were centralization of decision making and coercion; the instrument was the Communist Party and its front organizations. It was, in Huntington's terms, the institutionalization of political power in the all-embracing Party that made this process possible.[14] Within the ranks of Communist modernizers the Romanian Communist Party (RCP) must be considered as one of the classical cases.

The Communist Definition

The Communist modernizers produced a modernization program that was a curious mixture of classical Western concepts and generous doses of Marxism-Leninism. Industrialization, with higher productivity and thus greater output, urbanization, and especially improved education, were all accepted by Communist decision makers as genuine elements of modernization and progress. Similarly, in the social field major efforts were expended to increase medical services, services to children and to the elderly, and cultural offerings to the population. A major focus of the Communist elite was the eradication of regionalism, the integration of minorities, and the expansion of political participation (the latter only within carefully prescribed limits).

At the same time, ideological commitments produced a somewhat curious deviation from the model described above. It was postulated that increased production and improved productivity could only come in a socialized economy; public ownership was seen as a more "modern," and consequently higher, form of development than private capitalism, regardless of production figures and productivity tables in the interim periods of modernization. Similarly, Marxism-Leninism postulated that collective farming was superior to and more modern than private agriculture, and that state farms constituted the highest form of all, once again regardless of productivity. It is only very recently that Communist economists have started voicing cautious hints about the need for reorganization designed to increase production. By and large, public ownership of the means of production and collectivized or state-owned agriculture remain ideological givens in all Communist modernizing systems.[15]

Similar peculiarities exist in the Communist definition of political modernization. Increase in political participation is not a goal per se; the Communist leaderships only advocate political activity within the confines established by the Party. Thus political activity that falls outside these parameters will be considered "retrograde," "a remnant of bourgeois values"--generally a step backwards, compared to which political inactivity is seen as preferable.[16] There are indeed analysts who maintain that the goal of Communist leaderships is to depoliticize the citizenry and to separate politics, which is the arena of expertise for professional apparatchiki, from social and economic activity, which is an arena of legitimate concern for all citizens.[17]

Given such special interpretations, based on existing elite perceptions of Marxism-Leninism, it would be misleading to attempt to measure achievement by simply looking at statistics on productivity or political participation. The analyst must examine productivity within the preferred organizational forms (state farms, socialized industry) as compared to productivity in nonpreferred forms (private farms or plots, independent enterprises). Similarly, statistics on political participation must be examined in the context of the Party or outside of Party-approved limits.

The leadership of the RCP fits squarely within the Communist modernization model. At the time of Communist consolidation of power in 1944 Romania was one of the least developed countries in Europe. The overwhelming majority of the population lived in rural areas and made a rather miserable living tilling the soil. There was a high percentage of illiterates in the country, although some of the higher institutions of learning were on a par with similar institutions in more developed countries. Little industry existed, and most of the factories produced primarily consumer goods, directly dependent upon the agricultural raw materials markets. There was virtually no machine-building industry and only a few other firms in heavy industry; the only modern enterprises were the oil refineries, which were partly owned by foreign interests. Social conditions were often appalling and contributed to Romania's dubious distinction of having one of the highest infant mortality rates in Europe and also astonishingly low life expectancy. Widespread poverty and overpopulation on the land was coupled with absentee landownership and heavy concentration of wealth in a few hands. Even in agriculture, the mainstay occupation of the country, old-fashioned techniques prevailed, and there was a general lack of agricultural machinery; the result was extremely low yields per hectare. The same lack of skills contributed to very low productivity figures in other branches of the economy, notably in industry.

Much of the non-Romanian population lived in relative isolation from the majority group, either in urban ghettos (Jews and in some areas Germans) or in ethnically homogeneous rural areas interspersed with towns almost exclusively populated by the local minority (for example, Hungarians in parts of Transylvania, Germans in the Siebenburgen area and in the Banat). On the fringes of cities and in the villages lived the Gypsies, the pariahs of the country, despised and discriminated against by all others. Political participation by the masses was sporadic and in many cases closely controlled by the conservative and nationalistic elites that ran the country in the interwar period. Romania consequently belonged in the category of traditional, if not completely underdeveloped, societies.[18]

The Communist Party leadership set about the task of modernization with a single-mindedness characteristic of this kind of revolutionary elite. The process was carried forth through a series of integrated steps, chief of which were the following:

Destruction of existing political, social, economic, and cultural elites. This task was clearly a fundamental one, a sine qua non for the consolidation of Communist power and the development of the RCP modernization program. The elimination of political competition proceeded apace in the period 1944-47, according to a scenario that was played out in similar fashion all over Soviet-occupied Eastern Europe during the same time period. The first step was occupation by the Red Army and the promotion of the tiny RCP into the ranks of national leadership in a coalition of all "progressive" forces under the nominal leadership of Petru Groza, head of the Plowmen's Front.

Thereupon followed rapid Communist consolidation in all important mass organizations, such as the trade unions and the various agrarian organizations, in academia, and the armed forces and the police. This consolidation was carried out under the auspices of working-class unity and anti-Fascism: the RCP became the leader of a movement ostensibly designed to achieve unity of the working class through close cooperation between Communists and Socialists, and the fledgling Moscow-oriented party also became the self-appointed leader of anti-Fascist activity designed to liquidate "antinational" forces that had cooperated with the Germans and the Iron Guard during the war.

Third, the RCP, as leader of the anti-Fascist front, ruthlessly suppressed the bourgeoisie and its organizations, insofar as such structures could be termed "collaborationist"; and through confiscation of property, control and nationalization of banks, and various monetary reforms the organized power of the middle and upper classes was broken.

Fourth, the Communist Party proceeded to build out its own organization, primarily at the expense of other organized groups on the left; thus infiltration of trade unions and virtually complete control with anti-Fascist committees boosted the power of the RCP, produced fantastic increases in membership and organizational development, and propelled the Party into unquestioned leadership in the still mixed political system of Romania. By 1947-48 the Party was ready to do away with pretenses. The monarchy, which had been retained in a much-reduced form, was abolished, political parties were forbidden, and forcible unification of Socialists and Communists produced a united workers' party with a monopoly of political power.[19]

The destruction of social and economic elites could be only partly achieved through liquidation of their political organizations. Complete success in this endeavor depended upon a fundamental restructuring of society at the grass roots, a social revolution. It was this task that was inaugurated by the RCP with its ambitious industrialization programs in the late 1940s and continuing throughout the 1950s. As a result of the uprooting of traditional social and economic relationships and the establishing of a new order, controlled and sustained by the Communist Party, remnants of old elites would surely disappear.[20]

At the same time, the RCP set about structuring the countryside. Collectivization of agriculture was started already in 1947-48 and proceeded apace for the next decade and a half. This process was no less a social revolution than the concomitant industrialization and urbanization processes; it fundamentally altered human relationships in the countryside and created a new agricultural organization, which could more easily be controlled than the amorphous mass of individual peasants and landless laborers hitherto in existence in the country. Meanwhile a process had been started that resulted in organization forms (collectives) considered to be superior in an ideological sense to the private holdings of earlier regimes. This, then, was a truly dialectic process: the destruction of the old produced something new and normatively better.[21]

While social and economic policies of the RCP in the 1940s and 1950s were designed to destroy existing (and competing) elites, massive efforts were made to produce a new allegiance among the masses of the population. This was done through expanded and improved social services of all kinds and through a vast expansion of educational facilities, with a view toward increasing social mobility for individuals while at the same time producing the skills required by industry. The educational expansion clearly resulted in improved skill levels for the population and created a relatively large group of upwardly mobile individuals who owed their personal success to the regime. These cadres of the new intelligentsia could also reasonably be counted upon to provide strong support for the Party, and in due time they would be numerous enough to make it possible for the regime to dispense completely with the services of the bourgeois intelligentsia, which had been allowed to continue its existence while new cadres were developed.

The new Communist regime faced numerous obstacles in overcoming remnants of the bourgeois-landowner period. Religion continued to exercise a major influence over large sectors of the population, and ethnic particularism showed no sign of abating even after the establishment of the new political order. The RCP launched vigorous repressive campaigns against the organized churches, particularly the Protestant, Roman Catholic, and Jewish religious hierarchies. A massive atheist campaign was pressed among all levels of the population, but particularly youth, to convince the citizenry that religion was indeed the opium of the people, totally unnecessary in the age of enlightenment as supervised by the new breed of modernizers. By the mid-1950s the RCP had clearly managed to destroy the capacity of any religious organization to effectively oppose the political regime, although religion remained as an important spiritual force, especially among the rural masses.[22]

Ethnic particularism remained a troublesome phenomenon during this period. The RCP had to struggle with a legacy of ethnic animosity, so frequently manifested in Romania in earlier periods. The fact that the bulk of the top RCP leadership in the early period (1944-53) was made up of non-Romanians tended to increase the hostility to the new regime so clearly present among the ethnic Romanians during the consolidation period. When the massive leadership changes of 1952-53 propelled mostly "home Communists" of Romanian origin into the foreground, the sweep was so complete that other ethnic groups soon voiced complaints concerning discrimination. Among the masses of Hungarians, Germans, and Jews, the repressive policies emanating from Bucharest, whether promoted by a Pauker or a Gheorghiu-Dej, seemed a true sequel to similar approaches in the past; for them, the new order represented more efficient subjugation, not a new order. And for these ethnic groups, which had traditionally been more highly developed than Romanians in education, status, occupation, and general literacy, the accelerated modernization process had troublesome overtones of leveling, which would tend to reduce their relatively privileged position while propelling thousands upon thousands of Romanians up to their level. Thus there was little evidence of integration and assimilation following the modernization process undertaken by the RCP. But it was also true that the ethnic minorities could offer no meaningful threat to the new regime, especially since many of their political and economic organizations were disbanded during the Communist consolidation. The newly inaugurated modernization process may not have produced positive integration, but it certainly prevented any ethnic group from successfully challenging this new order.[23]

Laying the basis for multilateral development. The period of consolidation during which effective control was established in all areas of political, social, economic, and cultural life came to an end in the mid-1950s. Now started the task of laying the foundation for subsequent rapid modernization or "take-off." This stage, which lasted for approximately a decade, involved the following major policies: First, the RCP engaged in a vigorous campaign designed to expand its organization, especially in the countryside, which had been insufficiently covered up to this time. There was also a major effort to upgrade the skills, both technical-organizational and ideological, of Party cadres; and major campaigns were carried out for similar upgrading of the rank and file of members. The control over mass organizations was expanded, and special groups such as the Party youth organization Uniunea Tineretului Muncitoresc (UTM) and women's sections were strengthened. This was clearly a major effort of the institutionalization seen by some analysts as the perfect route to modernization.[24]

Second, and concurrently with the organizational expansion, came continued and indeed accelerated industrialization, especially in Category A (heavy industry). There was broad agreement within the Party leadership that sustained and broad modernization was only possible after a certain level of heavy industrial production had been reached. Thus the period 1955-65 is marked by uneven development in which heavy industry made giant strides while light and consumer goods industries experienced only slow growth. The educational system was expanded, especially in the technical fields, and ever-increasing cadres were turned out with the skills necessary for expanding industrial needs.[25]

Third, agricultural policy during the decade was characterized by continued collectivization, while investments in this branch of the economy were relatively small and certainly inadequate to the task of significantly raising output. The RCP leadership was consolidating its organizations in the countryside and completing the all-important transformation into collective farms. The disruptions in production frequently associated with the collectivization drive were not perceived as a setback in the modernization but rather as necessary and temporary problems that would be overcome once the correct organizational structures had been established. Collectivization of agriculture was completed in 1962 (with only a few private farms remaining, especially in the mountain areas where the terrain did not lend itself to large-scale farming). The period 1962-65 saw further consolidation of this new agricultural organization and a rather rapid development of state farms, which were considered the highest organizational form in the countryside.[26]

By 1965 the RCP leadership considered Romania ready for sustained and multilateral development toward modernity, which was termed "the multi-laterally developed society." Heavy industry had been rapidly expanded to a point that it was thought it could furnish much of the equipment and expertise for the development of other industrial sectors. In the countryside the stage was set, organizationally, for increased production. The increased revenues that were expected to flow from industry and agriculture could be used for rapid improvements in the social sector, especially in medical care, increased pensions, and educational aid. The Romanian modernizers also considered the foundation to have been laid for a new educational drive at the grass-roots level, which would propel the masses of the citizenry to a higher skill plateau, while the production of university-trained experts could be accelerated. And, above all, by 1965 the RCP had solidified its organization to a point that the leadership considered the Party ready for the task of leading society onto the path of multilateral development.[27]

Toward the "multilaterally developed society." The transition from laying the foundation for multilateral development to actually starting the process coincides fairly well with the coming to power of Nicolae Ceausescu. It is under Ceausescu's leadership that the drive toward modernity has been expanded, and it is during this period that the RCP leadership, especially its First Secretary, has clarified the goals of the modernization drive and the processes that Romania will undergo on its road toward modernity.

The Ninth Congress of the RCP, held in the summer of 1965, constituted the crucial point of Ceausescu's consolidation of power and the first major attempt to thoroughly define the long-term goals of society in operational terms. The First Secretary's report at the Ninth Congress was replete with references to multilateral development, and virtually every other speaker dwelt on the subject in great detail.[28] The program of development was further amplified in the five-year plan for 1966-70, at the 1967 RCP national conference, at the Tenth Party Congress in 1969, in the 1971-75 five-year plan, and in numerous Party meetings throughout this period.[29] The themes and goals remained basically the same throughout all these meetings, and this conformity to certain formulas makes it possible to produce a fairly cohesive breakdown of the Romanian elite's conception of this stage of modernity and the road toward it. The following elements of the RCP conceptualization are crucial.

SOCIOECONOMIC MODERNIZATION

"The multilaterally developed society" stage is to be reached through a two-pronged approach that can best be characterized as socioeconomic and political modernization. In the socioeconomic field modern Romania would exhibit the following characteristics:

Sustained Industrialization

The country would be predominantly industrialized, with the industrial branch of the economy constituting the main occupation for a majority of the work force. All branches of industry would be developed; heavy industry would still constitute a mainstay within this category, but light and consumer goods industries would also have reached very high levels of performance. Of particular importance at this stage would be the high level of development in the electronics industry, which would furnish computerization, automation, and rationalization of production. Economic planning at the central level, as well as output parameters at the county, regional, and factory levels would be improved through extensive use of data programming. It is envisioned that much of this electronic equipment and expertise can be developed and produced domestically.

A fundamental characteristic of the industrial sector in the stage of modernity is the interrelated character of all branches. A high performance level of heavy and extractive industries will provide the machinery and raw materials for sustained growth in the refining and finishing industries. Romanian industry will have reached a stage in which products receive the highest possible quality and processing, while semifinished products will decline in importance. The currently prevailing tendency for Romanian industry to act as a major producer of raw materials and semifinished goods for more highly developed countries will therefore be drastically changed. The economy will reach a stage of self-sustaining growth; that is, production will be so high that continued development can be assured through profits realized rather than through forced savings and investment allocations based on low consumption. Self-sustained growth, as defined, will permit large sums to be transferred to consumption and sociocultural programs designed to raise the standard of living. It is envisioned that Romania in the multilateral stage will have achieved a standard of living comparable or superior to that of the most advanced states in the West.

While the stage of modernity would have high performance levels in all sectors of industry, the road to this stage would still lead through a major emphasis on heavy and extractive industries, which would in turn pull Sector B (light and consumer goods) up to the high performance levels expected.

Continued industrialization is to be based on centralized planning and supervision, with some room for initiative at the regional and local levels. It is clear that Romania will not attempt to reach the goals outlined above through major economic decentralization or large-scale reform, as has been done in Hungary. Flexibility and initiative in Romania will rather be furnished through increased Party involvement at all levels of economic activity; Party activists will act as catalysts for new ideas and higher performance and will become essential links or "transmission belts" for planning, supervision, and information exchange. It is worthy of note that Ceausescu envisions the modernization process as directly linked to increased political institutionalization via the Party at a time when some other Communist systems exhibit a low Party profile in the economy. The Ceausescu vision therefore takes on rather distinct characteristics in Eastern Europe.

Sustained industrialization will inevitably bring with it related processes such as urbanization, pollution, traffic congestion, and excessive growth of some population centers. The Ceausescu regime plans to produce multilateral development in these fields by centrally directed industrial expansion that will tend to disperse plants all over the country, limit the growth of Bucharest, Ploiesti, Galati, Constantza, and other major industrial and commercial centers, and in general retain the big cities at an "optimum population level." The introduction of new antipollution techniques, conservation of raw materials and fuel, and systematic traffic planning will presumably enable Romania to reach the economic levels of the United States and West Germany (frequently mentioned as examples of modern societies at the present stage) without the uneven performance and growth-related problems besetting these two Western systems.[30]

Agricultural Productivity

Even within the multilaterally developed society agriculture will continue to play a major economic role. This sector of the economy will furnish much of the raw material for the expansion of consumer goods industries, and increasingly high output figures for the dairy industries and meat production must be achieved to help meet the ever-increasing needs of a citizenry whose standard of living has reached Western consumption levels. "Industrial" crops, such as cereals, must meet the needs for increased domestic consumption as well as major exports. Production of fruits and vegetables, now a weak spot in the agricultural sector, must be expanded considerably. Inland fisheries, as well as the catch from the Black Sea, will be considerably increased, and ocean-going fleets of trawlers will bring home much-needed protein from distant areas such as the fishing banks of western Africa and Latin America. In forestry output must continue to rise in order to meet major export commitments; domestic consumption of wood products will also rise considerably. In short, agriculture, fishing, and forestry will be capable of meeting the needs of an increasingly consumption-oriented public with money to spend for such products, while at the same time Romania's position as a major agricultural exporter will be maintained, indeed strengthened.[31]

Since development toward modernity will involve massive out-migration from the rural areas to the cities, the projected increase in agricultural production can only be achieved through rationalization, automatization, and higher productivity per employee. To this end the long-range plans for the period 1971-90 envisage considerably expanded investments in agriculture, especially in education of technical specialists, machinery, and fertilizers. The chemical industry is going to make major strides in fertilizer production; so Romania by 1990 will have reached U.S. standards in application of this commodity per acre of arable land.[32]

The ever-increasing use of tractors, harvesters, and other complicated agricultural machinery requires a major expansion of technical personnel to design, produce, and service such vehicles. Collective and state farmers must become familiar with the use of machinery and achieve a higher general level of knowledge so that they can apply their specialized skills to the best possible societal use. Short-term courses with both general and specialized subject matter must be organized as a frequent occurrence all over the country. Once again, U.S. agriculture, with its phenomenal productivity, is often mentioned as a model for multilaterally developed Romania.[33]

Expansion in the Domestic Raw Materials Base

In this age of fuel shortage and dwindling reserves of raw materials it is interesting to note that Romania's leadership intends to become self-sufficient in the production of all major raw materials available in the country and to establish itself as a supplier to the rest of the world in some fields such as petroleum, oil, and petrochemicals. It is indeed true that Romania is the richest country in Eastern Europe in raw materials and fuels (the USSR excepted). "Multilateral development" in this context simply means exploration of all available resources with subsequent exploitation. By 1970-2000 all major sources will have become workable and will have produced considerable quantities of coal, oil, and various important minerals.[34]

Foreign Trade Based on "Mutual Advantage"

In the stage of economic modernity Romania will play an important part in "international exchange and division of labor." Since Romania's industry and agriculture will have reached a high level of development, Bucharest will increasingly become a supplier of finished products (including fuels), technology, and organizational know-how, while imports will increasingly consist of raw materials, albeit with high technology imports on an exchange basis, primarily from the United States, Western Europe, and, to some extent, the USSR. In order to achieve this kind of status, Romania must greatly expand and modernize its merchant marine. Export of know-how is based on an increasingly sophisticated educational system and electronic expertise. Although some of this educational expansion will be "imported" through scientific exchanges and so forth, much of the projected achievement will be a result of domestic efforts (see Chapter 4, pp. 114-18).[35]

Education of the Citizenry

As indicated above, a major feature of Communist-sponsored modernization is the emphasis on achieving ever-increasing skill levels among elites and masses alike. In the stage of modernity there will be "virtually universal" intermediate education, with ample possibilities for specialization. A major feature of Romanian education at this level will be so-called vocational training, in which the student will combine theoretical studies with practical work in factories, commercial institutions, or on the farm. This combination of theoretical activity with manual work will contribute significantly to the eradication of functional and status differentiation between workers of the brain and workers at the bench, which is a major contemporary problem in all East European countries.

While mass education will be significantly expanded, the training of technical experts and other specialists needed in the sophisticated economy will be developed and considerably improved. Not only will there be more new experts but older scientific cadres will undergo periodic retraining designed to introduce new ideas and techniques at this level. Of major importance is the projected expansion of middle-level technical cadres, who can put theoretical knowledge directly to work in production. Higher scientific research personnel are also primarily charged with activities which can be of immediate benefit to production; there is a curious tendency to downplay basic research, although it is frequently stated that this field of endeavor will be of some importance in the stage of multilateral development.[36]

While acquisition and application of functional skills constitute the most important task of modern education, it is envisaged that all citizens will benefit in other ways as well. The most important achievement of the expanded educational effort will be the mass acquisition of a new outlook on society, nature, and the individual. The modernized citizen will discard traditional ways of thinking, and will use his skills for societal improvement rather than for petty, selfish gain. Social integration will be based on recriprocity and common effort for common goals, while old superstitions and prejudices will be left behind. Above all, the modernized citizen will tend to look upon the world and nature as malleable, as objects that can be changed through human will and action. This outlook will supersede widespread passivity, now admittedly a major problem among part of the population. Human beings will be free--free to interact with others, free to choose their educational paths, free to develop to their fullest creative capability. This kind of freedom does not include the opportunity to question the political order; the current Romanian definition of modernity precludes such an opportunity, since it states that personal freedom in the functional sense can only be achieved under the leadership of the RCP.[37]

The emphasis on new activist values as contrasted to old passivist views of nature is typical of modernizing elites, as indicated by several students of modernization. Only through a major reorientation of such values can the masses of the citizenry be mobilized for realization of the goals so clearly set forth by the modernizing elite. And only through full-scale mobilization can the modernizers hope to succeed in the frontal, simultaneous attack on all aspects of perceived underdevelopment, so characteristic of Communist regimes.

The multilaterally developed society is not only characterized by high levels of functional skills and modern, activist outlooks; it is also a highly cultured stage of development. The citizen in this society will have access to high quality literature, theatrical and cinematic productions, and sculpture and paintings, as well as other art forms, and will know how to appreciate such values of socialism. The cultured citizen will consciously break with boorishness, drunkenness, and boisterous behavior and will become a model citizen with proper regard for the finer things in life. The emphasis on a cultured life is already a factor of major importance in Romanian society; to be considered uncultured is one of the worst insults imaginable. Once again, the stress on a rounded personality is an integral part of the modernizers' goals, designed to break down old value systems with subsequent introduction of a new set of outlooks that belongs to the "new society." The RCP clearly understands the importance of culture as an agent of social mobilization and has therefore taken steps to ensure that all cultural manifestations are "socialist in kind and content." By this definition, literature and paintings that do not conform to the established norms (which will be discussed in detail in Chapters 3 and 4) are considered "old-fashioned" and "retrograde."[38]

In socioeconomic and cultural terms, then, the modernized society is made up of citizens harmoniously interacting within a framework of regime-sponsored goals and prescriptions. A modern citizen lives modernity in everyday life, and those who do not fit are guilty not merely of personal aberration but, more importantly, of activities that slow down the societal move to the higher stage entitled "multilaterally developed society." The individual is thus prevented from opting out of the modernizing process, let alone questioning it. The incessant mobilization efforts of the Communist elite must be seen against this backdrop of ideas.

Central Planning and Management

Although the final goal of socioeconomic and cultural modernization is to lay the foundations for a Communist society, which is still envisioned as a classless and stateless construct, the multilaterally developed society will be managed by political cadres and technical experts and the decision-making process will continue to be centralized. Decentralization is envisioned only in administrative functions. Thus, modern society will essentially be run by a well-oiled central bureaucracy, aided by a disciplined and functionally skilled, active and enthusiastic citizenry, which will be superbly prepared to carry out assigned tasks. Increased effectiveness and efficiency will be achieved through better skills, better planning, and harder work by central bureaucrats and higher productivity by the producers. The main difference between this stage of modernity and previous developmental epochs is the congruence of elite goals and mass views in the multilaterally developed society, as compared to the earlier disequilibrium. Clearly, with such general acceptance of all-important questions, economic productivity can be expected to rise dramatically.[39]

POLITICAL MODERNIZATION

The socioeconomic and cultural modernization process is to be matched by similar developments in the political field. In addition to having achieved the functional skills necessary for improved economic performance, a truly modernized citizen must also exhibit some crucial political behavior patterns, chief among which are the following.

Acceptance of the Communist Party as the Supreme Political and Socioeconomic Force

The modern citizen will be a conscious and willing participant in the political processes guided by the Party and will unquestioningly accord the RCP the right to lead society in all fields of decision making. Thus political participation is severely circumscribed and can only be permitted within the parameters established by Party decisions and the most important documents emanating from RCP congresses and national conferences. During the last five to six years personal pronouncements by General Secretary Nicolae Ceausescu have apparently become integral parts of formal Party decisions, which subsequently are routinely ratified by the Central Committee. The citizen, who is expected to participate within the limits set by the RCP, must therefore be conversant with the particular flavor of Ceausescu's unique mixture of orthodox Marxism-Leninism, populism, and Romanian nationalism.[40]

The citizen participating within the carefully prescribed limits outlined above is expected to give overwhelming endorsement to candidates put up by the RCP and the Socialist Unity Front (SUF) at the time of elections to the Grand National Assembly and judet (county) popular assemblies. Furthermore, the citizenry is expected to participate in mass meetings on special holidays, or in political "campaigns," when the political organs at the grass roots will attempt to mobilize large numbers for the completion of limited and specific tasks, such as "voluntary" contributions of time and effort to electoral campaigns or ratification of nominations. An important task devolving upon the citizenry is a supervisory function, in which the man-in-the-street examines the performances of political and administrative cadres and acts as a voice of complaint and rectification, an important input mechanism that can provide invaluable information for the central political leadership. An important mass function is also the funneling of new ideas of an administrative and economic nature, which can often lead to improvements in administrative input.[41]

Although this kind of political participation is relatively widespread, one basic element of participation as commonly understood in pluralistic democracies is missing: The citizenry cannot actively attempt to change the political elite or any basic element of its program. Leadership turnover is decided within the elite itself without recourse to public opinion, and the long- and short-range political programs are established as the result of elite interaction within a rather small circle. One cannot, therefore, speak of political participation per se but rather of political mobilization for already established ends. This fundamental aspect of Romanian political life will not change in the multilaterally developed society; on the contrary, circumscribed participation will become even more synchronized at that stage, since old-fashioned "bourgeois" and "anti-State" views will have disappeared. The modernized citizen will participate not because he feels a sense of duty or perhaps even compulsion but because he is thoroughly integrated into the new society and enthusiastically endorses it.

Central to both the contemporary and the future-oriented definitions of political participation sponsored by the RCP is deep mistrust of what Western scholars consider genuine political activity. Any action that falls outside the Party-established parameters is considered not merely erroneous but a serious break with the social and political unity that is supposed to exist in the country. A major element of modernizing Communist systems is this severe discouragement of real participation and the concomitant substitution of mobilization and synthetic political activity. At the contemporary stage the regime freely admits to massive problems associated with citizen passivity, indeed cynicism, in the face of such truncated participation. In the multilaterally developed society such cynicism is expected to give way to enthusiastic acceptance.[42]

Acceptance of the Right of the Communist Party to Mobilize for Regime-defined Goal Fulfillment

Central to the successful completion of the modernization process as envisaged by the RCP elite is its ability to mobilize the citizenry for socioeconomic activity.

In the earlier "breakthrough" stage of modernization mobilization was frequently achieved through coercion. The regime has increasingly discarded this method as relatively dysfunctional, especially if massive coercion is required. Instead, mobilization will be achieved through successful political socialization, which in turn will produce a set of societally functional values among the rank and file. This new set of values will include acceptance of the elite's right to mobilize part of society or all of it for fulfillment of regime-perceived goals. The modern society will be one in which the citizenry willingly forsakes privacy, consciously abstains from group formation that might isolate the individual from the political leadership, and enthusiastically undertakes any duty laid upon it by the unquestioned leader. Thus the fullest expression of human achievement is the successful carrying out of societal tasks, not individual definitions of what the task should be.[43]

Acceptance of a "Romanian" Communist System, with Equal Rights and Duties for All "Cohabiting Nationalities"

One of the most important elements of the RCP modernization effort is its strong nationalistic content. The multilaterally developed society is one in which Romania can face the world from a position of equality, not relative underdevelopment and subjugation. Nicolae Ceausescu clearly considers himself a national leader in the tradition of Stefan the Great and Michael the Brave, who is going to gain for Romania its rightful place among nations. This kind of nationalism is popular among the Romanian majority of the population but may not be quite as acceptable for the ethnic minorities, chief of which are the Hungarians, Germans, and, to some extent, Jews. Despite such divergence among minorities, there is little to indicate that Ceausescu (or anybody else within the Romanian-dominated RCP elite) will be willing to reduce the nationalistic overtones of the political goals associated with modernity. Instead, the Romanians in the political leadership express the hope that in the stage of modernity ethnic particularism will become unimportant or may even vanish completely. People will be committed to Socialist Romania first and will retain only minimal ties with their ethnic base, chiefly in cultural matters. Ethnic particularism is seen as a "bourgeois" and consequently old-fashioned value, whereas integration to a common goal of "Socialist Man" in modern society is considered a progressive process. The higher commitment is thus to the multilaterally developed society. Furthermore, the modernization process will eradicate the current contradictions between city and country, will raise the standard of living for everybody, and will therefore remove any socioeconomic reasons for particularism. Modernity becomes the great equalizer.[44]

This equalization and assimilation process must be carried forward through the socioeconomic improvements discussed above and through an accelerated rate of Party institutionalization, in which the RCP, by means of a vastly expanded network of grass-roots organizations, can help combat old-fashioned views of particularism and promote common socialist values. This scheduled institutionalization has been quite noticeable during the last four or five years, especially among Hungarians and Germans.

The strong element of Romanian nationalism in the concept of multilaterally developed society does not indicate that a purely one-sided acceptance of "Romanianization" is required of other ethnic groups. Romanians must assimilate to modernity as well as all others, and within the framework of society at this stage minorities will have equal rights with Romanians. Since most citizens will have accepted modernity with all of the ramifications explained in this chapter, such minority rights will be perceived as unimportant and cannot cause major problems in any field.

The ethnic concept of modernity is of particular importance in a multiethnic society such as Romania. Ceausescu's concept of intergroup relations in the multilaterally developed society is an important, if somewhat utopian, contribution to Marxism-Leninism in the contemporary world.

Struggle Against "Old-fashioned" Views and Checks on Deviant Elite Behavior

Since modernity is as much a state of mind as an actual socioeconomic and political condition, values must reflect the transformation of society. Thus all values that are considered old-fashioned, that is, belonging in the premodern stage, must be eradicated; and remnants of such views must be combatted wherever they appear. Particularly pernicious in the multilaterally developed society are values such as selfishness, greed, self-admiration, and adherence to "bourgeois nationalism"; similarly, all views that hinder the integration of individuals into the society must be destroyed. Antisocial views and behavior and "Westernism" and "cosmopolitanism," as well as "imperialism" and "chauvinism," have always been the objects of concerted regime attacks, and such values must be ruthlessly destroyed if modernity is to be achieved.[45]

The RCP elite is not oblivious to the side effects of rapid modernization; in fact, much of the current preoccupation of Ceausescu and his colleagues is focused on undesirable tendencies that develop within Communist systems in transition to multilateral development. A concerted struggle is carried out against careerism, corruption, formalism, and sloganeering. "Careerism" refers to the tendency of modernizing cadres, especially in the economy and in academic life, to become enamored with their particular tasks and the prestige and material benefits that go with them. For such cadres there is insufficient vision of the relationship between their own position and the rest of society. Careerism is also conducive to insulation from politics and real life, a condition that is particularly obnoxious to a political elite with visions of value penetration even to the grass roots. Isolation of technical and academic cadres from political realities already constitutes a major problem in contemporary Communist systems. In the multilaterally developed society these barriers will once again have been removed, both because of increased political-organizational penetration of such cadres and because of a significant value reorientation among the technocrats.[46]

Corruption is seen as a contemporary problem of some magnitude, and isolated instances will occur even in the stage of modernity. Regime concern with this kind of aberrant behavior clearly reflects the continued existence of old values and practices, in which corruption was a major factor in all walks of life in most of the Balkans, particularly Romania. Even though there will be little corruption in the multilaterally developed society, the political leadership will not be satisfied that Romania can move into socialism and communism until all such vestiges are removed. Total eradication of this cultural tradition must be successful.

"Formalism" has become an increasingly important problem in all walks of life, particularly among technical experts, academic personnel, and even Party cadres.

According to frequently repeated charges by Nicolae Ceausescu, formalism is a purely verbal commitment to slogans, especially of an ideological nature, with no real understanding of the meaning behind the formulas and no realization of how such formulas should be carried out in real life. Ideological activity under such circumstances becomes arid and bereft of practical results, serving as a screen for the narrow professionalism of the intelligentsia. Among Party cadres sloganeering is frequently seen as a shortcut to political power and the advantages that go with it. Ceausescu has made it clear that in the multilaterally developed society formalism will be superseded by real commitment to Party theory and ideology. The remnants of this old-fashioned value must be finally eliminated at this stage.[47]

A major element in the liquidation of negative values and behavior in modern society is citizen control. The citizenry, trained in socialist values, equipped with the economic and political skills necessary for this high level of development, will act as control mechanisms, checking on the performance of elites and thus performing a crucial task of balancing the increasing societal power among specialists, especially managers and technocrats. The Ceausescu style of political leadership has important elements of populism, with frequent forays from Bucharest into the countryside and regional industrial centers, during which the Party leader consistently attempts to establish contact with the rank and file. Such contact can, in turn, be used as an important check on intermediate elites. This kind of direct citizen control (within carefully established parameters emanating from the Party center) will be considerably expanded by the time Romania reaches the multilaterally developed society. Thus a form of decentralization of the Party apparatus can be expected; the control cadres at all levels can be considerably reduced in number, and this manpower can be used for other purposes. It is important to note, however, that this is decentralization of administration and control, not of decision making. The latter activity will remain centralized until full communism is achieved.[48]

A Projected High Level of Anticipatory Socioeconomic and Political Activity

The projected reduction in control personnel within modernized society is based on a high level of anticipatory citizen activity in all fields, especially in the economy and within carefully established political limits. Since the modern citizen presumably will have achieved a level of consciousness approaching that of the political elite, he will anticipate elite actions and reactions. This does not mean that the political elite has been rendered obsolete; on the contrary, the tremendous energy released through voluntary mass activity must be harnessed for maximum benefit and in conformity with the program established by the Communist Party. This is particularly important in the political field, where the Party program sets definite limits concerning organization, ideology, and day-to-day activities. The end result, socialist activity by socialist man, will be the crowning achievement of the modernization process.[49]

Need for Universal Acceptance of the End Result--A Communist Society

One of the strongest sources of legitimacy in a Communist system, as seen from the vantage point of elite values, is the close correlation between the practical Party program and the inevitable march of history, which will result in a highly desirable end--a Communist society. This inevitable outcome must be perceived by elite and mass alike. In order to ensure such close correspondence between mass perceptions and elite values a massive socialization effort must be undertaken, with emphasis on "socialist morality and consciousness." Since it is a maxim of the Party leadership that political consciousness, as interpreted by the RCP, and historical necessity are closely correlated, individual citizens do not have the right to "opt out" of the modernization process, let alone oppose the direction of this development under Communist leadership. The most important and most frequently condemned societal and political sin is active opposition to the regime; the second vice is conscious isolation from the Party program and its implementation. Pockets of alienation or apathy cannot be accepted in the multilaterally developed society; universal acceptance of the goals, procedures, and methods of the regime are crucial.

This extraordinary emphasis on penetration into mass consciousness represents one of the hallmarks of the Ceausescu approach. The general secretary in this respect has gone much further than some of his colleagues at the top of the RCP pyramid, whose chief concern has been simply to achieve citizen tolerance of the Party program.[50]

CONCLUSION

It seems clear that the current definition of the multilaterally developed society, sponsored by Nicolae Ceausescu, is an important contribution to contemporary Communist theory. The emphasis is clearly on expansion of human skills, both in the economic field and also in the political arena. The methods for such skill transmission are many, but can be classified chiefly as political socialization and expanded technical and moral-ideological education. In both cases the Ceausescu vision emphasizes the enormous importance of institutionalization through the continued expansion of the Communist Party. Party organizations will be instrumental in transmitting the moral, ethical, and political values that must go hand-in-hand with the technical skill dissemination carried out primarily by the educational establishment. The Party must also act as the chief agent of social mobilization and control. The staffing of this crucial organ of modernization thus becomes a major question, to which we will now turn.

NOTES

1. See, for example, S. N. Eisenstadt, "Varieties of Political Development: The Theoretical Challenge," in Building States and Nations 1, ed. S. N. Eisenstadt and Stein Rokkan (Beverly Hills, Calif.: Sage Publications, 1973), pp. 41-73.

2. Ibid.

3. Samuel P. Huntington, Political Order in Changing Societies (New Haven: Yale University Press, 1968).

4. Ibid.

5. Stein Rokkan, "Cities, States and Nations: A Dimensional Model for the Study of Contrasts in Development," in Building States and Nations, pp. 73-99.

6. Karl W. Deutsch, "Social Mobilization and Political Development," The American Political Science Review, September 1961, pp. 493-575.

7. Ibid.

8. Huntington, op. cit.

9. Ibid.

10. For a good overview see both volumes of Eisenstadt and Rokkan, Building States and Nations.

11. The Soviet experience ran along these lines, as described by Robert Conquest, in The Great Terror: Stalin's Purge of the Thirties (New York: Macmillan, 1973).

12. For a description of East European experience, see Zbigniew K. Brzezinski, The Soviet Bloc (Cambridge, Mass.: Harvard University Press, 1969), pp. 67-155.

13. For example, Charles Gati in "Modernization and Communist Power in Hungary," East European Quarterly, September 1971, pp. 325-60.

14. Huntington, op. cit.

15. This is certainly the case in Romania, reiterated by General Secretary Nicolae Ceausescu at the 1972 National Conference of the Romanian Communist Party (RC). See Scinteia, July 20, 1972.

16. As stated by Ceausescu in his speech to the Tenth RCP Congress, in Congresul al X-lea al Partidului Comunist Roman (Bucharest: Editura Politica, 1969), especially pp. 64-74.

17. See, for example, Ivan Volgyes, "East European Socialization," Problems of Communism, January-February 1974, pp. 46-56.

18. A good historical overview of Romanian development is found in Stephen Fischer-Galati, Twentieth Century Rumania (New York: Columbia University Press, 1970), especially pp. 1-90.

19. This process is described in some detail by Kenneth Jowitt in his Revolutionary Breakthroughs and National Development (Berkeley: University of California Press, 1971), especially pp. 73-159.

20. Ibid., pp. 159-98.

21. The collectivization process is described in Fischer-Galati, op. cit., pp. 46-128.

22. For a description of religion in Socialist Romania, see Kurt Hutten, Iron Curtain Christians (Minneapolis: Augsburg Publishing House, 1967), pp. 385-400.

23. For a discussion of the position of ethnic minorities in Socialist Romania, see my "Ethnic Minorities in Romania under Socialism," East European Quarterly, January 1974, pp. 435-64.

24. See Jowitt, op. cit., pp. 92-159.

25. For an excellent analysis of economic development in Socialist Romania, see John Michael Montias, Economic Development in Communist Romania (Cambridge, Mass.: The M.I.T. Press, 1967).

26. Ibid.

27. See Nicolae Ceausescu's statements to the Ninth RCP Congress, in Congresul al IX-lea al Partidului Comunist Roman (Bucharest: Editura Politica, 1966), pp. 32-66.

28. For example, Gheorghe Rosu, delegate from the Bacau region, at the Ninth RCP Congress, in Congresul al IX-lea, pp. 120-28.

29. The Tenth RCP Congress was reported in Congresul al X-lea, and the 1971-75 five-year plan was extensively discussed in the month of October 1971 in Scinteia and other press organs.

30. The guidelines presented here are summaries of major policy pronouncements by the RCP as published in Congresul al IX-lea, Ceausescu's speech to the RCP expanded Central Committee meeting (published in Scinteia, November 3 and 4, 1971) and the General Secretary's speech to the RCP National Conference, July 1972, in Scinteia, July 20 and 21, 1972.

31. Ibid.

32. Especially Ceausescu at the 1972 RCP National Conference, in Scinteia, July 20, 1972.

33. Ibid.

34. Ibid.

35. The long-range goal of foreign exchange was spelled out by Nicolae Ceausescu at the Tenth Congress; see Congresul al X-lea, pp. 42-44.

36. A thorough discussion of Romanian education at all levels is found in Nicolae Ceausescu's speech at the opening of the academic year 1972-73, published in Scinteia, October 3, 1972.

37. This definition of freedom has been discussed frequently. See Ceausescu's speech to the Tenth RCP Congress, in Congresul al X-lea, pp. 69-74.

38. This theme is repeatedly hammered home, for instance, at the 1972 Writers' Union meeting (Le Monde, May 20, 1972).

39. The latest major policy statement along these lines is found in Nicolae Ceausescu's speech to the 1972 RCP National Conference, as reported and discussed in Scinteia, July 20-29, 1972.

40. There has never been any doubt about the unquestioned position of the Communist Party in Romanian society; one of the most forceful declarations of this position came in a Ceausescu speech to the RCP Central Committee during the initial stages of the campaign for ideological orthodoxy in 1971. See Scinteia, November 4, 1971.

41. See my discussion of the Ceausescu style of leadership in Problems of Communism, July-August 1974, p. 29.

42. Ceausescu to the RCP Central Committee, in Scinteia, November 4, 1971.

43. An extremely forceful recent statement of this concept is found in the general secretary's speech to the RCP Central Committee in ibid.

44. See the Tenth Party Congress resolution, in Congresul al X-lea, pp. 736-49.

45. One of the most eloquent statements on this in Ceausescu's report to RCP Tenth Congress, in Congresul al X-lea, pp. 74-89.

46. Much of the discussion of the November 1971 RCP Central Committee Plenum on ideology revolved around this point, as reported in Scinteia, November 4-10, 1971.

47. See the General Secretary's thunderous denunciation of formalism in Scinteia, November 4, 1971.

48. For a discussion of the Ceausescu style, see my article in Problems of Communism, July-August 1974, op. cit.

49. This point is made in virtually all major speeches by RCP top leaders, for example, in Scinteia throughout July, 1972, in connection with the RCP National Party Conference of that year.

50. Compare Ceausescu's speech to the November 1971 RCP Central Committee Plenum (Scinteia, November 4, 1971) and Ion Gheorghe Maurer's speech on ideology and society in ibid., October 1, 1971.

CHAPTER 2

THE AGENTS OF MODERNIZATION: THE COMMUNIST PARTY AND ITS AFFILIATED ORGANIZATIONS

The main vehicle for achieving socioeconomic and political modernization in Romania is the Romanian Communist Party (RCP). This instrument is used in a multitude of ways, chief among which are organization, mass mobilization, control of elite structures and personnel as well as of the general citizenry, and the setting of specific political and socioeconomic parameters through planning and projection. The RCP is by definition not only the only legitimate political party in the country but also the recognized "leading force in society"; its style of operations, the characteristics of its leadership, and its formalized and informal decision-making processes therefore become crucial factors in the modernization process.

ORGANIZATION

One of the main goals of the RCP in its quest for social and political transformation is organizational coverage in the general population and in the most important social groups of the citizenry. Of particular importance is organizational penetration of the main socioeconomic elites that have developed in the country during the last 25 years. The special status of the military and the security police as instruments of coercion and supervision necessitates major Party efforts to ensure control by structural means and, through the vehicle of individual RCP membership, penetration in these two structures. Tables 2.1 and 2.2 explore various elements of organizational coverage and penetration in the period 1944 to the present.

TABLE 2.1

Growth of the RCP Structure, 1944-73

Year	Full Members	Candidate Members	Total Membership
1944	--	--	approx. 1,000
1955	538,815	56,583	595,398
1960	686,600	148,000	834,600
1965	--	--	1,450,000
1969	--	--	1,924,000
1972 (July)	--	--	2,231,000
1972 (31 December)	--	--	2,281,372

Sources: 1944: Kenneth Jowitt, Revolutionary Breakthroughs and National Development: The Case of Romania, 1944-1965 (Berkeley, Calif.: University of California Press, 1971), p. 78; 1955: Ghita Ionescu, Communism in Romania 1944-1962 (London: Oxford University Press, 1964), p. 242; 1960: ibid., p. 318; 1965: 1968 Yearbook on International Communist Affairs (Stanford, Calif.: Hoover Institution Press, 1969), p. 508; 1969: Virgil Trofin's report to the Tenth RCP Congress, in Congresul al X-lea al Partidului Comunist Roman (Bucharest: Editura Politica, 1969), pp. 127-28; July 1972: Scinteia, July 20, 1972; December 31, 1972: ibid., June 22, 1973.

The figures in Table 2.1 show an astonishing increase in RCP membership from an insignificant core of 1,000 before the coup d'etat on August 23, 1944, that set Romania on its course toward Communist domination to almost 2.3 million members at the end of 1972. The figure represents considerably more than 10 percent of the total population of Romania. Proportionally the RCP is one of the largest Communist parties in the world.

Table 2.2 explores the social composition of the RCP, 1955-73.

Table 2.2 shows developmental trends that are familiar to students of ruling Communist parties. It is extremely difficult to achieve a social composition of the Party that accurately reflects its claim to the title "Vanguard of the Proletariat"; only in 1960 did the official statistics show more than half the membership as workers, but at least one prominent analyst has charged

TABLE 2.2

Social Composition of the RCP, 1955-73

	Workers		Peasants		Intelligentsia	
	Number	Percent	Number	Percent	Number	Percent
1955	--	42.61	--	--	--	--
1960	--	51.0	--	34.0	70,000	--
1965	630,000	44.0	500,000	34.0	145,000	--
1969	--	43.0	--	28.0	--	23.0
1972 (July)	1,023,000	45.9	534,000	24.0	511,000	22.8
1972 (31 December)	1,060,658	46.5	526,589	23.1	430,000	18.8

Sources: 1955: Ghita Ionescu, Communism in Romania 1944-1962 (London: Oxford University Press, 1964), p. 243; 1960: ibid., p. 319; 1965: Nicolae Ceausescu's report to the Ninth RCP Congress, in Congresul al IX-lea al Partidului Comunist Roman (Bucharest: Editura Politica, 1966), pp. 71-72; 1969: Virgil Trofin's report to the Tenth RCP Congress, in Congresul al X-lea al Partidului Comunist Roman (Bucharest: Editura Politica, 1969), pp. 127-28; July 1972: Scinteia, July 20, 1972; December 31, 1972: ibid., June 22, 1973.

that this figure was the result of statistical falsifications.[1] In other years the percentage of workmen has hovered in the 42-46 percent range. An interesting development is the recent influx of workers, which is connected with Ceausescu's current campaign to "proletarianize" the RCP (see Chapter 3, pp. 81-83).

The proportion of peasants in the RCP is low considering that approximately half of the total population is located in the countryside and primarily occupied in agriculture. The lack of organizational penetration of the countryside is a major problem that the RCP shares with its sister parties in Eastern Europe.

Up to last year the Romanian Party also followed the traditional pattern of ruling Communist parties by steadily increasing its proportion of intellectuals and funtionaires. During the last year, however, a massive organizational offensive by the general secretary has been aimed against the bureaucratization of Romanian life; many functionaires have been removed from administrative to productive "line" jobs, and the representation of the intelligentsia in the Party has been reduced.[2] The socioeconomic and intellectual elites of Romania thus face the prospect of decreasing political representation at a time when their societal importance is increasing sharply. Here is surely potential for considerable political conflict in the future.

Just as the RCP has experienced considerable difficulties in penetrating certain social strata, such as the peasantry, it has met with considerable adversity in organizing cells and other Party bodies in certain occupational groups. Increasingly the organizational emphasis has turned to key groups, such as workers in heavy and extractive industries, machine building, transport and telecommunications, higher education, and the armed forces and the police. Thus, in 1967, 42 percent of all academicians and individuals with doctoral degrees were members of the RCP;[3] 54 percent of all high school teachers and university professors and fully 85 percent of all military officers carried Party cards.[4] By 1968 Party penetration of the metallurgical, coal, petroleum, chemical, and machine building industries fluctuated between 27 and 36 percent of the total labor force, a considerable achievement indeed.[5] Subsequent membership drives have essentially reinforced these penetration patterns. There are continued problems in the field of agricultural recruiting.

A major claim by Communist parties everywhere is that under socialism formerly disadvantaged groups such as women and youth will receive full representation. A major goal for the modernizers of Eastern Europe has been the mobilization of the younger generation, both for increased economic activity and for the purposes of political education and indoctrination. Thus, in 1955, 37.21 percent of the delegation to the Second Congress of the Romanian Workers' Party (RWP) were under 35 years of age; 17.31 percent were between 41 and 50; and 12.4 percent were 50 or over.[6] The delegate figures probably corresponded roughly to the age distribution in the Party itself; First Secretary Gheorghe Gheorghiu-Dej in his report emphasized that the Congress delegates represented a "true picture" of the Party membership. By the time of the Ninth Congress of the Romanian Communist Party in July 1945, 64 percent of all Party members were under 40 years of age, while 36 percent were classified as over 40.[7] At the Tenth RCP Congress, August 1969, Ceausescu reported that those under 30 comprised 24 percent of the total membership and those in the 30-40 bracket 36 percent.[8] Recently there has been much less publicity about representation of youth in the Party, perhaps an indication that this segment of the population has been less than enthusiastic in joining.

The emphasis on increased representation for women has had an important effect on recruitment. In 1965, 21 percent of the total membership was made up of women.[9] Since that time a major recruitment drive has been carried out. In 1972, 29.58 percent of all admissions to the Party were women.[10] That the female component is still low, reflects a general phenomenon in Communist parties as well as the important element of traditionalism still manifest among the rural population of the country. Women are simply not as available in political terms as are men in this kind of setting. The recent elevation of Elena Ceausescu, the general secretary's wife, to the RCP Executive Committee may signal a new drive for female representation in the political arena.[11]

One of the most frequently cited claims of Communist parties everywhere is that they will be able to solve the nationality problem, so often a major obstacle to national integration in the interwar period. The Communist approach to the nationality problem has centered on a number of specific remedies, chief among which are socioeconomic improvements and the extension of national services to all citizens, regardless of ethnic backgrounds, and improved political representation. One form of political representation often identified in such systems is membership in the Party.

This problem is clearly of major importance to Romania, where a large number of nationalities coexist, with especially large and important groups such as Hungarians and Germans in certain areas of the country. From the very beginning of Communist rule the RCP has been scrupulous in its attempt to establish a balanced nationality representation in the Party, whereby the ethnic distribution in the population would be reflected in the rank and file of the only legitimate Party organization. Table 2.3 examines this distribution for the period 1955-73.

TABLE 2.3

Ethnic Distribution of Party Membership in the RCP, 1955-73

Year	Romanians (Percent of Total)	Hungarians (Percent of Total)	Germans (Percent of Total)
1955	79.2[a]	--	--
1965	87.0	9.0	3.0[b]
1971 (31 December)	89.3	8.1	1.2
1972 (30 June)	88.0	8.0	3.0
1972 (31 December)	89.5	8.0	1.2

[a]Delegates to the Party Congress.
[b]Officially "Germans and other nationalities."

Sources: 1955: Ghita Ionescu, Communism in Romania 1944-1962 (London: Oxford University Press, 1964), p. 243; 1965: Congresul al IX-lea al Partidului Comunist Roman (Bucharest: Editura Politica, 1966), pp. 72-73; December 31, 1971: Scinteia, April 25, 1972; June 30, 1972: Nicolae Ceausescu at the RCP National Conference, July 19-21, 1972, in Report Presented by Comrade Nicolae Ceausescu, General Secretary of the Romanian Communist Party (Supplement to Romania Today, no. 8/213, 1972), p. 28; December 31, 1972: ibid., June 22, 1973.

The ethnic distribution of Party membership is roughly in correspondence with the distribution in the general population, with a slight overrepresentation of Romanians and a small underrepresentation of Hungarians and Germans. The national picture at the rank and file level of the

Party is therefore more favorable than the social composition, which has shown consistent overrepresentation of the intelligentsia, as described above. This kind of representation is of little value unless it can be shown that it has a real effect on policy. A subsequent chapter will examine the question in detail.

GROUP REPRESENTATION AT THE TOP IN THE RCP

The representation of various groups among the rank and file of the RCP is impressive testimony to the attempts at "ticket balancing" so prominent in Communist parties everywhere. Ideologically, the Communists' claim that their party is the vanguard of the proletariat demands a certain representation of workers. The recent ideological emphasis on Communist parties as "Parties of the Whole People" necessitates representation according to social stratum, sex, and nationality roughly corresponding to the breakdown of the general population. Such representation at the grass roots is of only limited importance, however; in centralized political systems, decision making takes place at the intermediate and top levels. Meaningful group representation with a view toward decision making is therefore only possible in the top RCP organs. Unfortunately, there are major gaps in our information on many of the present RCP leadership cadres. Thus, among 41 members and candidate members of the RCP Executive Committee, Permanent Presidium, and Central Committee Secretariat, the social background of fully 35 has not been established. Only 25 of the educational patterns in this group are clear, and there are some difficulties in establishing nationality backgrounds for several individuals. In most cases a birthdate is known, and generalizations can therefore be made concerning age distribution. The question of sex can of course be readily determined.[12]

In the spring of 1973, the most important Party bodies were staffed as follows:

Permanent Presidium: Nicolae Ceausescu, Emil Bodnaras, Manea Manescu, Ion Gheorghe Maurer, Paul Niculescu-Mizil, Gheorghe Pana, Gheorghe Radulescu, Virgil Trofin, and Ilie Verdet.

Central Committee Secretariat: Nicolae Ceausescu, Stefan Andrei, Iosif Banc, Cornel Burtica, Miron Constantinescu, Ion Dinca, Mihai Gere, Gheorghe Pana, and Dumitru Popescu.

Executive Committee of the RCP: Full members: Nicolae Ceausescu, Maxim Berghianu, Emil Bodnaras, Gheorghe Cioara, Constantin Dragan, Emil Draganescu, Janos Fazekas, Petre Lupu, Manea Manescu, Ion Gheorghe Maurer, Paul Niculescu-Mizil, Gheorghe Pana, Dumitru Popescu, Gheorghe Radulescu, Leonte Rautu, Gheorghe Stoica, Virgil Trofin, Ilie Verdet, Vasile Vilcu, Stefan Voitec, and Florian Danalache. Alternate members: Constantin Banalau, Iosif Banc, Petre Blajovici, Cornel Burtica, Miron Constantinescu, Mihai Dalea, Miu Dobrescu, Aurel Duca, Mihai Gere, Ion Iliescu, Ion Ionita, Ion Patan, Vasile Patilinet, Ion Stanescu, Mihai Telescu, Iosif Uglar, and Richard Winter.

Some of the full and alternate members of the Executive Committee had been in important central RCP positions earlier. This group included Mihai Dalea, who had been in the Secretariat in 1954-55, 1960-62, and 1965-69; Ion Iliescu, Central Committee secretary from February to July 1971; Vasile Patilinet, in the Secretariat from July 1965 to February 1972; and Leonte Rautu, likewise in the Secretariat, 1965-69. It seems fair to conclude that these cadres suffered personal demotions. However, Manea Manescu, who had held positions in the Secretariat in 1965-69 and again from late 1961 to late 1972, was not demoted; he has been in the Permanent Presidium since February 1971. Similarly, Paul Niculescu-Mizil lost his secretaryship in April 1972 (he had held this position since 1965) but remained in the Presidium. Virgil Trofin, who was removed from the Secretariat in February 1971, is still on the Presidium, to which he was admitted in 1968, and Ilie Verdet, a secretary for about five months in 1965, has been on the Presidium since June 1966.

Further changes took place during 1973. At a plenum of the RCP Central Committee on June 18-19 Iosif Banc and Ion Dinca were removed from the Secretariat and were given regional Party posts. Aurel Duca was released from his position as alternate member of the RCP Executive Committee.[13] Rather puzzling were the transfers of Niculescu-Mizil and Trofin, who were both removed from the Secretariat and given rather obscure government positions but nevertheless remained on the Permanent Presidium.

On the basis of the personnel listed above (Banc, Dinca, and Duca included), the following generalizations can be made about this leadership group:

Only two of the leaders whose social background at the time of entry into the RCP is known can be classified as working class (Mihai Gere, member of the Central Committee Secretariat, and Paul Niculescu-Mizil, a member of the RCP Permanent Presidium and a former Central Committee secretary). General Secretary Ceausescu is of peasant background; Miron Constantinescu, member of the Secretariat, from the bourgeoisie; Ion Gheorghe Maurer, premier and member of the RCP Presidium, and Gheorghe Radulescu, member of the Presidium, stem from the middle class and the prewar intelligentsia. Official sources are conspicuously silent on the family background of the others, an indication that the working class is seriously underrepresented at this level. There are only two women in the high Party bodies--Elena Ceausescu (wife of the general secretary) and Lina Ciobanu, both promoted to positions on the Executive Committee in the summer of 1973.[14]

The Romanian Party elite is relatively old. Of the 34 leaders for whom adequate information is available only two were born in 1930 or later (Stefan Andrei, member of the Secretariat, born 1931 and Ion Iliescu, alternate member of the Executive Committee, born 1930). Fourteen of the elite representatives were born in the decade 1920-30: Maxim Berghianu, full member of the Executive Committee, born 1925; Petre Blajovici, alternate member, Executive Committee, born 1922; Ion Dinca, member of the Secretariat, born 1922; Constantin Dragan, full member of the Executive Committee, born 1922; Janos Fazekas, full member, Executive Committee, born 1926; Ion Ionita, alternate member of the Executive Committee, born 1924; Petre Lupu, full member of the Executive Committee, born 1920; Paul Niculescu-Mizil, a one-time member of the Secretariat, Executive Committee, and Presidium, born 1923; Gheorghe Pana, occupying the same positions as Niculescu-Mizil, born 1927; Ion Patan, alternate on the Executive Committee, born 1926; Dumitru Popescu, Secretariat and full membership on the Executive Committee, born 1928; Ion Stanescu, alternate member of the Executive Committee, born 1929; Virgil Trofin, full member of the Secretariat (till 1972), Presidium, and Executive Committee, born 1926; and Ilie Verdet, full member of all these leading bodies, born 1926.

Of the remaining group, Ceausescu was born in 1918; Emil Bodnaras, a member of the Presidium and the Executive Committee, was born in 1904; Emil Draganescu, full member of the Executive Committee, was born in 1919 and the same year as Mihai Gere (Party secretary and alternative member of the Executive Committee). Manea Manescu, who is represented on all three top bodies, was born in 1916, while Ion Gheorghe Maurer, premier and member of the Presidium and Executive Committee, was born in 1902. Even older are Gheorghe Stoica and Stefan Voitec, both born in 1900 and full members of the Executive Committee. Finally, Vasile Vilcu, another full member of the Executive Committee, was born in 1910. An examination of the Presidium (highest Party body) reveals a relatively old group: the members Ceausescu, Bodnaras, Manescu, Maurer, and Radulescu were born before 1920, while Niculescu-Mizil, Pana, Trofin, and Verdet were born in the 1920s. Of the latter group, Niculescu-Mizil and Trofin have been demoted, thus leaving the older group around Ceausescu in firm control of the Party.

Data on educational backgrounds is also scarce. There is no information on 16 of the 41 persons examined here. These leaders probably joined the Party as activists and gained their promotions through work in the fields of organization, supervision and control, or cadre activities of different levels of the RCP, without much formal education. Among the remaining 25 top leaders two educational patterns prevail, engineering or a combined political-economic course, primarily at the Academy of Economic Studies in Bucharest. The engineers in the group include Stefan Andrei, Constantin Babalau, Gheorghe Cioara, Emil Draganescu, Ion Iliescu, and Stefan Voitec. Nicolae Ceausescu, Petre Blajovici, Florian Danalache, Constantin Dragan, Petre Lupu, Gheorghe Pana, Ion Patan, Dumitru Popescu, Virgil Trofin, and Ilie Verdet all graduated from the Academy of Economic Studies. Maxim Berghianu holds a degree from the Economic Sciences and Planning Institute, while Miron Constantinescu has a doctorate in economics. Petre Lupu graduated from the Academy of Political and Social Studies and is thus the only social scientist in the group. Paul Niculescu-Mizil and Gheorghe Radulescu both attended the Academy of Higher Commercial and Industrial Studies. Leonte Rautu's university degree is not specified. There are two individuals with military educations, Ion Ionita and Ion Gheorghe Maurer (the latter also attended the University of Bucharest). Finally Emil Bodnaras holds a law degree, and also has some training in military schools.

Among the nine members of the Presidium four have attended the Academy of Economic Studies (Ceausescu, Pana, Trofin, and Verdet). This educational institution is primarily designed to train general Party apparatchiks in more specialized topics such as economic management and political economy. Bodnaras (law), Maurer (military and University of Bucharest) represent single career patterns, while two members (Niculescu-Mizil and Radulescu) were educated at the Academy of Higher Commercial and Industrial

Studies. The ninth member, Manea Manescu, is an "unknown" in terms of education, probably indicating an apparatchik career. Thus five of the nine members have essentially similar career patterns within the Party apparatus. Even the specialists have been apparatchiks for a very long time and are now considered close associates of the general secretary. It seems clear that there is little influx of specialists at the very top of the RCP.

Further insights are gained by an analysis of the term of membership in the RCP among this leadership group. Unfortunately we lack this information on 23 persons, and generalizations therefore become hazardous. Among the remaining group of 18, seven joined the Party before August 23, 1944 (the date of legalization of the Party and its participation in the government). Eight individuals joined the RCP in the period 1944-50; two joined in the 1950s; and Aural Duca, who now holds the position of alternative member on the RCP Executive Committee and a Central Committee secretaryship in charge of the Propaganda Section,* has had a very rapid career, having joined the Party in 1960. Despite some upward mobility of such latecomers, the top Party organ, the Presidium, is staffed by individuals who have long-standing memberships (Ceausescu since 1936, Bodnaras since 1940, Maurer since 1936, Pana since 1947, Radulescu since 1933, and Verdet since 1945; there is no information on this point for Manescu, Niculescu-Mizil, and Trofin).

Although career background information yields valuable insights, it should be noted that many top leaders in Communist systems were coopted into the Party machinery at early stages of their careers, and were prevented from practicing their specialties. Therefore the dichotomy between specialists and general apparatchiks may become moot in functional terms; all these individuals are in fact apparatchiks, and many have had this occupation for a long time. It would be reasonable to expect that if such long-standing association with the Party apparat did in fact exist, social background and educational achievements attained at time of entry into a responsible Party post would be of relatively minor importance.[15]

Available biographical information indicates three main career tracks, which can be classified roughly as Party, Government, and Mixed. A Party career is essentially associated with primary tasks in regional or

---

*Duca was removed from this position in 1973.

central RCP organs for the greater part of the productive life span. Due to the tendency in Communist systems to establish a great deal of functional overlap, it is possible, indeed likely, that individuals with Party career tracks will hold occasional government positions as well; but the latter category of occupations is secondary in importance to apparatchik functions.

A government career, on the other hand, usually starts out in the state administration; and this field continues to be the main area of function, although prominent members of the state apparatus will usually end up with Party positions as well. However, such individuals achieve high Party positions primarily after considerable service in the government, and the state track continues to be the most important for them.

Mixed careers are a combination of the two patterns described above, in which there is a considerable switchover from Party to state functions and back again.

Among the 41 individuals examined, the career pattern breakdown was essentially as follows:

- Party track (time of first major Party position in parentheses): Ceausescu (1945); Andrei (1965); Babalau (1960); Banc (1954); Danalache (1952); Dobrescu (1966); Dragan (1954); Duca (1961); Gere (1960); Iliescu (1956); Lupu (1944); Pana (1958); Patiline (1952); Rautu (1948); Telescu (1965); Trofin (1947); Uglar (1954); Verdet (1948); Vilcu (1944); Winter (1956); Patan (not known). The most common career pattern in this group was service in the regional Party apparatus, followed by appointment to the RCP Central Committee, with subsequent promotions at the center. (In this category fall Babalau, Banc, Danalache, Dobrescu, Dragan, Duca, Gere, Lupu, Pana, Patilinet, Telescu, Uglar, Verdet, and Vilcu). The second most prominent pattern is service in the Party Youth Organization with subsequent promotions at the center (Ceausescu, Iliescu, Trofin, Winter). Leonte Rautu, one of the oldest members of the central hierarchy, had a long career in the underground between the two world wars, and in 1948 was already promoted to the Central Committee. Patan's career is not adequately known. Andrei appeared in written sources in 1965 already in the Central Committee; his previous career is not known.
- Government/state administration track (time of first major government position in parentheses): Burtica (1963); Cioara (1954); Constantinescu (1947); Dalea (1947); Dinca (1960); Draganescu (1951); Macovescu (1945); Radulescu (1944); Voitec (1949). The career patterns in

this group are much more diverse, ranging from service in economic ministries to diplomatic activity abroad. In all of them appointment to central Party positions came after a considerable period of service for the state.

- Mixed pattern (first major government and Party position indicated in parentheses): Berghianu (Party 1955, government 1956); Blajovici (Party 1952, government 1965); Bodnaras, (RCP Central Committee 1945, Secret Police 1944); Fazekas (Party 1951, government 1961); Ionita (Party 1955, government 1962); Maurer (Party 1945, government 1947); Niculescu-Mizil (Party 1958, government 1955); Popescu (Party 1956, publishing 1956); Stanescu (Party 1964, government 1967); Stoica (Party 1948, government 1953).

The information provided above clearly shows that the present elite have been in top politicial position, either in the Party apparatus or in the state administration, for a considerable period of time. The "representativeness" of such a group in relation to the general population can therefore be seriously questioned. The RCP central leadership is not representative of the Romanian population and may indeed be in considerable danger of isolation, a problem besetting the bureaucrats of all modern societies, perhaps more severely in the mobilization regimes of the Communist countries. The Romanian leadership must rely on their ability to utilize the myriad of organizational structures in the country to gain information about major trends, problems, prospects, and opportunities in the masses and the emerging social and economic elites; and they must rely upon the same organizations to act as transmission bases of command and enforcers of Party decrees at the level of implementation. This need for information and assistance in implementation is particularly acute in the modernization process; bureaucratic, political elites are primarily possessed of managerial and organizational knowledge but are lacking in the highly specialized skills required in an increasingly sophisticated economy and in a social system that is becoming more stratified and complex every year. Apparatchiks cannot maintain their hold over modern society and further guide its development without the army of experts organized and mobilized throughout the country.

At the same time, a successful implementation of the Party's program among the masses of the population requires a host of organizational networks directed toward various audiences. The most important mass organizations are the Party youth organization, Uniunea Tineretului Comunist (UTC); the trade unions; and the Socialist Unity

Front (FUS). Much of the technical expertise required is organized in governmental ministries and in various professional organizations that are strongly influenced by the RCP. The artistic and literary elite is organized in a Writers' Union, a Union of Plastic Artists, and various other groups with functionally determined membership.

THE GOVERNMENTAL APPARATUS

Common to all Communist political systems is the coordination of function between the Party structure and governmental bodies and a great deal of control by the former over the latter. Such control is exercised in a myriad of ways; the most important are direct control through Party bodies within governmental structures, overlapping of membership, the practice of staffing all important functions by use of the party-controlled _nomenklaturea_, and secret police supervision of governmental personnel. This kind of control is quite prevalent in Romania.

As of mid-1972, the most important governmental posts were staffed as follows:[16]

State

State Council	
Chairman (head of state):	Nicolae Ceausescu
Vice-Chairmen:	Emil Bodnaras
	Manea Manescu
	Stefan Peterfi
	Vasile Vilcu
Grand National Assembly	
Chairman:	Stefan Voitec
Deputy Chairmen:	Maria Groza
	Gyoergy Kovacs
	Ilie Murgulescu
	Gheorghe Necula

Government

Council of Ministers	
Chairman:	Ion Gheorghe Maurer
First Vice-Chairman:	Ilie Verdet
Vice-Chairmen:	Iosif Banc
	Emil Draganescu
	Janos Fazekas
	Mihai Marinescu
	Ion Patan
	Gheorghe Radulescu
	Leonte Rautu

Ministers (early 1973):

Agriculture, the Food Industry and Waters	Iosif Banc
Armed Forces	Ion Ionita
Chemical Industry	Mihai Florescu
Education and Instruction	Mircea Malita
Electric Power	Octavian Victor Groza
Finance	Florea Dumitrescu
Foreign Affairs	Corneliu Manescu
Foreign Trade	Cornel Burtica
Forestry Administration and Construction Materials	Vasile Patilinet
Health	Dan Enachescu
Industrial Construction	Matei Ghigiu
Interior	Cornel Onescu
Internal Trade	Nicolae Bozdog
Justice	Teodor Vasiliu
Labor	Petre Lupu
Light Industry	Ion Craciun
Machine Building	Ion Avram
Metallurgy	Nicolae Agachi
Mines, Oil, and Geology	Bujor Almasan
Technical-Material Supply and Control of Fixed Assets	Mihai Marinescu
Tourism	Ion Cosma
Transport and Telecommunications	Florian Danalache

First Secretary (with rank of Minister for Youth Problems), Communist Youth Organization	Martian Dan
Chairman, Council on State Security	Ion Stanescu
Chairman (ministerial rank), General Confederation of Trade Unions Central Council	Virgil Trofin
Chairman, National Council on Scientific Research and Technology	Gheorghe Cioara
Chairman (ministerial rank), National Union of Agricultural Producers' Co-operatives	Gheorghe Petrescu

Chairman, State Committee on the Economy and Local Administration	Petre Blajovici*
Chairman, State Committee on Planning	Maxim Berghianu
Chairman, State Committee on Prices	Gheorghe Gaston-Marin
<u>Under Jurisdiction of State Council</u>	
Chairman, Economic Council:	Manea Manescu
Chairman, National Defense Council:	Nicolae Ceausescu
Chairman, State Committee on Nuclear Energy:	Ion Ursu
<u>Under Direct Control of Central Committee</u>	
Chairman, Council on Socialist Culture and Education:	Dumitru Popescu
Chairman, National Council on Romanian State Radio and Television Networks:	Dumitru Popescu

All top governmental officials listed above are members of the RCP Central Committee; in addition, Ceausescu, Bodnaras, Manescu, Maurer, Verdet, Radulescu, and Trofin were on the Presidium in 1972; Ceausescu, Banc, Burtica, and Popescu were current members of the RCP Secretariat, while Manescu, Verdet, Rautu and Patilinet had held Secretariat positions during the 1960s. In addition to the personnel mentioned above, Vilcu, Voitec, Draganescu, Fazekas, Patan, Ionita, Lupu, Cioara, Blajovici, and Berghianu were members of the RCP Executive Committee (the personnel occupying seats in the Presidium and the Secretariat were also members of the Executive Committee).

Thus, of 54 government positions listed fully 26 were occupied by persons in the very top Party bodies, and this overlap was conspicuous in the most important government departments. Overlapping membership at the top of the Party and government pyramids is therefore important in Romania.

Late in 1972 and throughout 1973 important organizational changes took place in the government apparatus.

---

*Later removed.

The Council of Ministers was somewhat revamped, in that Virgil Trofin was released from his position on the RCP Secretariat and became a vice-chairman on the Council; Manea Manescu was transferred from the State Council to the Council of Ministers; Trofin and Manescu were also given specific governmental jobs (Trofin became minister of Internal Trade, while Manescu was made chairman of the State Planning Committee, giving up his position as vice-chairman of the State Council). Manescu relieved Maxim Berghianu at the State Planning Committee; Berghianu was moved to the Ministry of Technical-Material Supply and Control of Fixed Assets. Emil Draganescu, already a vice-chairman on the Council of Ministers, in addition took on the Ministry of Transport and Telecommunications. Trofin was replaced in the Trade Unions by Mihai Dalea, while Florian Danalache, who had yielded the Ministry of Transport and Telecommunications to Emil Draganescu, in turn became chairman of the Union of Handicraft Cooperatives. (Its former head, Ilie Alexei, was replaced without being given another assignment.) Miron Constantinescu took over as chairman on the Economic Council, and Paul Niculescu-Mizil, already on the RCP Presidium and the Council of Ministers, also became minister of Education.[17] In addition, Petre Blajovici has been released as chairman of the State Committee on Local Economy and Administration; his successor was not immediately named.[18]

The numerous personnel changes at the top of the governmental hierarchy have had an unsettling effect on this apparatus but have in no way reduced Party control over the state administration. In most cases the reorganization represents a reshuffling of personnel whose positions in the Party are well established, and Ceausescu's personal control over both Party and state bodies was never questioned. Indeed, one may argue that the reorganization underway has enhanced his personal power. No matter what views one may have on these recent organizational changes, the ability of the RCP to control the state administration and to harness it for its mobilization program remains essentially intact, perhaps enhanced. This is certainly a factor of major importance in contemporary Romanian politics.

THE UNION OF COMMUNIST YOUTH (UTC)

The UTC has grown from a modest beginning of 7,800 members in 1922 to a total of 2,400,000 in 1973. This structure has undergone numerous reorganizations and was disbanded between 1939 and 1944. From August 1944, when the Antonescu regime was overthrown, until early 1946 the UTC was part of a large coalition consisting of the UTC, the UTS (Uniunea Tineretului Socialist), The Union of Patriots (Uniunea Patriotilor), the Ploughmen's Front (Frontul Plugarilor), the Hungarian People's Union (Uniunea Populara Maghiara), ARLUS (The Patriots' Union), National-Liberal Youth (Tineretul National-Liberal [Tatarascu]), and National-Peasant Youth (Tineretul National-Taranescu [Anton Alexandrescu]).[19] This coalition was designed to represent all "progressive" youth in the country, and the Communist subgroup, although important, did not play a dominant role in this progressive front.

By mid-1946 it was becoming clear that the RCP, in conformity with developments elsewhere in Eastern Europe, was on the verge of a massive political offensive designed to increase its power at the expense of its partners in the coalition government of Petru Groza. This Communist offensive was mirrored in the youth movement as well; the UTC was formally reestablished in February of that year, under the name Uniunea Tineretul Muncitoresc (UTM), The Union of Working Youth, with the express purpose of providing a revolutionary organ for the completion of the political revolution in the country. By 1947, the Communist youth organization had grown considerably in size and influence, and by 1948 its competitors on the left, especially the Socialist group UTS (Uniunea Tineretului Socialist) had been brought under control. This consolidation of Communist control over the youth movement closely paralleled the development in the so-called progressive coalition, which was dismantled in early 1948 in favor of a pure Communist government.[20]

Since 1948 the UTC has been the only legal political youth organization in the country. It is now a massive structure, with more than 75,000 branches throughout the country.[21] It is well represented in the major industries and in the armed forces, but a considerable problem exists in the countryside, parts of which are only weakly covered by both the Party and the UTC. On the other hand, key youth groups such as students and pupils in technical schools are subjected to much more forceful organizational efforts by the UTC and its sister organization, the Union of Students' Associations of Romania (UASR). The close coordination of the UTC and the UASR can be clearly seen in the formal constitution of the latter, which states

> The Union of Students' Associations of Romania is the single, representative,

> political and professional organization of university youth, inspired by the noble ideals of socialism and communism.
>
> The Union of Students' Associations of Romania is an integrant [sic] part of the Union of Communist Youth--the revolutionary organization of our homeland's entire youth. The Union of Students' Associations of Romania, in full unity with the younger generation of the homeland, stands for the implementation of the policy of the Romanian Communist Party, the leading political force in the Socialist Republic Romania.[22]

Correspondingly, an important section in the UTC constitution specifies that

> the Students' associations are the specific form of organizing the activity of the Union of Communist Youth in higher educational institutes. The associations share their contribution to professionally training and rearing the university youth in a communist spirit, they organize cultural--art, sports, tourist activities and drilling in defence of the homeland, they see to solving the students' socio-administrative problems, actively participate within professors' councils and university senates in steadily perfecting the instruction-educational process.
>
> The Union of Students' Associations in Romania is an integrant [sic] part of the Union of Communist Youth and has its own Rules. The Council of the Union of Students' Associations in Romania carries on its activity under the guidance of the Central Committee of the Union of Communist Youth.[23]

Both organizations recognize that the RCP is the leading political and socioeconomic force in society, and therefore pledge their allegiance to, and cooperation with, the Communist Party:

> The Union of Communist Youth is the main reserve of the Romanian Communist Party, its helpful companion in educating the

> youth in the spirit of communism, in mobilizing them in the struggle of the entire people for building the socialist multilaterally developed society, for fulfilling the Party's fundamental goal--the building up of the communist society. The Union of Communist Youth carries on its entire activity under the leadership of the Romanian Communist Party.[24]
>
> The Union of Students' Associations of Romania carries on its entire activity under the leadership of the Romanian Communist Party.[25]

Furthermore, the UTC maintains special branches in the armed forces and has supervision of the Pioneers, a political organization for the youngest generation. This close collaboration is further enhanced by the fact that the top personnel of both organizations are important members of the RCP and hold high positions in the Party. Thus, Ion Iliescu, secretary-general of the UTC from 1967 to 1971, is a member of the Executive Committee of the RCP Central Committee and has also had the position of party secretary in charge of youth matters.[26] Similarly, Traian Stefanescu, head of the Students' Union, was promoted to full membership in the Central Committee in 1972. Stefanescu is now the secretary-general of the UTC, another testimonial to the close coordination between the organization and the RCP.[27]

THE TRADE UNIONS

Stalin once characterized the Soviet trade unions as "transmission belts" carrying orders and directives from the political leadership to the organized working class, while carrying implementation and production back. This function, so drastically different from the tasks of representation taken for granted in the West, is also the main task for contemporary Romanian trade unions. In a centralized economy virtually all workers are organized in trade unions; this complete coverage provides the unions with a unique penetration effect for the largest single occupational group of citizens--industrial workers. Workers in state farms are also organized in professional groups, while the collective farmers are reached through other structures. Artisans and small independent service personnel are formed into cooperatives with a trade union structure.

Romanian trade unions are structurally similar to their counterparts elsewhere; there is a hierarchy of functionally specialized unions, which are horizontally coordinated in regional councils and a General Council at the national level. The General Council is staffed by high RCP officials. In the mid-1960s the head of the Uniunea Generala a Sindicatelor (UGSR) was Florian Danalache, an old RCP apparatchik. Upon the dismissal of Danalache the position fell to Virgil Trofin, whose Party career was discussed above. The unexpected dismissal of Trofin from the post of general secretary of the UGSR in 1972 ushered in another prominent RCP leader, Mihai Dalea, as trade union boss.

The present leadership of the UGSR[28] is as follows:

Chairman:	Mihai Dalea
Main Vice-Chairmen:	Gheorghe Petrescu
	Oliviu Russu
Secretaries:	Larisa Munteanu
	Stefan Pavel
	Paul Nagy
	Constantin Mindreanu

Dalea is an old apparatchik who was RCP Central Committee secretary in 1954-55, and 1960-69; he is currently on the RCP Executive Committee. Petrescu is an alternate member of the RCP Central Committee (he was a full member in 1965-69). Russu, on the other hand, does not have membership on the Party Central Committee but heads the Scientific Association of Engineers and Technicians, an organization that is closely supervised by the RCP. Munteanu's career is essentially within various trade union structures, and she apparently is not on any top Party body. Pavel has had full RCP Central Committee memship since 1969, while Nagy became an alternate member of that Party body; the latter now apparently heads a Central Committee section. There is virtually no biographical information on Mindreanu.

The members of UGSR leading organs represent some of the most important functional unions in the country. While Dalea is a Party apparatchik, Petrescu started his career in the Union of People's Councils and Communal Administration Workers, an important group in a socialist state, with its centralized control of economic and administrative activity. Russu is an engineer and thus envisioned as a representative of the technical intelligentsia. Munteanu's career was in the Consumer Goods Workers' Union and also in the Textile, Clothing and Leather Workers' Union. In this "balance concept" of representation in the UGSR Munteanu presumably represents the consumer goods industry and also the sizable female labor force in Romania. Nagy's profession falls within the literary intelligentsia (he was head of the Tirgu Mures branch of the Writers' Union). Mindreanu's career is not known, but he is chairman of the UGSR Council for Political, Cultural and Educational Mass Activity. This is an important function indeed, and it seems likely that a trusted Party apparatchik would be put in charge of this vital section.

The only individual on the UGSR Secretariat whose main career has not been in the trade unions or the Party is Stefan Pavel. Pavel was Minister of Forestry, then Minister of Internal Affairs (1952). Subsequently he became Deputy Minister of the Armed Forces and then headed a regional People's Council (in Bucharest). After demotion for "opportunism," he reappeared in governmental activity (deputy minister of Road, Marine and Air Transport, 1966, then minister of Transportation, 1964, and finally in 1971, head of the Ministry's section on Road, Marine and Air Transportation). He became a secretary in the UGSR in March 1971.

Pavel's many-sided career is hard to classify, and it is not clear what kind of group he is presumed to represent; his extensive governmental career may indicate that his function on the UGSR is representation of and supervision over the vast state administration personnel of Romanian labor.

The close coordination between the trade unions and the RCP is further strengthened by the membership of many workers and most trade union officials at all levels in the Communist Party. Furthermore, the Party cells in factories and other economic production establishments exercise close control over all union matters, as do the local and regional "People's Councils," representative structures closely controlled by the RCP. All in all, the trade unions are a major organizational outgrowth of the Party, the influence of which extends beyond the formal parameters of the RCP. During the last few years the unions have been invested with new tasks, such as the supervision of the actual production process, in a clear move by Ceausescu to reduce the power of the technical intelligentsia and the production managers. Add to those powers the trade union functions of supervision of bonus distribution, pension funds, vacation assignments, housing, recreational facilities, and child care centers, and a picture emerges of an organizational apparatus with considerable political, economic, and social power, which combine to make the trade unions one of the most formidable mobilization agents available to the Commumist Party.

THE SOCIALIST UNITY FRONT

In addition to the mass organizations discussed above, numerous other structures are directly controlled by the Communist Party (such as women's groups, Pioneers, and various nationality organizations). Even those groups that are not directly controlled by the RCP are members of the overarching Socialist Unity Front (Frontul Unitar Socialist--FUS) formally established in the late 1960s. The FUS is an umbrella organization that incorporates virtually all political, social, cultural, and economic organizations in the country, including the RCP, the UTC, and the trade unions.

The FUS leadership is closely controlled by the Party, both through overlapping membership at the top and through various control mechanisms, chief of which are Party discipline for those FUS members who are also enrolled in the RCP, and Party cells within virtually all organizations affiliated with the FUS. Nicolae Ceausescu is chairman of the FUS. Other prominent Party figures in the FUS hierarchy include Florian Danalache (member of the FUS Executive Bureau); Janos Fazekas (also on the FUS Executive Bureau); Mihai Gere (secretary of FUS Central Council); Ion Gheorghe Maurer (vice-president of the FUS); Paul Niculescu-Mizil, Gheorghe Stoica, Virgil Trofin, Vasile Vilcu, and Stefan Voitec (all members of the FUS Executive Bureau). Virtually all members of the RCP Central Committee are members of the FUS National Council, and all regional (Judet) RECP first secretaries either head the regional FUS branch or are members of the respective executive bureaus. There is thus little doubt that the Party has penetrated this mass organization, and FUS activity from the start has been completely coordinated with the Party's policies.[29]

THE GRAND NATIONAL ASSEMBLY, PEOPLE'S COUNCILS, AND OTHER ELECTIVE BODIES

The Romanian political system maintains a strict formal separation of administrative, executive, and elective functions, with the Communist Party formally occupying a different position as the only legal party and the "leading force" of society. These elective bodies are the so-called People's Councils at the local and regional levels and the Grand National Assembly (Marea Adunarea Nationala) at the national level. Both the Grand National Assembly (GNA) and the People's Councils are designed to represent the broad masses of the population, not just the Party, and there is considerable non-Party representation in these structures. The leading organs of the elective bodies are nevertheless strongly penetrated by Party personnel, as evidenced by the following breakdown of the top GNA organs:

Chairman	Stefan Voitec
Deputy Chairmen:	Maria Groza
	Gyoergy Kovacs
	Ilie Murgulescu
	Gheorghe Necula

Of the GNA leadership Stefan Voitec is on the RCP Executive Committee and Gyorgy Kovacs, Ilie Murgulescu, and Gheorghe Necula are full members of the RCP Central Committee. (Necula also has considerable government experience.) Maria Groza apparently is not on the Central Committee.[30]

Further evidence of RCP penetration of the elective bodies is the fact that virtually all major Party leaders are also deputies in the GNA; of the 41 top RCP personnel discussed earlier in this chapter only Stefan Andrei, Constantin Babalau, Cornel Burtica, Gheorghe Cioara, Miron Constantinescu, and Ion Patan were not members of the national legislature. In addition, virtually every regional first Party secretary was also a GNA deputy.[31]

Party control over the People's Councils is as tight as the supervision of the GNA. Of the 41 top leaders examined, Cioara, Dobrescu, Dragan, Telescu, Uglar, Vilcu, and Winter are chairmen of the Bucharest, Suceava, Brasov, Timis, Satu Mare, Constanta, and Sibiu County People's Councils; all other regional first Party secretaries have the same position in their respective People's Councils. The RCP Central Committee plenum, June 18-19, 1973, also established two coordinating bodies that will further strengthen the role of the Party in the People's Councils. The first of these bodies is the Congress of Deputies to the People's Councils, which is to meet every five years. There will also be national conferences of Council chairmen in city and communal councils every four years and judet (county) conferences every two years.[32] Second, a committee designed to handle problems of the People's Councils was established by the plenum and promulgated by the GNA almost immediately. The new committee includes the chairmen of the Executive Committees of all County People's Councils (all of whom are prominent Party leaders); some important municipalities, planning offices, and mass organizations will have representatives on the committee. All appointments are to be approved by the RCP Central Committee, the Council of Ministers, and the State Council. (As shown above, all these central bodies are controlled by the Communist Party.)

These new organizational measures will undoubtedly expand RCP control over the People's Councils and make them better suited for the task of carrying out Party policies at the local and county levels. Nicolae Ceausescu indeed foresees an expanded role for the People's Councils in the modernization process, and it was therefore logical that Party control of these structures would be expanded.

PARTY DIFFICULTIES IN ORGANIZATIONAL MATTERS

The evidence presented above shows an impressive organizational coordination of major mass organizations, governmental structures, elective bodies, and umbrella organizations with the Communist Party. The Party maintains clear control over all these structures and can therefore harness them for the fulfillment of the ambitious modernization plans discussed in the preceding chapter. A mere reading of the organizational synchronization discussed in this chapter would surely yield a clear impression of the Party juggernaut harnessing the multitude of organizations in a modernizing society for the execution of its will through monolithic decision making and unquestioning administration. Modern scholarship on Communist systems has shown that decision making and execution do not follow such neat, clear-cut lines but instead somewhat resemble the complexities of Western, pluralistic processes.[33] There are numerous reasons for this lack of actual performance; scholars have pinpointed such diverse factors as institutional conflict, bureaucratic delays, "strata animosity," individual incompetence or sabotage, or simply general inefficiency.[34] All of these factors will be discussed in due course, but at this point the examination will turn to another factor especially germane to the previous examination of organizational synchronization--the problems associated with frequent organizational changes in Romanian society during the last few years. The organizational instability within the Party itself has produced considerable uncertainty among the very cadres who were presumably in charge of supervision with socioeconomic and lower level political organs. It seems likely that continuation of these reorganizations will ultimately have a detrimental effect on the Party's ability to fulfill its own ambitious modernization plans.

The current personnel changes in the RCP started in February 1972, with the removal of Vasile Patilinet, who was tied to the conviction of General Ion Serb for spying "for a foreign power" (it was made clear in Bucharest that that power was the Soviet Union).[35] In April, Ilie Fasui, first party secretary in Caras-Severin County (judet) was dismissed from his position in the judet, and he also lost his position on the Central Committee. Karol Kiraly, first party secretary in Covasna Judet, was released from his duties, ostensibly at his own request. Dimitru Popa, a secretary in the Bucharest Party Committee, was sharply criticized and removed. Gheorghe Cioara became head of the Bucharest Party branch and was also promoted to the RCP Executive Committee.[36]

Patilinet's replacement in the Secretariat was Cornel Burtica, a newcomer to the top bodies of the RCP.[37] Since Burtica was inexperienced in Party matters, he probably did not take over Patilinet's functions involving internal security but rather assumed more general tasks in this august body. That Burtica's appointment did not solve the general secretary's problems in the security and mass supervisions fields was further confirmed by the removal of Miu Dobrescu, who had headed the Central Committee Propaganda Section from 1971 to late 1972. Dobrescu's replacement was Aurel Duca.[38]

In October Manea Manescu was replaced as secretary by Miron Constantinescu. Manescu maintained his position on the Party Presidium, however, and also became head of the powerful State Planning Committee. Constantinescu, an old Party leader with considerable expertise in economics, made a comback at the top after several years in the political wilderness during the 1960s.[39]

During the summer of 1973 two members of the Secretariat, Iosif Banc and Ion Dinca, were removed from their positions and made first Party secretaries in Mures and Arges counties respectively.[40] Ion Coman, a colonel-general, was promoted to chief of the Central Committee Section for Military Affairs in May, 1973.[41]

Further changes in the top bodies of the RCP took place in June 1973. Elena Ceausescu and Lina Ciobanu were promoted to full membership on the Executive Committee, and Magdalena Filipas and Aurelia Danila* to alternate membership in this body.[42] Furthermore, Aurel Duca lost his position as alternate member of the Executive Committee.[43]

The many personnel changes in the top Party bodies involve transfer of members of the Secretariat to county Party positions (Banc, Dinca); transfer of secretaries to important government posts (Manescu) and to less important positions (Trofin, Niculescu-Mizil). Duca apparently is slated for an ambassadorial post. At the same time, several section chiefs in the Central Committee have been replaced, and other personnel changes below the top level of this apparat probably have taken place. The principle of "rotation of cadres" is officially invoked to justify this procedure, but it seems likely that such constant reshuffling increases Ceausescu's personal power, while creating considerable problems with execution of Party policy in several fields.

Institutional reshuffling is magnified in the state administration. (Some of the most important personnel changes here have been noted in Chapter 2. But the personnel changes are of much larger magnitude.) Especially in the Ministry of the Interior and the Ministry of Justice, frequent changes have taken place at the top and intermediate levels. There is a purge in the military. All these institutions, as well as virtually all other ministries and agencies, state committees, and planning bodies, are also experiencing massive transfer of personnel from administrative posts to production jobs "in the

---

*Elena Ceausescu is the general secretary's wife, whose earlier career was primarily in the youth organization; Lina Ciobanu is an apparatchik in a Party district of Bucharest; Magdalena Filipas a trade union official in the Light Industry Unions; and Aurealia Danila an activist in the Cluj Judet women's organization. (See Radio Free Europe Research, Rumania 18, 29 June 1973.)

field." This dramatic reshuffling has clearly reduced the political power of the state apparatus; but it has also lessened efficiency in many areas, thus possibly producing major difficulties for continued socioeconomic modernization. Seen against this backdrop of institutional change, the impressive organizational control established by the Party appears less formidable as a vehicle for mobilization and modernization.

CREATION OF NEW PARTY-STATE BODIES

The problems of bureaucratic centralization and sluggishness, on the one hand, and incessant institutional reshuffling, on the other, have created increased needs for coordinating bodies that can bring together Party and state personnel associated with modernization plans and procedures. A number of such bodies have been created recently in Romania. First, the general secretary in his speech to the RCP National Conference, July 1972, proposed the establishment of three central, coordinating bodies, closer cooperation between county Party bodies and the respective People's Councils, and new structures for coordination and cooperation at the local levels.[44] In conformity with this proposal, the Supreme Council for Socio-Economic Development, the Council on Economic and Social Organization, and the Financial Control Court were established during 1973.

The Supreme Council for Socio-Economic Development consists of approximately 250 members, nominated by trade unions, scientific organizations, elective bodies, ministries, and the RCP Central Committee. The Supreme Council has a chairman, who is the president of the State Council, Nicolae Ceausescu; and there is a first vice-chairman, several chairmen, and secretaries of various sections. The numerous specialized sections deal with important socioeconomic matters such as raw materials, energy, specific industries, science and technology, education, research, and many other fields.

The composition of the Supreme Council is as follows:[45]

Chairman:	Nicolae Ceausescu
First Vice-Chairman:	Ion Gheorghe Maurer
Vice-Chairmen:	Ilie Verdet
	Manea Manescu
	Gheorghe Cioara
	Iosif Uglar
	Gheorghe Oprea

Secretary-General (of the Supreme Council):	Emilian Dobrescu
Section Chairmen:	
Raw Materials, Fuel and Power	Maxim Berghianu
Metallurgical Industry and Machine Building	Gheorghe Oprea
Chemical Industry	Miron Constantinescu
Construction, Building Materials, and Forestry	Janos Fazekas
Consumer Goods	Leonte Rautu
Agriculture, Food Industry, and Water Management	Gheorghe Pana
Transportation and Telecommunications	Emil Draganescu
Foreign Economic Relations and International Cooperation	Ion Patan
Science, Technology, and Environmental Protection	Ioan Ursu
Standard of Living, Internal Trade, and Tourism	Virgil Trofin
Demography, and Labor Force, Social and Health Problems	Emil Bodnaras
Education and Culture	Paul Niculescu-Mizil
Regional Planning, Economic and Social Development	Gheorghe Cioara
Finances	Gheorghe Radulescu
National Defense	Ion Ionita

The Supreme Council is made up of familiar names; all but Gheorghe Oprea, Emilian Dobrescu, and Ioan Ursu are members or candidate members of the RCP Executive Committee, with all members of the Permanent Presidium and several Party secretaries represented as well. Given the overlap of Party and government posts at the top, the Council of Ministers is also well represented on the Supreme Council. Even the three men who do not belong at the very top of the RCP have impressive credentials. Gheorghe Oprea is counselor to Ceausescu in the latter's capacity as president of the State Council. Oprea was listed as a candidate member of the RCP Central Committee in 1969.[46] Emilian Dobrescu is a first vice-chairman of the State Planning Committee; he was also listed as a candidate member in the Central Committee at the Tenth Party Congress in 1969;[47] Ion Ursu is chairman of the National Council on Scientific Research and Technology and full member of the Central Committee in 1969.[48]

The Supreme Council is charged with the task of economic planning for the economy as a whole and coordination of economic activities in all important sectors. It is to report to leading Party and governmental bodies. The law establishing the Supreme Council envisions it as one of the chief vehicles of modernization and development, which can cut through the bureaucratic problems of centralized administration, thus speeding up the decision-making process and helping with the quick identification of major problem areas in socioeconomic and political development. The extremely strong representation of top Party personnel is an indication of the Supreme Council's projected importance. Since it has been in operation for only a few months, it is a little hard to assess its functioning.

The Council on Economic and Social Organization is composed of the following cadres:

Chairman:	Gheorghe Pana
First Vice-Chairman:	Petre Lupu
Vice-Chairman:	Ion Romanu
Secretary-General:	Aurel Ionica

The full membership is 45.[49]

Of the permanent staff of this body, Pana and Lupu are top RCP leaders, whose careers have been discussed above. Ion Romanu is a counselor to the RCP Central Committee. He was listed as a candidate member in that Party body in 1969.[50] Aurel Ionica, a deputy director-general in the Ministry of Foreign Trade, was not among the full or candidate members listed at the end of the Tenth RCP Congress in August, 1969.

The Council on Economic and Social Organization was established to improve the administrative functions of both Party and state bodies, to find ways to streamline organization, and also to reduce the administrative "overhead" in the centralized system that clearly prevails in Romania. The tasks of this council are therefore geared more toward political and administrative matters, whereas the Supreme Council for Socio-Economic Development is primarily concerned with economic modernization. The specialized sections of the Council on Economic and Social Organization deal with organization of economic activity, organization of sociocultural activity, and organizational coordination. The Council is advisory to the top Party bodies but can give compulsory recommendations to the state structures.[51]

The Financial Control Court is designed to check on public expenditures and investigate the use of funds by state bodies as well as by the GNA and the People's Councils.

The personnel of this court includes representatives from various governmental agencies such as the Legislative Council, the Supreme Court, the UGSR (trade unions), and the Central Bank. The personnel staffing the positions of chairman, secretary-general, heads of sections, and "Juristic Collegium" have not yet been formally announced, but it is highly likely that direct Party representation from top RCP bodies will be important here.

In addition to these new structures, the Economic Council, formerly a state body, has been reorganized as a joint Party-state organization and renamed the Workers' Central Control Council of Socio-Economic Activities. Its head is Miron Constantinescu, a member of the Party Secretariat and the RCP Executive Committee. This body seems to have functions that overlap with both of the new councils.

The reorganization of some institutions and establishment of others have transferred considerable power over socioeconomic modernization from state functions to that of joint groups controlled by the Party. There is little doubt that these organizational measures have appreciably strengthened the power of the RCP to control the modernization process in Romania.

New political bodies were also established at the regional and local levels during 1972 and 1973. First, secretaries in county Party organizations were to be appointed vice-chairmen of the People's Councils. (The first Party secretary in each county is already chairman of the Regional Council.)[52] This was done in order to coordinate planning and economic activity as well as political education among the masses. In addition, so-called "Workers' Control Councils" were established by the RCP National Conference in July 1972. These councils were to be staffed by qualified workers, engineers, technicians, and other specialists for the purpose of promoting increased participation in productive life, as well as exercising added control over existing bodies (especially management and the trade unions).[53] The control councils are under the direct supervision of the local Party organization and thus represent yet another vehicle for mobilization and control.

CONCLUSION

The constant reshuffling of personnel and structural reorganization in already existing structures, the expansion of Party control over all existing socioeconomic bodies in the state administration, and the establishment of numerous new councils and other administrative organs with joint Party-state jurisdiction represent Nicolae Ceausescu's most recent attempt to get at the intractable problems of modernization. In the early stages of modernization, centralization of decision making and a dose of coercion were necessary ingredients. As society developed and the economy became more complex, with resulting stratification of the social system, centralization became detrimental to continued rapid development. A decentralization of socioeconomic and political organization was inaugurated (in 1967 in the economy), but the trend during the last five to six years has been toward recentralization. The resulting bureaucratized system is once again under attack, especially through the transfer of administrative personnel to production jobs.

The Party's power is also being expanded to ensure greater control of the myriads of interactions in the increasingly sophisticated economic and social systems. The establishment of joint bodies, designed to supervise further development, is a bold attempt to cut through the "parallelism" and sluggishness of entrenched bureaucracies, but the establishment of new supervisory bodies will not necessarily do away with bureaucratism. Instead, new bodies with jurisdictions that frequently overlap with areas already covered by others could lead to insecurity, confusion, lack of initiative, and ultimately dissent.

This is the dilemma now facing the entire modernizing elite of Romania. In many ways, it seems that the country stands before an important crossroad, where the paths of continued strict political control and further socioeconomic development take off in somewhat different directions. It is the very success of socioeconomic modernization in Romania that has brought about this dilemma. It therefore seems appropriate to examine the methods employed in propelling the country to its present stage, as well as the approaches designed for the future in this field. The following six chapters will deal with these methods of modernization.

NOTES

1. Ghita Ionescu, Communism in Rumania (London: Oxford University Press, 1964), p. 319.

2. This reorganization was reported in the RCP press throughout the spring and summer of 1973, for example, in Scinteia, March 23, 1973.

3. Yearbook on International Communist Affairs, 1968 (Stanford, California: Hoover Institution Press, 1969), p. 308.

4. Ibid.

5. 1970 Yearbook on International Communist Affairs (Stanford, California: Hoover Institution Press, 1971), p. 75.

6. Ionescu, op. cit., p. 243.

7. Congresul al IX-lea al Partidului Comunist Roman (Bucharest: Editura Politica, 1966), p. 72.

8. Scinteia, August 7, 1969.

9. Congresul al IX-lea, p. 72.

10. Scinteia, July 20, 1972, and June 22, 1973.

11. Elena Ceausescu was promoted to the RCP Executive Committee in 1973; for a discussion see Robert R. King, "Unresolved Questions Concerning Personnel Changes in the Rumanian Party Leadership," in Radio Free Europe Research, Rumania/8, 29 June 1973.

12. The raw information on the top RCP leadership is taken from Radio Free Europe Research, Rumania/4, 30 March 1973 (Introduction by Robert R. King, charts and individual chronologies by Unity Evans).

13. These changes were reported in Scinteia, May 16 and 19, 1973.

14. See Radio Free Europe Research, 29 June 1973.

15. For a discussion of "cooptation," see Frederic Fleron, "Representations of Career Types in Soviet Political Leadership," in Political Leadership in Eastern Europe and the Soviet Union, ed. R. Barry Farrell (Chicago: Aldine Publishing Co., 1970), pp. 108-40.

16. Source: Radio Free Europe Research, "Communist Party-Government Line-up" (March-April 1972).

17. Changes reported by Agerpres, October 11, 1972.

18. Radio Bucharest, April 21, 1973.

19. C. Barbulescu et al., File Din Istoria U.T.C. (Bucharest: Editura Politica, 1971), pp. 225-81.

20. Ionescu, op. cit., pp. 147-97.

21. Report by Ion Iliescu, then general secretary of the UTC, to the UTC Ninth Congress (1971) in Romania's Youth, 1971, p. 26.

22. Ibid. (Supplement).

23. Ibid.

24. Ibid.

25. Ibid.

26. Radio Free Europe Research, 30 March 1973, p. 56.

27. The promotion of Stefanescu took place at the RCP National Party Conference, July 1972, as reported in Scinteia, July 22, 1972.

28. The information on the UGSR Leadership is gleaned from a number of sources during 1972 and 1973, chief of which are Munca (Chief organ of the UGSR); Scinteia, and Radio Free Europe Research.

29. Information on leadership positions from Radio Free Europe Research, 30 March 1973.

30. Ibid., March-April 1972.

31. See my "Regional Political Leadership in Romania: The Case of the Judet Party, 1968-1973," East European Quarterly (January 1975).

32. Reported in Scinteia, June 22, 1973.

33. For example, Richard Cornell, ed., The Soviet Political System: A Book of Readings (Englewood Cliffs, N.J.: Prentice-Hall, 1970).

34. See, for example, William Taubman, Governing Soviet Cities: Bureaucratic Politics and Urban Development in the USSR (New York: Praeger Publishers, 1973).

35. For a discussion of this development see Trond Gilberg, "Ceausescus Kleine Kulturrevolution" in Osteuropa, October 1972, pp. 717-28.

36. Ibid.

37. Burtica's appointment was announced by Radio Bucharest, February 16, 1972.

38. Duca was also fired from this position. See Scinteia, June 22, 1973.

39. Agerpres, October 11 and 17, 1972.

40. Scinteia, May 16 and 19, 1973.

41. Coman's appointment was confirmed by the RCP Central Committee Plenum, June 18-19, 1973 (Scinteia, June 22, 1973).

42. Ibid.

43. Ibid.

44. Scinteia, July 20, 1972.

45. Ibid., May 17, 1973.

46. Congresul al X-lea al Partidului Comunist Roman (Bucharest: Editura Politica, 1969), p. 755.

47. Ibid.

48. Ibid.

49. The personnel on this body was revealed throughout May 1973. See, for example, _Scinteia_, May 17, 1973.

50. _Congresul al X-lea_, p. 755.

51. The guidelines for this body's activity were established at the RCP Central Committee Plenum, February 28-March 2, 1973, published in _Scinteia_, March 8, 1973.

52. See Ceausescu's detailed speech on those bodies, in _Scinteia_, July 20, 1972.

53. Ibid.

CHAPTER

3

DECISION MAKING FOR MODERNIZATION

The impressive machinery of the RCP and state bureaucracies, described in the preceding chapter, is geared to rapid socioeconomic and political modernization through constant involvement in the creation and implementation of policies designed to produce such societal change. The RCP and state apparats are fundamentally involved in all crucial steps in this process, such as decision making, planning, investments, budgeting, supervision of the implementation at all levels, and also in meting out sanctions for faulty performance. This chapter will deal with these processes of decision making.

INTERNAL DECISION-MAKING PROCEDURES

Decision making for socioeconomic modernization in a centralized Communist economy is to a large extent a political process. The Communist Party will set the broad parameters of the economic plans, will supervise the actual planning performed in the economic ministries, planning agencies, and in plants and on collective farms; and, in the end, Party-controlled bodies will supervise actual production. The Communist Party is clearly a crucial part of the economic decision-making process in Romania, as specified by the RCP "Directive of the Ninth RCP Congress Concerning the Socio-economic Development Plan for Romania in the Years 1971-1975 and Guidelines for the Development for the Period 1976-1980." The latest (Tenth) RCP Congress in August 1969 stated:

> During the last four years, the creative energy and efforts of our people have been

> directed by the implementation of the great program established by the Ninth Congress of the Romanian Communist Party for the Development of the productive forces, perfectioning of socialist relations, of the entire social and economic life of the country.
>
> The balance sheet of completion in the period 1966-1968 shows that the five year plan established on the basis of the Congress directives and including its superior foresight--is completed with success, [in which] great performance was achieved in all sectors of activity.[1]

The Tenth Congress directives go on to specify in great detail the main direction of the 1971-75 five-year plan in all fields of economic activity.[2] This general commitment was further amplified by the fact that the detailed five-year plan (promulgated in 1970 and ratified by the Grand National Assembly, thus becoming formal law) as well as each yearly subplan was first thoroughly debated in various Party bodies before formalization.

On this basis, it is clear that internal decision-making procedures in the RCP are important in the modernization process. A myriad of factors clearly interact to produce decisions within the Party, and any attempt to describe this complicated interaction will of necessity fall short of completeness. The main steps in the procedures are nevertheless fairly clear and permit rather rigorous analysis.

The Goal-setting Process

The major social and economic goals clearly originate in the top RCP leadership. During the first five to six years of Communist domination in Romania, the so-called "Muscovites" around Vasile Luca and Ana Pauker closely followed the Soviet model of modernization, which emphasized forced industrialization and collectivization of agriculture. The initiatives for decision making were therefore largely a product of Soviet control and perceptions, and much of the information necessary for planning and implementation was transmitted to the RCP leaders through inter-Party channels, through the Soviet ambassador, and by means of the administrative structure of the notorious joint Soviet-Romanian companies, the so-called

Sovroms.[3] After the ouster of Pauker and Luca in 1952, the new leadership under Gheorghe Gheorghiu-Dej continued its close reliance on the Soviet model but with increasing signs of limited autonomy toward the end of the 1950s. By the early 1960s even the "Stalinist" Gheorghiu-Dej had opted for increased autonomy for Romania, both in foreign policy and in economic decision making. This semi-independent line has been continued and expanded by the present Party head, Nicolae Ceausescu. Contemporary economic decision making is thus a highly complex mix of specific national conditions in Romania and more general factors common to all of the command economies run by Communist parties. We shall here be concerned mainly with goal-setting in the "Nationalist" period, that is, from 1960 to 1973.

The economic goals are by and large preset by the leadership's commitment to rapid socioeconomic modernization and political development, as analyzed in Chapter 1. The formulation of the broad outlines of the five-year plan, as well as each yearly subplan, starts in the top RCP bodies--the Permanent Presidium, the Secretariat, the Executive Committee, and occasionally the Central Committee Plenum, as much as a year and a half before implementation is envisioned. The fairly detailed outline for each major sector of the economy is established. This process is facilitated by the presence among the top RCP leadership of several technical or economic experts, who can contribute much in terms of specialized knowledge at this stage. (See Chapter 2.) The Secretariat and the Central Committee apparats are also well staffed with knowledgeable personnel, whose counsel is often sought. In recent years the increasing personal power of Nicolae Ceausescu has produced a situation in which much of the early decision making consists of the general secretary's initiative.

In many cases, the consultative process at this stage involves discussions with key personnel from ministries and planning agencies. This interaction is facilitated by the close coordination of Party and state bodies and the overlapping of membership, especially in top positions. During the last few years a major drive toward "unification" of Party and state organs has created even stronger coordination at this level.*

---

*This drive became especially forceful after Ceausescu's speech at the 1972 RCP National Conference, published in Scinteia, July 20, 1972.

Major economic planning usually also involves the regional Party leadership, primarily the judet (county) first RCP secretaries, who are called upon to give reports on the productive capacity in their districts as well as to comment on suggestions from the rank and file and economic managers, trade union leaders, and other "responsible cadres" in their areas. The deliberations of these early planning sessions take place against the backdrop of fulfillment figures for the existing year plans, together with projections for sector fulfillment by the end of the planning period. Such evidence is naturally important in the planning for investment and execution on a sectoral basis.

After the draft "theses" on economic development have been established by the top Party bodies, a massive information campaign is started, in which the directives are thoroughly discussed in the general press and in more specialized media. The judet secretaries bring the proposals back to their regions and submit them to discussions at the grass-roots level; at this stage, trade unions, local Party branches, sections of the Socialist Unity Front, and a host of other groups are mobilized for discussion. At the national level large organizations, such as the trade union federation, discuss the draft. There is considerable input from ministries, planning bodies, and academic personnel.[4]

The "open discussion" stage is usually expanded by large meetings and congresses of specialist groups such as collective farm managers, industrial managers, technical experts, and trade union functionaries, to name but a few. Elements of the draft proposals pertaining to each group's specialty will receive further discussion at such meetings.[5]

This second stage, in which considerable input is fed back to the top political leaders, is followed by plenums of the RCP Central Committee, in which the specifics for each planning sector are set down. There are occasional major amendments to the original draft proposal, but most frequently changes pertain to specifics and questions of implementation, not to the basic allocations of funds and tasks. The final decision of the Central Committee is called a "decree" (hotarea), which is binding on Party bodies.* The decree is submitted to rather perfunctory

---

*A typical Central Committee meeting on July 7, 1972 debated a number of economic issues and passed a decree on the 1973 economic plan, which was sent to the Grand National Assembly for approval (Scinteia, July 8 and 9, 1972).

debate in the Romanian Parliament, the Grand National Assembly (GNA). After passage here the decree becomes law, binding on all agencies, Party or state, as well as individual citizens.

An Alternative Process: The "Bubbling Up" Syndrome

Although the decision-making process sketched above seems to be the normal one, there are variations on this theme. One of the alternative processes is the so-called "bubbling up" syndrome, in which suggestions, recommendations, and demands start at the grass-roots level and filter through various bureaucratic layers to the top echelons of decision makers. In a socialist country like Romania such bubbling up is not a result of spontaneous public participation but primarily a carefully orchestrated outpouring of "citizen concern," which always falls well within the development parameters set by the political leadership. The initiative for such grass-roots participation therefore comes from the Party leadership. (Ceausescu has on numerous occasions made the claim that he is responding to "legitimate inputs" from the citizenry in economic decisions.)[6] Occasionally, grass-roots initiative will also come about because of factional strife; in this scenario a faction of the Party leadership will send up a trial balloon from the "working class" in a given judet or city in order to promote their own interests at the center. In either case, real grass-roots initiative seems to be lacking; rank and file activity in the planning process is primarily limited to reactions and responses to the plans already formulated at the center (as described above); in this field public reaction can lead to important modifications of implementation goals.*

In the bubbling up process grass-roots initiative can follow basically two paths to the top leadership. One would be the staged movement from the rank and file to the local Party or trade union organization to the RCP judet leadership and on to Bucharest. During Ceausescu's reign

---

*Some of the modifications of the 1971-75 five-year plan approved throughout 1973 came about as a result of "grass-roots initiative" to complete the five-year plan in five and a half years. This led to upward revisions of the plans, as shown in Scinteia, March 3 and 4, 1973.

such grass-roots input often by-passes intermediate stages entirely and reaches the general secretary directly, either through telegram campaigns sponsored by local groups or through direct interaction with the Party leader during one of his frequent visits to factories, schools, or farms. This direct pipeline provides Ceausescu with important information that can be used to offset the Party's growing reliance on technical and managerial expertise in the planning process. It also fits well with the general secretary's pronounced preferences for plebiscitarian rule, in which the disdained bureaucrats can be by-passed in a direct dialogue with the people.[7]

After the initial input from the rank and file, the decision-making process is rather similar to the stages outlined above. Central Party bodies debate the proposals, confer with experts in the requisite fields, and provide for a round of discussion at lower levels of the hierarchy. In the end the Central Committee issues a "decree," which becomes law after promulgation by the GNA.

A Second Alternative: The Expert Input

Although the grass-roots initiative is an important political device for Nicolae Ceausescu's political leadership, its practical value for actual decision making is quite limited. Of considerably greater importance is a variation of the bubbling up process, in which a sector of the technical or managerial intelligentsia will launch an initiative for the purpose of furthering certain goals. Because of the Party leadership's dependence on technical expertise, advice emanating from the intelligentsia cannot be lightly dismissed. In many cases, such trial balloons sent up by technical experts reflect the views of fairly well-established groups, whose membership crosscuts the functional-administrative distinctions between Party apparat, state administrators, academic personnel, and leaders of non-Party mass organizations. In some cases, such elite inputs result from the formation of less stable groupings of individuals whose views correspond on one or a few issues.[8] In either case, the expert inputs provide many opportunities for factional involvement on the part of the RCP apparatchik as well.

The initiative emanating from expert sources may travel the Party path from local bodies to regional or functional RCP groups and on to the center. A more likely route would be through the many "councils," which are joint Party-state bodies with informational and advisory functions in matters socioeconomic and political. The most important joint body in the field of socioeconomic modernization is the newly established Supreme Council for Socio-Economic Development, which is headed by Nicolae Ceausescu with ample representation of the top RCP bodies. The express function of the Supreme Council is to gather information from all available sources and to issue recommendations to both Party and state bodies. It appears that these recommendations have now been made binding on state agencies but are only advisory to the RCP; this is another step in the direction of increased Party control with socioeconomic development.[9] In any case, the joint councils provide a channel for expert input into the decision-making process that is likely to become increasingly important in the future as the general secretary continues his quest for streamlining of the cumbersome bureaucratic structure so far characteristic of the Romanian government.

Conflict in Decision-making Structures

The complex procedures outlined above provide many opportunities for conflicting views to emerge. There is no scarcity of information on such conflict; Nicolae Ceausescu speaks rather freely about differing perceptions at various levels of the Party and state hierarchies, although most of the emphasis is on conflicts over implementation and execution rather than basic goals.[10] The most important differences at the very top of the RCP hierarchy seem to be on the question of continued investment bias in favor of heavy industry. Ceausescu has frequently voiced concern about low yields in agriculture, and his solution has been increased investments in the chemical industry, which produces fertilizers. More money has also been pumped into agricultural machine building. There are some indications that others in the Permanent Presidium, notably Premier Ion Gheorghe Maurer, are somewhat reluctant to accept such investment decisions.* On

---

*Maurer has usually emphasized technical and managerial expertise more than mere quantities of production, as illustrated by his speech to the RCP Tenth Congress, in <u>Congresul al X-lea al Partidului Comunist Roman</u> (Bucharest: Editura Politica, 1969), pp. 91-120.

the whole, however, there is relatively little dissent at this level, since the general secretary remains strongly in favor of heavy industrialization as well.

Some opposing voices can be found at lower levels of the Party hierarchy or in some ministries, as well as among specialist groups. Meetings of collective farm leaders in 1971 and 1972 strongly called for increased investments in agriculture, although the final resolutions endorsed the general economic policy of Nicolae Ceausescu and the Party leadership.[11] On several occasions academic personnel have also spoken out on the investment problem in agriculture.[12] The most visible opposition has nevertheless materialized among technical experts at various levels. The pages of specialized journals such as Viata Economica (Economic Life), Finante si Credit (Finance and Credit), and Probleme Economice (Economic Problems) have been filled with much discussion of planning and investment, especially during the intermediate period of information feedback following the proclamation of Party draft theses on the economy. Some of the contributions have been critical of elements of the budgeting process, although all contributors give routine endorsements of the overall program.[13]

Some of the topics most frequently discussed include the following:

Investments in consumer goods versus heavy industry. Although virtually all commentators in the specialized journals have endorsed the general industrialization program, perceptional differences do persist and emerge in veiled references to the need for development of consumer goods industries "in step with" the producer goods fields. Furthermore, some of the spokesmen of light industry refer to the need for more "balanced" development of the economy. The lengthy discussion on material incentives in the economy carries an undertone of differences over planning and investment. While most of the top RCP leaders, including the general secretary, increasingly emphasize moral and ideological incentives, strong voices have been raised in favor of the argument that incentives must be material and only increased emphasis on consumer goods production can provide such incentives.*

---

*Such arguments have apparently had some effect on actual policy; in late 1971, the Ministry of Agriculture, the Food Industry and Waters was reorganized in order to improve the supply of foodstuffs to the population (Buletinul Oficial, December 31, 1971).

Import of technology versus domestic development. Nicolae Ceausescu has recently complained about the tendency among technical experts and planners to engage in excessive importation of foreign technology, without any serious attempt to develop such resources domestically. The general secretary's emphasis on domestic achievements in this field reflects his concern with Romania's unfavorable trade balance with its most important Western trade partners, especially West Germany. There is considerable concern that Romania will revert to its traditional position as an exporter of raw materials and an importer of technology and know-how. The result of this outlook has been increasing investments in domestic research and constant exhortations to personnel in institutes of higher learning to produce more.[14] This view has been implicitly challenged by those who emphasize the need for a division of labor in science and technology; arguments in this area have pointed out that Romania can increase production in many fields through expanded use of foreign licenses and joint companies.[15] Once again, the lines are not tightly drawn; Ceausescu's recent emphasis on domestic technology has not prevented him from trading extensively with the West, and there have been several joint company ventures in Romania lately. Once again, the controversy revolves around emphasis rather than different economic directions.

The position of technocrats in the planning and budgeting process. Communist systems everywhere are faced with a very basic dilemma. Economic development is perceived as a crucial part in the move toward Communism; indeed, there can be no Communist society without a material "base." The development of the economy requires technical and managerial expertise, and the political leaders are therefore confronted with the problem of maintaining control over indispensable technocrats. During the Stalinist period, indeed up to the end of Gheorghiu-Dej's reign, the political leadership by and large maintained tight control over the technical experts. During the period 1965-69, in which Nicolae Ceausescu consolidated his personal power in the Party apparatus, the technocrats in economic planning and management attained a certain autonomy. During the 1970s, however, this relative autonomy has been drastically curtailed, through increased emphasis on ideology, expanded Party control at all levels, and, lately, massive reorganizations. However, the experts have not accepted their lessened stature without struggle; in many instances spokesmen for the technical and managerial intelligentsia have voiced their concern for planning and budgeting, strongly hinting that more input is needed from those who have the skills and the know-how. An example of this kind of reasoning is an article by G. Siclovan in Probleme Economice of July 1972 in which he criticizes the present system of economic indicators used for planning purposes. Maxim Berghianu, head of the State Planning Committee, was making similar criticisms to the RCP National Conference in July, 1972.[16] Many other examples could be cited. Despite such concern by technical experts, the current trend in Romania is toward increased Party control over all aspects of planning. Such tendencies could produce considerable conflicts in the future.

CONTROL OF IMPLEMENTATION

Close Party control over the planning process is matched by tight supervision of the implementation of economic plans. This control is exercised through a multitude of channels, the most important of which include supervision at all levels by Party bodies.

Due to the practice of overlapping membership of Party and economic cadres at all levels, the RCP maintains a direct command link in all implementing organs. The top RCP leaders are also prominent, indeed controlling, members of the governmental apparatus, as shown in Chapter 2. There is direct Party control at the very top of all planning agencies, economic councils, academic institutions, and mass organizations. Furthermore, Party organizations exist in all societal groups at any intermediate and local level. The judet Party branches control the staffing of regional economic "centrals" as well as branches of central economic ministries. The regional People's Councils (broadly elective structures) are under direct supervision of the judet Party leadership, both through overlapping membership and parallel RCP control organs. At the local level RCP cells are active in all economic enterprises, farms, and residential areas, thus providing controls over non-Party personnel at the managerial and production levels. Staffing of managerial posts is undertaken in cooperation with relevant Party bodies. Finally, local branches of mass organizations such as trade unions perform an important function of "workers' control" at the grass-roots level.* This awesome control

---

*This control system has been expanded as a result in organizational measures proposed by Ceausescu at the 1972 National Conference (Scinteia, July 20, 1972).

mechanism can be expected to prevent major deviations from the established line. On the other hand, the control apparatus is so large and cumbersome that unnecessary rigidity is produced, thus resulting in much waste and slow implementation. Despite the many criticisms of excessive control voiced by the general secretary and others, the cumbersome apparatus continues to exist and may even be considered to have expanded during the last two years.

Party Control over the Ideological Belief System

Although much has been written about the "end of ideology," considerable evidence indicates that Communist political elites tend to accept a set of beliefs and values commonly called Marxism-Leninism. The main elements of the RCP's modernizing ideology have been described in Chapter 1.

In addition to having a fairly systematic pattern of views on politics, economics, and social life, a Communist party enjoys the tremendous advantage of controlling actual behavior within the ideological parameters of Marxism-Leninism. Thus the Party can determine the contents of the doctrine and also metes out punishment to those who are seen as violators of the code. This monopoly of ideological definition and supervision of its execution provides the Party leadership with a major advantage over any societal elites whose expertise may become politically dangerous.

The RCP has always attempted to guard its monopoly status in ideological matters and has frequently resorted to drastic measures against groups and individuals whose behavior was considered ideologically faulty. During the period 1944-49, massive purges of "bourgeois" elements, "individuals with old-fashioned, land-owner mentalities," and fellow-traveler groups such as the Ploughmen's Front and the Social Democrats decisively established the RCP as the sole legitimate political group in society.[17] In 1952 a large-scale purge of the "Muscovites" around Ana Pauker and Vasile Luca was carried out on ideological grounds.[18] Collectivization of agriculture, completed in 1962, was partly an ideological confrontation between much of the peasant class, on the one hand, and the Party leadership, on the other. Both during the Stalinist period and during Gheorghiu-Dej's regime, ideological struggles were waged against "nationalistic elements," especially the remnants of the pre-Communist middle class, and organizations such as the various churches were brutally suppressed, all in the name of ideological orthodoxy.[19]

In the Ceausescu era ideology has been primarily a weapon used to ensure Party control over all aspects of the decision-making process. Ideological campaigns primarily have been employed to check the influence of the emerging social and economic elites in a rapidly modernizing society, especially the managerial and technical intelligentsia, artists, writers and other intellectuals, and academic personnel. Furthermore, ideological campaigns are launched periodically in order to combat widespread political apathy among the masses.

One of the most important ideological campaigns in recent years was the so-called "little cultural revolution," which was launched by Nicolae Ceausescu in the summer of 1971. The little cultural revolution was a clear attempt to reimpose Party control over societal elites such as economic managers and planners, technical experts, academic personnel, and the literary intelligentsia. The campaign was furthermore aimed at the Party cadres at all levels, whose ideological vigilance was seen as appreciably weakened.[20]

The little cultural revolution ran through several stages. The first step was sharp denunciation of ideological work by the general secretary at the RCP Central Committee plenum in June 1971. This speech was almost immediately followed by a major press campaign, in which the main elements of Ceausescu's speech were discussed and elaborated upon. Then followed meetings of Party activists at all levels, and mass organizations such as the trade unions also met to discuss the new criticisms emanating from the center.[21]

By November 1971 the campaign swung into high gear. Another Central Committee Plenum assessed the results of the campaign so far. Ceausescu, obviously unhappy with the conduct of the campaign, castigated the Party apparatus for faulty ideological work, lax enforcement of the control functions entrusted to it, and dangerous tendencies toward corruption and the resurrection of bourgeois-landowner mentality. Even stronger criticism was meted out to the economic managers, technical experts, and much of academia; in these fields, Ceausescu said, ideological work frequently degenerated into empty sloganeering, a "chanting of litanies" without any attempt to relate ideology to Romanian life. "Professionalism," defined as emphasis on one's specialty without regard for Party policy and the goals of creating a new socialist society, was also identified as one of the greatest dangers to the development of the country in the only possible direction, namely the road defined by the Party. The general secretary indignantly described cases in which experts had attempted to resist Party control on the assumption that apparatchiks would not understand the technical problems involved and should therefore stay out of decision making in these fields. Ceausescu vowed that such deviations would be dealt with ruthlessly so that the cardinal principle of Party control would be reestablished.[22]

The general secretary's scathing criticism was followed by much self-criticism by major political figures. Ion Iliescu, then head of the youth organization UTC, admitted mistakes in his ideological work with youth. Virgil Trofin, head of the trade unions and a member of the RCP Permanent Presidium, spoke of faulty ideological work in mass organizations. Paul Niculescu-Mizil, a Party secretary in charge of education and propaganda, was very contrite in his description of "serious mistakes" in his field of activity.[23] Virtually every other speaker at the plenum admitted some mistake or oversight in this important field.

Subsequent to the November plenum, the campaign took a familiar turn. Ceausescu toured the country, spoke to mass audiences, castigated local and regional RCP cadres, and supervised a publicity blitz in the press.[24] Ideological plenums were called at all levels of the Party structure; all such plenums ended with "unanimous and enthusiastic" endorsement of the general secretary's program. Virtually all of the Party-controlled mass organizations met and generally endorsed the new ideological guidelines. An exception to this unanimity was found among the writers; the scheduled congress of the Writers' Union had to be postponed several times and finally met in May 1972. In the meantime, a lively debate had taken place in the ranks of the writers. Several books and plays were published that indirectly took issue with the renewed emphasis on ideology and "Socialist realism"; some writers even went so far as to suggest that each individual has the right to decide for himself whether he is to become part of the development process as established by the Communist Party, and the right to "opt out" of this process was forcefully reiterated.*

---

*Such views were apparently expressed by Ceausescu when he met with many of the top leaders in the summer

By May the Party had successfully overcome the opposition of some of the most prominent writers. The congress of the Writers' Union was an exercise in conformity, in which many of the recalcitrants were purged and pliant union leadership was installed. One of the first acts of this new leadership was to reiterate Ceausescu's words on the need for Party control and the importance of arts and literature designed to aid in the developmental process.[25]

Meanwhile the ideological campaign had engulfed the central and regional Party bodies and had also spilled over into several governmental ministries. During the winter of 1971-72 two regional first secretaries were removed from their positions for reasons of ideological mistakes or lack of zeal (Ilie Fasui in Caras-Severin judet and Dimitru Popa, head of the Bucharest City Party Committee). Another judet first secretary, Carol Kiraly of Covasna, was removed "at his own request." Vasile Patilinet, RCP Party secretary in charge of military and security matters, was transferred to a minor ministry and some of his subordinates followed suit. Ideological shortcomings seemed to be the most important reasons for the transfer. In the governmental apparatus some personnel changes began, and this process has continued, especially in the ministries of Interior, Justice, and Foreign Affairs.[26]

The ideological campaign continues, although in a slightly muted form at the present. It is a vivid reminder that the RCP has full control over the ideological sphere and can indeed use this monopolistic position to ensure administrative and political control over other elites in society. The net result of the little cultural revolution has been a considerable strengthening of the Party vis-a-vis other groups.

The Party and the Nomenklatura

The power of the Party in ideological matters and its control over the top decision-making positions in the governmental apparats, planning agencies, and academia allow the top political leadership close control over lower levels of the elite structures as well. Individuals can be quickly rerouted, dismissed, or promoted in accordance

---

of 1971; the general secretary indignantly rejected such views (Scinteia, October 13, 1971).

with the Party's wishes. Reorganization and transfers can be accomplished relatively rapidly if not smoothly. The RCP is in charge of the "nomenklatura"* for all major societal elites, a fact that is of the utmost importance in ensuring decision making in correspondence with the Party program.

This tight control over the nomenklatura has frequently been exercised in Romanian politics. Change in political leadership at the top has been followed by massive reorganizations and transfer of personnel. During the early years of Communist dominance in Romania, RCP control over recruitment to intermediate and top political, social and economic positions helped emasculate the remnants of bourgeois elites. After the trials of Vasile Luca and Ana Pauker, massive reorganizations and purges at all levels swept the country.[27] Administrative reorganizations during the Gheorghiu-Dej regime were used to eradicate possible opposition and to unseat potential political rivals. During the Ceausescu period three major administrative changes have demonstrated the Party's ability to control personnel and therefore crucially influence decision making. First was the economic decentralization plan, launched in 1967;[28] second, the 1968 territorial reorganization of the country, which brought back the prewar administrative units of judets or counties;[29] and, finally, the massive reorganization of economic and administrative agencies, which started in earnest in early 1973 and is still going on.

During the current reorganization campaign top personnel in many departments and governmental agencies have been transferred to other positions, and their jobs have been taken over by important Party personnel. Thus Paul Niculescu-Mizil, full member of the RCP Secretariat, was appointed head of the Ministry of Education.[30] Virgil Trofin, formerly head of the trade unions, is now minister of Internal Trade.[31] Numerous other examples could be given.

The transfer of important Party personnel to governmental positions and the removal of state administrators from their usual positions serve several important functions. One of the most important effects is the merging

---

*Nomenklatura, a Russian word, essentially means the list of names of personnel and positions to be filled with reliable individuals; the list is under the control of the Party.

of Party and state positions, a trend that clearly enhances RCP control over the decision-making process. In addition, frequent reshuffling of personnel prevents any dangerous concentration of power in the hands of any of Ceausescu's lieutenants, thus vastly enhancing the general secretary's power.

Another major element of the reorganization campaign is the drive to remove large numbers of governmental bureaucrats from administrative positions to actual production work. Literally thousands of administrators have now been shifted over to production work, primarily as engineers, supervisors, and experts working directly for enterprises. The Romanian press has carried detailed coverage of these transfers, and departments and agencies periodically "check in" with progress reports on the reallocation process.*

While the expressed goal of reducing administrative overhead in a highly bureaucratized system is commendable, it cannot fail to arouse animosity and dissent in the ranks of the entrenched bureaucracy. There are indications that such dissent is crystallizing into more solid opposition to Ceausescu's reorganization schemes.[32] Despite such evidence, observers are struck primarily by the astonishing control exercised by the general secretary, which has permitted him to rearrange drastically a whole organizational network, apparently without serious challenge to his power. As long as the Party head can maintain such control over other elites in society, his grasp on the decision-making process remains strong. Decision making for modernization, then, is profoundly influenced by the Ceausescu style and personality. The main modernization goals, outlined in Chapter 1, are to a large extent a direct reflection of Nicolae Ceausescu's dreams and aspirations for Romania.

Ceausescu's Control over Decision Making

The predominance of the Party leader in socioeconomic decision making is somewhat tempered by his need to rely on technical experts and planners for the specialized information required in this field. In the political realm, however, Nicolae Ceausescu is himself the professional, a

---

*The June 18-19, 1973, RCP Central Committee plenum codified this practice (see Scinteia, June 20, 1973).

long-time Party apparatchik superbly skilled in the control of power. In this field he is without equal in Romania today.

Ceausescu's immense personal power over decision making stems from a multitude of factors. His control over the Party apparatus is unchallenged, and his position as head of state enables him to exercise predominant control in this field as well. As shown in Chapter 2, he is also in charge of the most important of the many joint Party-state councils that exist in Romania. These institutional safeguards of political power are further strengthened by his style of decision making and his personal charisma.

The problems of Party control over the technocrats, which stem primarily from the increasing need for specialized knowledge in decision making, will spill over into the political arena once the political leadership becomes committed to economic growth and efficiency as a primary goal. Under such circumstances, political leaders will be forced to make concessions to those who possess specialized knowledge. On the other hand, a political leadership that is willing to sacrifice some economic growth in order to maximize its political control is much less prone to engage in compromise with the technocrats. Throughout his rule in Romania, Nicolae Ceausescu has decisively shown that he considers continued Party control over political and socioeconomic decision making a necessity. Economic growth will take place under Party auspices; and if the RCP's control will be safeguarded through ideological controls, personnel change, and administrative reorganizations, the general secretary will emphasize such control factors, even at the expense of development in the socioeconomic field. This continued commitment to political power above all has been drastically illustrated by the little cultural revolution and the current reorganization campaign, both of which slowed down economic development and created insecurity and waste in the productive sector.

This overriding commitment to political power has made it possible for Nicolae Ceausescu to achieve a degree of personal control unknown in Eastern Europe in the post-Stalin period. The general secretary insists on being involved in virtually all aspects of decision making, and this commitment has brought about a situation in which most important decisions in Romania today are responses to Ceausescu's personal initiative. So strong is this tendency that the feedback process has been hampered, and initiative seems to be suffering at all levels of the Party structure. The apparatchiks either wait for an initiative from the general secretary or attempt to anticipate his wishes. Both of these procedures are dangerous, in that they tend to exclude whole problem areas from meaningful debate unless the Party leader perceives an interest in that field.[33]

The strong personal power of Ceausescu at times gives rise to a real cult of personality. During the celebrations of his birthday in 1973, the Romanian press was full of glowing accolades to the Party leader as the great national leader of Romania, a heroic figure in the league of Stephan the Great and Michael the Brave. Furthermore, Party apparatchiks hailed him as a great theoretician and ideological leader; some literati praised him as a great cultural inspiration and a promoter of arts and the theatre, and economic experts paid tribute to his great foresight and wisdom in economic management and planning. All these manifestations of personality cult are clear indications of Nicolae Ceausescu's undisputed power.

In addition to such personal control, the general secretary has also promoted several close family members to high political and administrative positions, thus further strengthening his grip on decision making. The most notable of these moves was the elevation of Ceausescu's wife, Elena Ceausescu, to the RCP Executive Committee in the summer of 1973.[34] Mrs. Ceausescu has been highly visible in many areas during the last few years. Perhaps this indicates that she is building a political platform of her own, not necessarily dependent on her marriage to the undisputed Party leader. Her influence on the general secretary is also said to be great, and it appears that the recent campaign to bring more women into high positions in political and socioeconomic life originated with the First Lady.[35]

The general secretary is clearly aware of the dangers associated with such enormous concentration of power. He has attempted to deal with the problem of relative isolation at the pinnacle of power through a political style, one of the hallmarks of Ceausescuism, that involves frequent forays into the provinces, where meetings are held with local Party leaders, economic managers and, above all, with the rank and file. This emphasis on direct contact with the masses provides Ceausescu with a channel of information that is highly valuable, given the predisposition of apparatchiks to react to initiatives from the center rather than to funnel inputs to Bucharest. Mass inputs give Ceausescu access to popular moods and public opinion, and he may also hear about many problems that the bureaucrats at various levels have attempted to keep from him. The Party head can also claim that he is a truly democratic leader, easily accessible. Such a claim is likely to heighten Ceausescu's personal popularity among the masses, and it provides him with a steady flow of criticism against Party and government leaders at all levels, which can be used for personnel control at any time. Some of the impetus for the little cultural revolution and the current reorganization program ostensibly came from mass criticism and suggestions.[36]

The reliance on mass inputs as a corrective measure fits well with Ceausescu's personal views on political decision making, which include a heavy dose of populism, plebiscitarian tendencies, and skepticism toward bureaucratic structures and procedures.[37] The general secretary would like to be considered a father figure for all citizens of Romania, with equal concern for the man in the street and the valuable expert. Apart from such idealistic factors, the use of the masses as a personal power base and supplier of information serves to keep the bureaucracies of Party and state on the defensive. After all, in a socialist society no one can object to a policy ostensibly in the interests of the people and a decision-making process that presumably relies heavily on the information received from the rank and file.

There is no possibility that the inputs from the masses of the population can become really decisive factors in Romanian decision making. Inputs are only permissible within carefully prescribed limits, and Nicolae Ceausescu acts as the chief interpreter of these parameters. Thus the main lines of socioeconomic development are preset by the RCP. The position of the Party as the leading force in society cannot be questioned. Any development must take place within the confines of Marxism-Leninism, primarily defined by Ceausescu. Mass input therefore concerns itself with the application of the Party program. Within such parameters the average citizen can reasonably expect to be able to communicate his grievances. This relative accessibility of the top Party leader is a rather unique factor in Eastern Europe, a distinctive Ceausescu touch.

PERSONAL LEADERSHIP

The combination of Party control with economic decision making and Nicolae Ceausescu's unprecedented personal power within the RCP clearly indicate the extent to which modernization in Romania during the last decade has been fashioned by the Party leader, just as the strong personal power of Gheorghe Gheorghiu-Dej before him was a decisive influence on this process during the 1950s and early 1960s. True, there are many other factors entering into the decision-making process for modernization, some of which are the prevailing values of the political elite, a broad commitment to progress among large strata of the population, and an administrative-bureaucratic system that encourages centralized decision making and implementation. But the most important factor has been the ability of a strong leader to fashion and synchronize the many facets of modernization into a coherent program. Subsequent chapters will deal with the specifics of that program in the socioeconomic and political fields.

The extremely heavy concentration of power in the hands of the general secretary makes it imperative that his belief system and his style of operation be examined in some detail. It is the personality of Nicolae Ceausescu that more than any other factor determines policy in contemporary Romania. A close examination of his major speeches and his actual behavior as Party leader during the last decade reveals an extraordinary complex personality whose major features at times produce somewhat contradictory behavior. First, Nicolae Ceausescu is the Party apparatchik par excellence. Virtually his entire political career has been spent in the Party youth organization, in underground activities, or in the apparat itself. The general secretary's higher education was in a Party-directed institute of economics, where the curriculum was heavily laden with orthodox ideology and political management concepts. This extremely close relationship with the apparatchik career pattern has had a profound effect on Ceausescu's conception of leadership and style of operations, and this conception is now being acted out, with great ramifications for the entire societal system in Romania.

Ceausescu's main political views represent an original blend of traditional Marxism-Leninism, Romanian nationalism, and a form of populism. The general secretary is a firm believer in the perfectability of man, and many of his writings are strongly reminiscent of the early Marx, with heavy emphasis on individual emancipation through the collective achievements of society. According to this view, an individual is only truly free when he is able to serve the greater whole, society and his fellow man; self-fulfillment is not achieving material goods for oneself but producing socially meaningful and positive behavior. Man is a social animal who can only reach his highest level through interaction with others. This strongly moralistic view of the relationship between man and society has resulted in continuous efforts of political socialization and indoctrination in Romania to an extent unknown in most other socialist states. According to Ceausescu, a modern, developed society includes a citizenry that act and think as socially responsible beings, with a firm commitment to a social and moral code of behavior set down by the political leadership. The frequent ideological campaigns in Romania are therefore more than mere Party manipulations designed to concentrate control in one apparat in opposition to other emerging elites; the campaigns represent the carrying out of a strong moral conviction on the part of the undisputed Party leader.[38]

It follows from this conviction that Ceausescu is not content to play the part of merely political leader. His program is moral and ethical as well, and the general secretary is constantly involved in discussions with, and exhortations to, educators, writers, artists, and playwrights in order to ensure that his wideranging views are clear to all citizens and moral-cultural elites. Ceausescu has become a self-appointed authority in fields that nowadays are generally left to others, even in socialist states. This heavy involvement in all fields by the Party leader is duly recorded in the arts, literature, and news media, and his contributions are heavily praised by politicos as well as song writers. This gives a strong impression of personality cult in contemporary Romania. The entire little cultural revolution can in fact be seen as a massive effort to impose some of Ceausescu's moral and ethnical convictions upon an artistic and technical elite that was primarily concerned with the problems of modern socialism and the need for increased production respectively. For Ceausescu, commitment to specialization became narrow "philistinism," which threatened to remove the technical intelligentsia and a substantial portion of the citizenry from the Party's direct control in moral and ethical matters. Novels and plays portraying the seamier side of socialist society became manifestations of "negativism." The cultural revolution was an attempt to reestablish the principle of positive thinking along lines set down by the Party and Ceausescu personally, a major effort to revive the flagging revolutionary spirit and enthusiasm of a leadership and citizenry grown tired of endless campaigns for remote goals.[39]

By the time Ceausescu had geared up the Party machinery for a frontal attack on the "sectarians" and "negativists" among the technical and artistic intelligentsia, some of the personnel had received the Party leader's message and were already beginning to behave in conformity with the new guidelines. This belated attempt at conformity could not prevent a massive Party attack on the autonomy of other elites, however. Throughout 1971 and 1972 Ceausescu castigated educators, the intelligentsia in all its specialties, and even the Party apparat itself. Thus, in the spring of 1972, the general secretary met with those members of the Writers' Union who were RCP Central Committee members and severely castigated them for their lack of commitment to a great moral-political offensive in modern Romania.[40] Similar conferences were held with technical experts in industry, agriculture, and transportation, and several major Party meetings took on the aspect of massive self-criticism sessions, in which Ceausescu would typically set the stage by a thunderous denunciation and then sit back to listen to admissions of shortcomings from every speaker. The protracted campaign culminated in the RCP National Conference of July 1972, where Ceausescu's program was accepted unanimously and in toto, and his personal power was further enhanced through several organizational measures.[41]

Ceausescu's moral-political program had become the overt standard for all societal elites, and the personality cult flowered. The general secretary is quoted in the introduction of virtually all books published, especially in the humanities and social sciences, and artists, sculptors, and playwrights habitually claim great inspiration from the Party leader.[42] Ceausescu clearly relishes this role and continues to take an active interest in all matters pertaining to the arts and literature. Since the beginning of the little cultural revolution this involvement has been particularly heavy and is designed to ensure the production of "socially valuable literature," which does its part in citizen education and description of the great achievements of Socialist Romania.

The close personal control exercised by the general secretary over all aspects of Romanian societal life is also a reflection of the ideological orthodoxy so firmly embedded in Ceausescu's mind and mode of operation. The Party leader is a convinced Marxist-Leninist with a firm grasp of the basics of the ideology, and his position in society allows him ample opportunity to attempt realization of the prevailing ideological program. Ceausescu also considers himself a genuine ideological innovator, capable of using the basic writings of Marx and Engels as a starting point for a searching, scientific analysis of contemporary society. In this manner, the general parameters set forth by the grand old men of socialist thought can be creatively applied to existing conditions in Romania. The concept of the multilaterally developed society is indeed one of Ceausescu's contributions to contemporary Communist ideology, and it is hailed as a major innovation in Romanian scholarly publications as well as the Party press. Another Ceausescu contribution, it is claimed, is the whole infrastructure of international relations theory built around the concept of "non-interference in internal affairs, peace, and mutual advantage," which is a stock phrase in virtually all of the general secretary's foreign policy statements.[43]

With this kind of personal commitment of the head of state to Marxism-Leninism it is small wonder that periodic ideological campaigns become major features of Romanian political life. Modernity is measured not only in output and economic efficiency but also in terms of ideological orthodoxy. In fact, the frequent reorganizations now besetting the whole administrative structure of the country, coupled with the continuation of the little cultural revolution, strongly indicate that ideology and Party control take a primary, not a secondary, position in Romanian politics today.

The personalized leadership of Nicolae Ceausescu, imbued with moral-political givens and a commitment to ideological orthodoxy, reveals an authoritarian form of leadership. The people must be led toward the goal of multilateral development, socialism, and communism; individual self-fulfillment consists of successful completion of tasks preestablished by an unquestioned political and moral leadership. There is little room for deviations, little toleration for other outlooks and approaches, in such a system. It seems unthinkable that a Nicolae Ceausescu could tolerate, let alone encourage, diversification in the interpretation of the modernization program or the meaning of multilateral development or socialism, as is taking place in Hungary. The RCP general secretary is a benevolent authoritarian leader who is seriously attempting to create a society according to his own vision of Romanian greatness and happiness for all.

With this kind of authoritarian approach, this penchant for leading the population along a predetermined path, goes a genuine form of populism. Nicolae Ceausescu is known for his rapid and extensive forays from the sheltered atmosphere of the capital out to industrial plants, agricultural enterprises, educational institutions, as well as to foreign capitals. During 1972 and 1973, for example, Ceausescu visited practically every county in Romania, was a frequent guest in major industrial plants, and on several occasions discussed educational matters with students and faculty at some of the major institutions in the country.[44] On such occasions, the general secretary engages in direct contact with the rank and file, actively encouraging direct communications with the man in the street. A frequent element of such "flying visits" is praise for the common man and his efforts and criticism of leaders and managers for mistakes made. This approach establishes the impression of a powerful leader genuinely concerned with the welfare of the masses, impatient with bureaucrats, and, above all, accessible. It provides Ceausescu with important sources of information that are not subject to checks by managers and other elites, and the "direct dialogue" can also be used as a device for control over social and economic elites. The masses in turn seem to be generally in support of the Party leader, an important source of legitimacy in any political system. Ceausescu's approach to the masses, often by-passing established channels, resembles Charles de Gaulle's "rule by plebiscite" in style. At the present time, the frequent contacts between the RCP general secretary and the rank and file constitute a source of considerable insecurity for officials and bureaucrats alike.

Ceausescu's tendency to approach the rank and file directly rather than through established channels reflects his distrust of bureaucrats and bureaucratic procedures. As an apparatchik with primary experience in Party affairs, the general secretary is unaccustomed to experts and their established ways of doing business; and he has on numerous occasions voiced fear that the Party may become ossified and bogged down in red tape, thus losing contact with the population.[45] Ceausescu is action oriented and believes in crash programs designed to achieve goals quickly and decisively. There are strong elements of "storming" and overcommitment of resources in this approach, and the application of these principles to daily political and economic practice tends to create systematic activity similar to the frantic efforts expended in the Soviet Union in the 1930s and 1940s in the field of modernization.

While Ceausescu distrusts bureaucrats per se, he is a firm believer in organizational and administrative solutions to problems. The solution to low labor productivity in Romania has been sought in frequent reorganizations of economic ministries and the establishment of committees and commissions to study the problem. The frequent mergers and separations of state and Party functions, with subsequent reshuffling of personnel, are other examples of this approach. The most recent attempt to overcome problems in the political and socioeconomic performance of Romania is the formation of several joint Party-state councils, such as the Supreme Council on Socio-Economic Development (see Chapter 2). Despite such efforts, problems of considerable magnitude do persist, as the following chapters will show.

NOTES

1. Congresul al X-lea al Partidului Comunist Roman (Bucharest: Editura Politica, 1969), p. 666.

2. Ibid., pp. 666-710.

3. Stephen Fischer-Galati, Twentieth Century Rumania (New York: Columbia University Press, 1970), pp. 109-28.

4. This process was well illustrated by the continuous campaign of information and discussion carried out in the Party press in October and November, 1971, in which the 1971-75 five-year plan was debated.

5. For example, the second Congress of Agricultural Production Co-operatives, January 12, 1972, which was addressed by RCP Presidium member Gheorghe Pana.

6. See, for example, an article in Scinteia, September 13, 1971, which discusses the "tens of thousands of proposals" originating from the rank and file of the working class.

7. For a discussion of this approach see the last section of this chapter and also my article on contemporary Romanian politics in Problems of Communism, July-August 1974, pp. 29ff.

8. An example of this kind of expert input is found in the discussions of the 1967 economic reform decrees and their implementation, for example, G. Sickovan in Lupta de Clasa, January 1968; G. Gaston-Marin in ibid., January 1972; and S. Arsene, Probleme Economice, January 1972.

9. The draft law on the Supreme Council for Socio-Economic Development was published in Scinteia, March 6, 1973.

10. See, for example, his speech to the RCP Central Committee plenum, November 3, 1971, printed in Scinteia, November 4, 1971.

11. In *Viata Economica*, September 18, 1970, inadequate investments in agriculture were directly tied to low production and low wages, which in turn resulted in mass migrations from the countryside to the cities.

12. See, for example, A. Verniceanu, *Probleme Economice*, March 1971.

13. Ibid., and G. Antonescu in *Finante si Credit*, January 1972; and *Viata Economica*, September 18, 1970.

14. See Ceausescu's speech to the RCP Central Committee plenum, November 1971 (*Scinteia*, November 4, 1971).

15. See, for example, Maurer at the Tenth Congress, in *Congresul al X-lea*, pp. 91-120.

16. *Scinteia*, July 21, 1972.

17. Kenneth Jowitt, *Revolutionary Breakthroughs and National Development: the Case of Romania, 1944-1965* (Berkeley: University of California Press, 1971), pp. 131-50.

18. Ghita Ionescu, *Communism in Rumania 1944-1962* (London: Oxford University Press, 1964), pp. 210-15.

19. Kurt Hutten, *Iron Curtain Christians* (Minneapolis: Augsburg Publishing House, 1967), pp. 385-96.

20. See my "Ceausescus Kleine Kulturrevolution in Rumanien," *Osteuropa*, October 1972, pp. 717-28.

21. Ibid.

22. *Scinteia*, November 4, 1971.

23. These speeches were published in ibid., November 5-8, 1971.

24. Trond Gilberg, "Ceausescus Kleine Kulturrevolution," especially pp. 723-24.

25. Important excerpts from the debates at the Congress were published in *Le Monde*, May 2, 1972.

26. See my "Ceausescus Kleine Kulturrevolution," pp. 723-24.

27. Ionescu, op. cit., pp. 210-25.

28. The reorganization was published by *Agerpres* in October 1967.

29. See my "Regional Political Leadership in Romania: The Case of the Judet Party 1968-1973" in *East European Quarterly*, January 1975.

30. Changes announced by *Agerpres*, October 11, 1972.

31. Ibid.

32. These are unconfirmed reports which have circulated in Bucharest and elsewhere for some time. No documentary evidence is available.

33. For a discussion of this general problem area see Frederic Fleron, "Representation of Career Types in Soviet Political Leadership," in *Political Leadership in*

Eastern Europe and the Soviet Union, ed. R. Barry Farrell (Chicago: Aldine Publishing Co., 1970), pp. 108-40.

34. Radio Free Europe Research, Rumania/8, 29 June 1973.

35. Ibid.

36. Statement by Ceausescu in Scinteia, November 4, 1971.

37. His views are well reflected in a collection of his speeches entitled Romania: Achievements and Prospects (Bucharest: Meridiane Publishing House, 1969).

38. Ibid.

39. Trond Gilberg, "Ceausescus Kleine Kulturrevolution."

40. Reported in Scinteia, February 5, 1972.

41. The Ceausescu program was reported in ibid., July 20, 1972.

42. See, for example, Ilie Radulescu, Functia Economica-Organizatorica a Statului Socialist (Bucharest: Editura Academiei Republicii Socialiste Romania, 1967), pp. 5-19.

43. For example, in his speech to the RCP National Conference, July 2, 1972 (Scinteia, July 20, 1972).

44. See, for example, ibid., September 8, 1972.

45. Most strongly voiced in his great ideological speech at the RCP Central Committee plenum, November 1971 (Scinteia, November 4, 1971).

PART II
MODERNIZATION PROCESSES

CHAPTER

4

EDUCATION

Both the social science literature in the West and the RCP ideological framework emphasize certain modernization processes as crucial for the achievement of "modernity" and "multilateral development." The most important of these processes are education (both for socioeconomic and political purposes), industrialization, the development of agriculture, and the expansion of the communications network and social services. In multinational societies, integration of ethnic minorities into a common, national culture is an important modernization process. In this and the next four chapters we shall examine each of these processes in detail and assess achievements and failures in each field.

The clear goals of modernization, consistently held by the Communist elite, are to be implemented through the formidable structures of Party, youth organizations, the Socialist Unity Front, the trade unions, and other groups under the control of the RCP, by means of centralized decision making and control. There has been considerable achievement in this process, especially in the socioeconomic fields, while many commentators, including Nicolae Ceausescu himself, have voiced concern over the performance of the system in the political field. Briefly, then, it can be said that the regime has been successful in socioeconomic mobilization of the population, while the desired political development that was to have created a citizenry that would willingly and enthusiastically participate in the Party's programs has been lagging. By its own admission, the regime has not been successful in creating the "New Socialist Man"; there are remnants of old "bourgeois-landowner" mentality in the population, while new sources of "antisocial" behavior have developed inside socialist society itself.[1] The same can be said of the other countries of Eastern Europe as well, and in some of those states the regime seems to have reconciled itself to the continuation of ideological lethargy and a citizens' morality that is less than the new ethics presumably forming as a result of the modernization process. In Hungary, for example, Party chief Janos Kadar has stated that the petty bourgeoisie will be allowed to exist as a social stratum as long as it does not actively work against the socialist system of political and economic decision making.[2]

For Nicolae Ceausescu such a position appears unthinkable. He has repeatedly stressed the need to work actively for the creation of a New Socialist Man, and numerous ideological campaigns have proved that he is serious. An evaluation of Romanian performance in the field of political development must therefore proceed along two paths: first, an examination must be made of the degree to which the regime has succeeded in instilling new values in the population; and, second, if that goal has been only partly achieved the investigation must attempt to determine whether a minimum levèl of tolerance, necessary for survival, has been established. At the same time, the socioeconomic performance of Romanian society since World War II must be investigated. The following four chapters will attempt such an assessment, both in the socioeconomic and political fields.

SOCIOECONOMIC EDUCATION

One of the most characteristic features of Communist modernization policies is the strong emphasis on education, both technical and political. It is recognized that improved economic performance hinges on the establishment of a well-educated citizenry and a reliable corps of technical and managerial experts who can administer the complex tasks of planning, output, and development in a centralized system. The political monopoly exercised by the Communist Party is to be buttressed by intensive and extensive political education, which is ultimately designed to help create a new set of values among the citizens of the country, values that will facilitate political control, ensure decision-making monopoly by the Communist elite, and, finally, help create the New Socialist Man whose values will make the transition into Communism possible.[3]

Educational Development in the Postwar Period

Educational development in Romania in the postwar period has been fraught with many difficulties. Although in prewar Romania there were some institutions of higher learning in which education and research were of high quality, general and secondary education left much to be desired. There were many illiterates; in 1930, for example, fully 40 percent of the total population was classified as unable to read or write.[4] It took more than ten years of intensive postwar educational development to eradicate illiteracy; as late as 1956, there were 1.5 million individuals without these essential skills in the population (8.6 percent of the total population or 10 percent of all citizens over eight years of age).[5]

Secondary education was even more woefully underdeveloped. Only the privileged few had a chance to go on to lycees or other forms of secondary schools. In 1938 only 1.6 million students in a population of some 18 million (with a birth rate considerably above that of Western Europe, where school attendance was much higher) attended such institutions.[6] That specialized secondary schools were of little importance represented a problem for the development of the economy, which simply lacked skilled manpower at the plant level. The most serious deficiency was in agriculture: the lack of agronomists, veterinarians, and botanists prevented meaningful modernization, with the result that Romanian agriculture operated with outdated methods and equipment, with a very low yield and productivity per worker.[7]

Higher education in Romania was on the whole of relatively high quality, particularly at such high prestige institutions as Bucharest University and the Technical Institute at Timisoara. Despite such quality, however, there were serious problems in this field as well. First, recruitment to the universities was almost exclusively from the ranks of the upper classes, and the manpower base was therefore extremely narrow. The production of specialists for the economy was too low to give any great impetus for modernization in this field. Reforms in education were clearly needed and would undoubtedly have been forthcoming even without the establishment of a Communist regime.

The RCP Educational Offensive

After August 1944 the RCP-dominated coalition moved decisively toward educational development on a massive scale. The educational offensive was a frontal attack on shortcomings at all levels. It involved large investments in education and research and a campaign to eradicate illiteracy, with a massive expansion of enrollment in elementary education, a considerable increase in secondary training, both general and specialized, and a decisive move toward a vast improvement of higher education, especially in the technical and science fields. Tables 4.1-4.4 examine various aspects of this educational offensive.

Table 4.1 shows that the Romanian regime has maintained a consistently high level of investments in education, culture and the arts, and science and related fields, with a proportionately very high investment level for science. A direct comparison between time periods is difficult since two different price bases have been used, but it is clear that a relatively large amount of total investments has been funneled into education and research activities.*

The considerable investment has had several major goals. First, primary education was to be extended to all inhabitants, and an attempt was made to expand the amount of general and specialized secondary training so that a large manpower pool could be established whose knowledge base could be used for economic and social expansion. Second, a major offensive was launched to ensure an adequate supply of middle-level specialists in the economy, with a view toward staffing the increasingly complex industrial and agricultural enterprises emerging as a result of investment policies in those areas. Third, higher education was given a massive infusion of funds, personnel, and students, and thousands of experts were turned out from expanding institutions every year. This expansion in primary education is well illustrated by Table 4.2.

---

*This investment is actually much higher, if funds used for salaries, stipends, and maintenance of buildings and equipment are included; estimates indicate that 25-30 percent of all funds expended in Romania go toward salaries and stipends in the field of education.

TABLE 4.1

Investments in Education, Culture, and the Arts and Sciences, 1945-72
(in millions of lei)

	1950 Costs				1963 Costs			
	1950	Percent of Total	1960	Percent of Total	1969	Percent of Total	1971	Percent of Total
Total Investments	5,663	100	24,422	100	67,529	100	82,617	100
Education	88	1.5	437	1.8	1,103	1.6	1,194	1.4
Culture and the arts	105	1.8	277	1.1	345	0.5	323	0.4
Science and science-related fields	106	1.9	321	1.3	433	0.6	578	0.7

Sources: Republica Socialista Romania, Directia Centrala de Statistica, Anuarul Statistic 1970 (Bucharest: 1970), pp. 458-59; Anuarul Statistic 1972, pp. 328-29.

TABLE 4.2

General Education, 1938-72

Year	Registered Students: General Schools	Graduates: General Schools	Graduates: General Lycees
1938-39	1,575,477	17,225	4,200
1950-51	1,777,987	81,987	8,339
1960-61	2,346,322	182,216	46,550
1969-70	2,934,222	316,963 (1968-69)	76,218 (1968-69)
1970-71	2,934,051	360,887	81,344
1971-72	2,823,749	--	--

Sources: Anuarul Statistic 1970, pp. 596-97; Anuarul Statistic 1972, pp. 446-47.

The steady climb of enrolled in general schools from 1938-39 to 1972 was partly a reflection of the expanding population but more so of the expansion of primary education to all citizens. Illiteracy was finally eradicated between 1956 and 1966, and from then on the number of registered students varied in line with the age distribution of the population. A further illustration of this expansion is provided by the fact that while the population of Romania increased by 8.6 percent in the period 1938-72 primary school enrollment increased by 84 percent.[8]

The dramatic improvement of education at this level is further illustrated by the increase in graduates, both from general schools and general lycees. This increase is so startling that it must be a product of several factors; first among these was the tendency in the prewar system to provide only incomplete primary and secondary education, which cut down on the number of graduates. Second, with the expansion of the Romanian school system came increased possibilities for education beyond the general schools--hence the tremendous expansion of graduates from general lycees.

The development of Romanian education under the Communist system was also aimed at the production of specialists at all levels for rapid infusion into the modernizing economy. Some of this expansion came through the development of specialized schools. Table 4.3 examines professional school enrollment by field, 1950-72.

TABLE 4.3

Professional School Enrollment, by Field, 1950-72

Enrollment	1950-51	Percent of Total	1960-61	Percent of Total	1969-70	Percent of Total	1971-72	Percent of Total
Total	99,257	--	127,224	--	202,048	--	210,364	--
Mines and petroleum	2,764	2.8	5,615	4.4	11,191	5.5	8,601	4.1
Electrical energy and electronics	7,216	7.3	512	0.4	6,352	3.1	6,447	3.1
Metallurgy and machine building	45,626	46.0	32,493	25.5	56,471	27.9	70,549	33.5
Chemistry	2,392	2.4	3,667	2.9	13,668	6.8	15,303	7.3
Woodworking	3,336	3.4	3,447	2.7	6,754	3.3	6,111	2.9
Consumer goods industries	9,524	9.6	23,071	18.1	21,392	10.6	21,152	10.1
Textiles and apparel	4,174	4.2	458	0.4	3,910	1.9	4,648	2.2
Construction and construction materials	7,416	7.5	12,489	9.8	25,416	12.6	26,233	12.5
Agriculture and forestry	6,377	6.4	35,135	27.6	25,834	12.8	19,487	9.3
Transport and tele-communications	4,950	5.0	5,186	4.1	17,019	8.4	18,591	8.8
Commerce and trade	4,108	4.1	5,151	4.0	7,696	3.8	7,881	3.7
Health and sanitation	--	--	--	--	5,760	2.9	4,798	2.3

Sources: Anuarul Statistic 1970, pp. 598-602; Anuarul Statistic 1972, pp. 449-50.

Professional school enrollment in this period clearly reflects the commitment of the political regime to expand the basis of heavy industry as rapidly as possible. The field of metallurgy and machine building alone accounted for almost one-half of all enrollment in 1950; by 1970 this proportion had decreased to roughly one-third, still considerably larger than any other field. In electrical energy and electronics, another field of large enrollment, there was a very drastic reduction in 1960-61 but a come-back toward the end of the decade. The initial heavy enrollment in this field probably reflects the attempt to expand electrical energy production rapidly in the early 1950s; by 1960 most of these projects were completed, and training in electronics had not yet reached significant levels. The upswing in this category during the 1960s is a reflection of the regime's determination to master the most modern technology available through improved domestic education.

Other fields in which there has been a considerable and steady increase in enrollment during this period are chemistry, construction and construction materials, transport and telecommunications, and mines and petroleum. Education for the consumer goods industries, as well as agriculture and forestry, registered conspicuous gains around 1960, but declined considerably in enrollment during the decade of the 1960s. Other areas remained static or declined in importance during the period examined.

These trends are further illustrated by Table 4.4, which shows the number of graduates in the same fields over the 20-year period. The breakdown of graduates naturally tends to follow the enrollment distribution but with minor differences due to the varying length of study programs in fields as disparate as metallurgy and agriculture. The most impressive finding emanating from Table 4.4 is the large number of trained specialists funneled into the economy every year. This massive skill infusion has been a major factor in the consistently high growth rate in Romania, especially in the heavy and extractive industries. But despite this decisive move toward a higher level of expertise and wider distribution of skills in the economy Romania still suffers from a drastic lack of experts at all levels, especially in the factories and on the farms. A continuation of the educational offensive is therefore envisioned for the next decade; the 1971-75 five-year plan called for a total investment of 4.5 billion lei in education and science, fully 1.5 percent of all investments proposed in this period. Of these investments, a considerable amount was set aside for professional schools in an effort to further improve performance.

TABLE 4.4

Professional School Graduates in Selected Fields, 1950-72

Graduated	1950-51	Percent of Total	1960-61	Percent of Total	1968-69	Percent of Total	1970-71	Percent of Total
Total	24,783	--	30,236	--	79,492	--	68,492	--
Mines and petroleum	730	2.9	1,535	5.1	4,391	5.5	3,563	5.2
Electrical energy and electronics	883	3.6	106	0.4	2,980	3.7	1,423	2.1
Metallurgy and machine building	9,578	38.6	6,050	20.0	17,275	21.7	17,373	25.4
Chemistry	450	1.8	606	2.0	4,889	6.2	4,742	6.9
Woodworking	1,993	8.0	1,173	3.9	1,621	2.0	2,297	3.4
Consumer goods industries	3,290	13.3	4,431	14.7	8,538	10.7	7,953	11.6
Textiles and apparel	537	2.2	209	0.7	1,364	1.7	1,553	2.3
Construction and construction materials	881	3.6	4,195	13.9	9,089	11.4	9,658	14.1
Agriculture and forestry	1,045	4.2	8,860	29.3	17,541	22.1	10,018	14.6
Transport and telecommunications	3,993	16.1	954	3.2	4,538	5.7	4,965	7.2
Commerce and trade	1,068	4.3	2,107	7.0	2,873	3.6	2,359	3.4
Health and sanitation	--	--	--	--	4,021	5.1	2,468	3.6

Source: See Table 4.3.

No field has been given more regime commitment than higher education. Table 4.5 examines the development of institutions in the most important fields of study, while Table 4.6 shows the expansion of student enrollment since the establishment of communist power in Romania. Table 4.5 provides further illustration of the educational offensive launched and sustained by the regime in certain high priority fields, such as electrical energy, metallurgy, construction, mathematics and physics, and economics. The rapid expansion of departments in pedagogy is a monument to the regime's attempt to train specialists in the field of teaching, clearly a necessity if the general educational level of the population is to be raised. The belated realization of the need for training in agriculture resulted in an expansion of departments in this field, and the traditional Communist concern with expanded social and medical services is reflected in the relatively large number of medical schools maintained. Economics has expanded rapidly in the 1970s, reflecting the regime's concern with better planning and forecasting, as well as business management, at a time when the old central indicators of performance are no longer sufficient in the increasingly sophisticated Romanian economy.

While high priority fields expanded considerably in the forming of new departments, certain fields remained underprivileged--especially the social sciences and humanities as well as fields related to consumer goods industries, services, and transportation. More attention has been paid to the performing arts, including music; but the imbalances in higher educational facilities remain, and it will take a considerable amount of time to overcome them. Multilateral development of all socioeconomic activities will be hindered by this imbalance.

There are signs that the social sciences now will receive more attention, especially disciplines such as sociology and social psychology that can be directly related to productivity and economic performance.[9] Even with this increased interest, however, Romania is one of the least advanced of all East European countries in modern social science teaching and research, several years behind Poland, the most highly developed socialist state in this field, not to mention West European countries and the United States.

The expansion of institutional facilities and increasing student enrollment at all levels of the Romanian educational system are only two of the most conspicuous developments in this field. The regime has also made a

TABLE 4.5

Higher Education, by Departments of Speciality, 1948-72

	1948-49	1950-51	1960-61	1970-71	1971-72
Total	129	136	131	175	187
Mining	3	3	2	2	2
Petroleum	2	3	4	4	4
Electrical energy and electronics	3	3	5	8	8
Metallurgy and machine building	7	9	8	11	12
Industrial chemistry	3	3	3	3	3
Wood industries	2	1	1	1	1
Light industry	1	1	1	1	1
Food industries	2	2	1	1	1
Transport and telecommunications	1	5	1	1	1
Architecture and construction	5	6	8	10	10
Agriculture	12	13	8	13	13
Veterinary medicine	2	2	1	4	4
Forestry	2	2	1	1	1
Human medicine	20	20	7	12	12
Pharmacology	3	4	3	4	4
Philology	4	4	6	7	9
Philosophy	4	4	1	4	4
History, geology, and geography	4	8	1	1	1
Natural and biological sciences	4	4	3	3	3
Chemistry	4	4	3	9	4
Mathematics, physics	4	4	3	9	9
Pedagogy	6	9	43	64	52
Law	4	4	3	3	3
Economics	5	5	3	11	13
Physical education	1	1	1	1	1
Plastic and decorative arts	3	2	3	3	3
Cinematography and theater arts	5	5	2	2	2
Music	5	4	5	6	6
Other specialties	8	1	--	--	--

Sources: Anuarul Statistic 1970, pp. 612-14; Anuarul Statistic 1972, pp. 459-61.

TABLE 4.6

Higher Education, by Student Enrollment and Fields, 1948-72

	1948-49	1950-51	1960-61	1970-71	1971-72
Total	48,676	53,007	71,989	151,885	148,428
Mining	380	889	919	1,308	1,288
Petroleum	274	769	1,582	1,562	1,667
Electrical energy and electronics	1,250	1,757	3,528	9,718	9,598
Metallurgy and machine building	1,667	3,576	5,574	13,370	13,578
Industrial chemistry	1,009	1,249	2,184	3,874	3,610
Wood industries	334	501	484	592	536
Light industry	824	582	468	1,170	960
Food industries	393	901	813	1,000	798
Transportation and telecommunications	316	965	1,075	1,106	1,063
Architecture and construction	2,430	2,055	5,563	10,818	11,208
Agriculture	2,813	5,947	6,889	6,258	7,290
Veterinary medicine	769	966	733	2,030	1,711
Forestry	253	664	684	786	720
Human medicine	8,815	6,763	7,058	8,366	9,182
Pharmacology	1,205	855	767	1,532	1,681
Philology	2,713	1,887	6,022	14,810	14,562
Philosophy	530	547	2,075	5,754	5,907
History, geology, and geography	1,667	2,065	663	690	689
Natural and biological sciences	792	939	2,861	3,395	3,577
Chemistry	1,286	1,587	1,606	2,979	3,011
Mathematics, physics	762	3,192	4,006	7,837	8,216
Pedagogy	1,321	4,474	5,774	20,605	17,423
Law	5,534	2,464	3,101	5,901	5,787
Economics	8,294	4,650	5,085	21,016	18,974
Physical education	218	465	744	2,038	2,001
Plastic and decorative arts	814	635	452	585	637
Cinematography and theater arts	581	619	305	277	281
Music	907	875	973	2,508	2,473
Other specialties	525	169	--	--	--

Source: See Table 4.5.

massive effort to strengthen the professional teaching staffs at all levels. In general schools and general lycees the number of teachers increased from 45,359 in 1938-39 to 149,604 in 1969-70.[10] Similar expansion occurred in professional schools, with the teaching staff increasing from 896 in 1938-39 to 11,527 in 1969-70.[11] Professional school training was also undertaken by factories and other economic units during the late 1960s; there are no figures for the personnel assigned to this job, but the commitment must have been substantial, since 61,318 students were enrolled in this program in 1969-70.[12]

The most impressive increase in teaching staff took place at the university level. In 1938-39, there were 2,194 staff members teaching at this level, but, by 1969-70, 13,166 individuals were classified as teachers in higher education,[13] a massive increase of 500 percent over approximately 30 years.

Indispensable elements in educational progress are adequate libraries and research facilities. Table 4.7 illustrates the impressive expansion in library holdings during the period 1947-70. Book production is also considerable, as indicated by Tables 4.8 and 4.9. Tables 4.8 and 4.9 are further illustrations of the heavy emphasis on science and technology in Romania during the last 20 years. The greatest number of book titles has consistently been in the fields of science and social problems as well as in technology, industry, agriculture, and medicine. In volumes printed the former category has maintained first place, while general literature has been a close second. This finding is clearly indicative of the policies established by the political leadership, who control publishing, in terms of titles, print runs, and content; publishing is primarily designed to help the political and economic development of the country, rather than providing entertainment through fictional works. (As will be seen in subsequent discussions, much of the fiction produced is in the vein of "Socialist Realism," designed to provide political education and indoctrination.)

Thus another important field of activity has been mobilized for the achievement of modernization and the establishment of the multilaterally developed society. Education and research are designed to help establish the material base for Communism. Romanian modernization theory recognizes that the achievement of political goals cannot be completed without a highly productive and diversified economy, and such a goal is in turn only feasible through massive educational efforts. The establishment of the

TABLE 4.7

Libraries, 1949, 1950, 1955, 1960-69
(volumes in thousands)

	State		University		Documentary		School		Public	
Year	Unit	Volumes	Unit	Volumes	Unit	Volumes	Unit	Volumes	Unit	Volumes
1949	7	1,590	56	2,668	1,133	736	14,862	3,909	14,352	5,641
1950	7	1,846	53	3,034	--	--	15,780	4,197	18,444	11,765
1955	6	3,959	40	6,612	4,623	5,589	15,572	7,825	19,670	26,505
1960	2	8,328	36	7,845	5,032	9,662	5,762	10,539	14,407	31,859
1961	2	8,722	42	8,305	4,889	10,179	5,497	11,003	13,595	33,929
1962	2	8,885	45	8,953	4,922	11,348	6,042	12,289	12,305	37,253
1963	2	9,150	46	9,474	4,997	11,517	6,779	13,582	11,801	39,791
1964	2	9,357	47	10,142	5,205	12,213	7,153	15,243	11,456	41,790
1965	2	9,727	47	10,467	5,321	12,777	7,785	17,198	11,240	43,136
1966	2	10,070	43	10,689	5,262	14,169	8,528	19,281	11,036	43,905
1967	2	10,422	42	11,315	5,061	14,184	9,094	23,319	10,478	45,186
1968	2	10,688	43	11,864	4,535	13,591	9,260	24,388	6,823	43,252
1969	2	10,846	43	12,297	4,475	14,078	9,452	27,217	8,134	46,516

Source: Anuarul Statistic 1970, p. 630.

TABLE 4.8

Books and Brochures Printed and Legally Registered in 1955, 1960, 1965-69
(volumes in thousands)

	1955		1960		1965		1966	
	Titles	Volumes	Titles	Volumes	Titles	Volumes	Titles	Volumes
Total	5,182	48,414	6,335	51,393	8,422	78,024	9,131	80,397
General	105	423	186	479	218	572	325	1,068
Philosophy	38	444	26	188	39	180	44	197
Atheism, religion	61	330	31	589	32	234	28	176
Science and social problems	1,198	19,324	2,082	24,588	1,980	36,736	2,246	38,391
Philology and linguistics	39	153	20	372	84	881	126	1,038
Natural sciences and mathematics	342	805	234	1,156	408	1,932	403	1,275
Technology, industry, agriculture, medicine	2,072	12,806	1,949	10,230	3,121	10,204	3,238	9,251
Art, plays-games, sports	347	1,291	897	1,728	1,158	2,566	1,298	5,160
Literature	873	12,013	768	11,599	1,123	23,190	1,162	22,188
History, geography, biography	107	825	142	464	259	1,529	261	1,653

(continued)

TABLE 4.8, continued

	1967		1968		1969	
	Titles	Volumes	Titles	Volumes	Titles	Volumes
Total	9,923	104,138	9,372	103,331	9,399	91,024
General	241	1,278	205	754	249	811
Philosophy	105	321	47	238	85	488
Atheism, religion	39	194	50	169	20	224
Science and social problems	2,280	46,095	1,857	35,947	2,080	33,645
Philology and linguistics	109	1,374	117	1,061	85	1,245
Natural sciences and mathematics	628	1,653	468	1,723	510	1,413
Technology, industry, agriculture, medicine	3,218	10,843	3,385	16,616	3,054	10,666
Art, plays-games, sports	1,733	8,759	1,551	11,822	1,683	8,139
Literature	1,314	31,958	1,444	32,250	1,444	33,162
History, geography, biography	256	1,663	248	2,751	189	1,231

Source: Anuarul Statistic 1970, p. 643.

TABLE 4.9

Books and Brochures Printed and Legally Registered in 1969

	Titles			Thousands of Volumes		
	Total	Books	Brochures	Total	Books	Brochures
Total	9,399	5,085	4,314	91,024	69,953	21,071
General	249	107	142	811	275	536
Philosophy	85	61	24	488	430	58
Atheism, religion	20	15	5	224	211	13
Science and social problems	2,080	1,325	755	33,645	27,467	6,178
Philology, linguistics	85	82	3	1,245	1,244	1
Natural science and mathematics	510	281	229	1,413	1,347	66
Technology, industry, agriculture, medicine	3,054	1,393	1,661	10,666	4,998	5,668
Arts, plays-games, sports	1,683	344	1,339	8,139	1,798	6,341
Literature	1,444	1,335	109	33,162	31,050	2,112
History, geography, biography	189	142	47	1,231	1,133	98
Learning manuals[a]	832	832	--	21,807	21,807	--
Musical notes[b]	123	34	89	99	40	59

[a]Included in Science and social problems.

[b]Included in Arts, plays-games, sports.

Source: See Table 4.8.

multilaterally developed society requires a balanced production of skilled personnel, whose performance in the economy can ensure development in all fields. Given this commitment, it is somewhat surprising to find that the major educational effort is still in the fields of heavy industry. The impressive expansion of Romania in this area is at least partly related to educational investment; if balanced development is to be achieved, a considerable reorientation of educational priorities must take place. There is little evidence to indicate that such a reorientation is in fact taking place, and the Romanian school system will probably continue to emphasize technical and applied skills, to the detriment of other disciplines. This in turn will most likely ensure continuation of the severe imbalances currently besetting the economy (for a detailed discussion, see Chapter 5).

CONTINUING PROBLEMS

Even within the high priority fields of education many problems still remain. There have been frequent complaints by educators and political leaders alike that the productivity of Romanian universities and research institutes is low, and that it takes much longer to achieve a completed academic degree than in most of the other socialist states.[14] Similarly, contracted research projects are frequently delayed due to inadequate equipment and inefficient use of manpower.[15] As a result of this slow execution of research tasks often a completed project was outdated before its implementation, since social and economic change had outrun the basic premises upon which the work had been based.

The Ceausescu regime is considerably concerned over this problem. Thus, at the Ninth RCP Congress in 1965, the Party leader stated that

> academic institutions and departments, institutes of higher education, laboratories of major enterprises form a string group of units, which include the principal areas of research and [thus] permit multilateral scientific development of the country. <u>We need improvement of the system organizing scientific activity, concentration of cadres and material facilities for objectives with</u>

highest possible efficiency. [In order] to achieve this, it follows that a national Council for Scientific Research be established, which will elaborate directives of orientation and a unitary program of scientific research and training of cadres, thus ensuring coordination of activity in this field.[16] (Emphasis in original.)

Similarly, at the Tenth Party Congress four years later the need for increased efficiency and more judicious use of educational and scientific institutions was heavily stressed:

> The actual level of Socialist society, its developmental perspectives demand multilateral development of education, within a unitary concept, on the basis of the perspectives in the program for the preparation of cadres, in strict conformity to social and economic development. The directives of the Central Committee and the Law on Education, were adopted last year--to establish the orientation and the cadres of modernization in education over an extended time period. Of the highest priority now is organizational and practical activity; it is necessary for the Ministry of Education to act with speed and efficiency for concretization of the guidelines established by the Party.
>
> In conformity with the directives of the Central Committee [one] must continue the emphasis on the development of higher technical and economic education; in the five year plan attention is paid to the preparation of specialists in fields which represent priorities in technology and modern economic activities. It is also necessary to further develop other fields of university education, which will ensure the training of professors, medical doctors, and the establishment of research centers in social sciences and the humanities. The Ministry of Education, academic personnel, councils and university senators must permanently improve

> educational programs, each course, and systematically eliminate everything that is old fashioned and outdated, so that we can deal with the realization of the contemporary technical-scientific revolution, with necessary practice.[17]

The problems of inefficient use of the existing research facilities in Romania are compounded by the continuing need to keep up with developments in more advanced countries, particularly Western Europe and the United States. During the last two decades the veritable explosion of knowledge in all fields has made it increasingly more difficult for smaller countries to keep up in the race toward more and more advanced achievement in this field. Though Romania is not in a unique position, the tight ideological control in the country has made free exchanges of ideas impossible in many fields, particularly in the social sciences and the humanities but also in technical disciplines.

During the first four to five years of the Ceausescu era the problem of keeping pace with education and research achievements abroad was partly solved through importation of know-how and technology. Whole industrial plants were purchased abroad, and there was a considerable expansion of foreign trade, which also allowed some foreign business investment in Romania, in which the more advanced partner would contribute the kind of scientific knowledge that was not available in the host country.

Beginning in 1971, however, a marked turn took place toward domestic achievement and less reliance on imports of scientific patents and procedures. Ceausescu repeatedly stressed the need to develop Romanian research and produce high quality work in all fields, particularly in technology and the hard sciences.[18] Since 1971 the emphasis has also been heavily on applied rather than basic research. This approach may have some immediate benefits in increased industrial production; but basic research remains indispensable, especially if Romania is to make the leap into sustained growth and achievement comparable to that of most West European countries, not to mention the United States.

One of the most serious deficiencies of higher education in Romania is the underdevelopment of the social and behavioral sciences. Social science has been locked into ideological and political requirements, which have precluded systematic investigation of important social problems. Sociology is only now beginning to recover from its long hiatus under socialism, while political science is primarily concerned with Marxism-Leninism and the explanation of political phenomena within the context of ideology. Economics, long circumscribed by ideological parameters, is undergoing rapid change, in which some of the more advanced concepts developed in the West are examined for possible application in a socialist setting. Rural sociology is beginning to concern itself with social problems in the countryside, in an effort to stem the drastic outflow of skilled personnel from the farms and at the same time increase output in the crucial sector of the economy. But despite such encouraging developments, the social sciences remain relatively underdeveloped in Romania; and repeated Party intervention, designed to ensure continued ideological orthodoxy in this important field, has further hampered systematic work. Since the new ideological campaign (the little cultural revolution) was launched in the summer of 1971, direct Party control over education has once more become a fact of life; and the RCP Central Committee now directly supervises the teaching of social sciences in Romania as well as the research projects undertaken by personnel in these fields.[19]

Severe problems of student enrollment and understaffing of certain fields have also plagued the Romanian educational system. Until the early 1960s many students tended to prefer enrollment in the humanities, despite the fact that the technical disciplines were better equipped and jobs in the latter category were more plentiful.[20] It is hard to determine the reason for this discrepancy without survey studies, but one factor involved was probably the traditional Romanian emphasis on the classics and philosophy in the "real" academic disciplines, while technical subjects were seen as directly related to production, an endeavor often despised by the intelligentsia. It took a considerable amount of effort for the regime to break such traditional patterns, but by the 1960s it was abundantly clear to all students that a career in scientific or technological fields would be considerably more lucrative than traditional positions in the humanities and that, furthermore, the former category would offer relative autonomy and insulation from political control, a factor very much present in humanistic and social science disciplines.[21] Enrollment trends have therefore been considerably modified during the last decade, and there is now a sufficient manpower pool from which to select students in high priority programs. The biggest manpower problem in contemporary higher education seems to be the generally restrictive admissions policy at a time when economic and social needs demand more specialists. The RCP will soon be faced with the need to revise its admissions policy, including the political and ideological requirements, or else face a growing shortage of skilled personnel at all levels.

Another manpower problem arises from the predilections among parents and youth alike for academic studies, a view that has hampered the development of professional schools. There have been innumerable references to this problem in the Romanian press, and Nicolae Ceausescu has publicly castigated the "widely held notion" that only academic study can lead to self-fulfillment for individuals.[22] This tendency to view professional schools below the university level and the students in such institutions as second class in potential and achievement runs counter to both real needs of the economy and the egalitarian doctrines of the regime. During the last few years, educators and political leaders have attempted to stem the trend by widespread introduction of so-called "polytechnical" education, in which students (both in universities and in secondary schools) spend some time in actual production. This approach was measurably strengthened as a result of the ideological offensive in 1971, and it now represents the norm throughout the country.[23]

POLITICAL EDUCATION AND SOCIALIZATION

Communist regimes have established a two-fold educational task: not only must the citizenry be trained in all fields functional to the development of the socioeconomic system, but the rank and file must also achieve a high level of political consciousness. A major part of the educational drive in postwar Romania has indeed been directed toward this eradication of old political values and outlooks and the establishment of a new consciousness in this field. This offensive is carried out through a multitude of vehicles, both formal and informal. In Romanian terminology these processes are commonly called "political education."

Political education consists of several analytically separate functions. There is first of all the transmission of the fundamentals of Marxism-Leninism to all individuals in society, starting with informal vehicles such as the family and continuing through the kindergartens, elementary, and secondary schools, the specialized and generalized lycees, and finally the institutions of higher learning. Virtually all organized groups in society participate in this immense task. The most important vehicles outside the school system are peer groups such as the trade unions and the armed forces. The unions and the military are of particular importance because of their broad coverage; since virtually all urban and rural employees are organized in trade unions the regime can be sure to reach the employed population, and compulsory military training ensures coverage of the adult male population. As discussed in Chapter 2, a substantial part of the population can also be reached through the formal Party organization and the UTC.

A second task of political education is to ensure not only popular acceptance of the fundamentals of Marxism-Leninism but a thoroughgoing training in the main values associated with the Romanian variant of the ideological classics. This form of education is pursued primarily through intensive political socialization of the younger generation and resocialization of the older citizens whose childhood value systems were fashioned during the "bourgeois landowner" period.[24]

A third educational function is implementation of the symbols transmitted in political socialization and resocialization. It is an inadequate achievement to ensure popular internalization of major ideological values if this process does not lead to actual desired behavior. Political education in Romania is therefore submitted to instant reality testing by continuous regime scrutiny of individual and group actions. Such scrutiny in turn results in frequent alterations in methods of education, primarily in the form of ideological campaigns designed to rectify mistakes and improve on the shortcomings of previous approaches. Given such continuous testing, political education in Romania takes on a spirit of feverish activity coupled with periods of relative lethargy and relaxation of ideological demands. "Storming" and crash programs are part and parcel of political education in contemporary Romania. This aspect is a source of considerable worry to the regime, which would like to see a more sustained educational effort with steady returns. The multilaterally developed society would presumably reach such a level, in which a self-sustained educational drive in the political field would result in higher material production, which in turn would increase the possibilities for successful ideological training. The level has not yet been reached, and there is considerable discussion of whether Romania is even making meaningful progress toward this goal.[25]

The self-admitted deficiencies of political education in Romania have posed another alternative for the regime. Rather than attempting to effectively transform popular values on a massive scale, the regime might resign itself to the less formidable task of simply ensuring minimum popular acceptance of basic goals and a functionally adequate tolerance of the political system by the citizenry. Such limited acceptance would presumably ensure continued political and socioeconomic control by the Communist Party and would prevent major abuses and antiregime manifestations, as well as a meaningful organized opposition. It seems that some other socialist states in Eastern Europe have settled for this minimal goal of political education.[26] Nicolae Ceausescu's Romania, on the other hand, is still the scene of massive ideological campaigns that seem designed to go beyond the minimal legitimacy and tolerance levels of some fraternal Socialist states. This continued emphasis on a new socialist society with new "socialist individuals" is a result partly of the general secretary's personal views and partly of the still unsettled nature of the rapidly changing society in Romania. It is conceivable that the RCP too will become content with maintenance of limited legitimacy when its major socioeconomic goals have been reached. The more highly developed countries in the area, such as Czechoslovakia and Hungary, have experienced less "Sturm und Drang" in the quest for a thoroughly socialist society, probably because of the social and political complexities of highly modernized systems. Romania is not yet at that level of development, and the quest for fundamental political socialization goes on.

Socialization Symbols

In the educational and socialization efforts of the postwar regime one can distinguish between two sets of socialization symbols, each with a positive and a negative component. One set of symbols is directed at establishing mass values necessary for the rapid socioeconomic development of society and is therefore an integral component of the educational effort in various fields discussed previously in this chapter. The second value set can be termed "moral-political," aimed at the formation of views and behavior in the moral, ethical, and political fields befitting a new Socialist Man. The most important positive "moral-political" symbols are the following:

"Building of Socialism." Building of Socialistm has been a constant theme throughout the entire period. Imbedded in the concept is the emphasis on Socialist Man, free from alienation, greed, careerism, and "negative individualism," a human being fulfilling the classical Marxist dictum of contributing to society according to his means, receiving from it according to his needs. While this goal is considered a final product of Communism, several other "middle-range" elements have been emphasized. Chief among these are appeals for acceptance of Party supremacy and societal control, democratic centralism in decision making, mass participation in socioeconomic and political organizations for better popular understanding of societal needs, and increased commitment to elite goals through improved education and "citizenship training." At the same time, this concept has obvious economic connotations insofar as the Party press gives prominent coverage to planning, reporting of production results and problems, and new methods in the economy. Building of socialism means laying the material base for the sociopolitical relations befitting a higher stage of development, and in this context constant production increases and a rising standard of living are important goals. So far the regime has clearly opted for rapid expansion of heavy industry at the expense of consumer goods production, but this development is also seen as befitting the process of building socialism insofar as heavy industry must be the backbone of the material base on which "political-moral" socialism rests.

"Socialist Morality." Socialist morality clearly embodies many elements listed above under "Building of Socialism," especially commitment to society and its leadership rather than to individual advancement and well-being. But morality also includes other traits seen as desirable, especially trustworthiness, honesty, "a personal life befitting citizens of a Socialist society"; furthermore, discipline and a sense of duty to one's family and society are stressed. The themes subsumed under socialist morality seem to come close to the celebrated "Protestant work ethic," and they constitute an important regime effort to promote stabilizing and societally functional behavior in a country where corruption and self-seeking, as well as public inefficiency, have been endemic under previous regimes. Socialist morality as defined clearly has economic connotations as well, insofar as duty, discipline, and honesty are crucial factors in the struggle for modernization and efficiency in industry and agriculture.

"Patriotism." Patriotism, with generous doses of Romanian nationalism, has become a major symbol in the socialization media, especially in the 1960s and 1970s. "Building of Socialism" and "Socialist Morality" are increasingly interpreted as building Romanian socialism and establishing socialist morality fitting Romanian conditions. Legitimacy is also claimed by the RCP as a progressive, national elite rather than as part of an international working-class movement. Sacrifices in the modernization process are justified and should be accepted as a necessity for laying the foundations of national progress that will finally propel Romania into the ranks of modern states, claiming its rightful place in the concert of nations.

Patriotism as defined is clearly a powerful symbol for a regime whose policies have been unpopular with parts of the population because of the political control exercised and the material sacrifices endured by the masses. In emphasizing this symbol, the RCP is in the mainstream of developments in East Europe in the 1960s, where nationalism has become perhaps the most important fact of political life. The nationalist revival in Romania has of course manifested itself most strongly in foreign policy, and it seems that it is precisely Bucharest's foreign policy that has increased the legitimacy of the regime and made its emphasis on patriotism credible among the masses.

"Love of Socialist Commonwealth." In comparison with patriotism and nationalism, the symbol "Love of Socialist Commonwealth" has become a somewhat empty slogan. The emphasis on commonality of interests within the Soviet bloc was clearly a symbol with major political content in the period of Stalinism and indeed beyond, when Romania acted as a loyal member of the commonwealth. In the 1960s, however, Romania became a maverick in foreign policy, and acceptance of the commonwealth is now usually coupled with emphasis on noninterference in domestic affairs, respect for national sovereignty, and mutually beneficial relations. The Ceausescu regime is also increasingly insistent upon its rights to establish and maintain friendly relations with countries outside the commonwealth, without regard to social and political system. The usual press emphasis on Romania's unshakable faith in the close cooperation among socialist countries is therefore partly a coverup for relative independence in foreign policy. At the same time, Bucharest is realistic enough to continue to adhere to certain basic elements of commonwealth relations, such as close economic ties with the fraternal socialist countries, an "anti-imperialistic" stance primarily directed against U.S. involvement in Vietnam and elsewhere in the Third World, and domestic ideological orthodoxy.[27]

Negative Slogans. In addition to the major recurring positive themes discussed above, several negative slogans appear with some frequency and emphasis. Among these, "anti-individualism" is virtually the antithesis of "Socialist Man," the chief goal of the building process constantly hammered home in the RCP press. Individualism represents a pantheon of undesirable qualities such as selfishness, economic activity only for personal gain, lack of willingness to contribute to societal needs, careerism, lip-service to Marxism-Leninism but no real commitment to it, and negative views toward the Party and its leading role in society. Anti-individualism is often mentioned together with sharp criticism against remnants of "bourgeois-landowner mentality" and "bourgeois nationalism." Selfishness, greed, and exploitation are seen as major elements of political and social systems that preceded socialism in Romania, and the building process can only be successful if such remnants are completely erased.

Another negative remnant is "bourgeois nationalism," which bases itself on the differences in social and cultural traditions among ethnic groups in a multinational political system. The Communist regime in Romania has consistently maintained that relations among ethnic groups will be friendly and mutually beneficial in a socialist society; indeed, the task of building socialism will transcend old national animosities and lift social life onto a higher plane in this field. Continuing nationality problems are therefore attributed to remnants of bourgeois nationalism, and the struggle against such manifestations has been consistently waged in the RCP press. Patriotism, that is, commitment to building a socialist Romania, is therefore seen as a positive concept, while nationalism is viewed negatively.

Just as "Love of the Socialist Commonwealth" has been a positive theme in Romanian political socialization, "the Menace of Imperialism" has had consistently negative overtones. In this case, too, there has been an important, if subtle, change during the 1960s. Imperialism was traditionally identified with the foreign policy of major Western powers, especially the United States and West Germany.

This connection is no longer established as a matter of course; and, when it is made, it is likely to refer to specific cases (such as U.S. involvement in Vietnam) rather than to all policies emanating from Washington. Imperialism is now usually seen as a breach of the principle of noninterference in internal affairs and respect for national sovereignty, and the perpetrators are mostly identified as "big powers," a connotation that could fit the Soviet Union as well as the United States. In any case, the Romanian regime associates itself with anti-imperialism and always stresses that it stands for respect of sovereignty and mutually advantageous relations with all states, thus clearly promoting an image of peacemaker among the Romanian public.

Economic Themes. In addition to the major political-moral themes discussed above, the RCP press has consistently emphasized certain themes primarily oriented toward economic needs and the requirements of the modernization process. Several of these have been mentioned already (for example, discipline, commitment to societal goals, willingness to suffer present deprivation in order to promote accumulation and future well-being, and honesty) because of their partially moral connotations. Themes with primarily economic connotations include increased productivity in all branches of the economy, reduction of costs, reduction of waste, better quality in production, and better utilization of existing resources. By the same token, loafing, shirking, sloppy work performance, overcommitment of resources, excessive idle time of expensive machinery, and underutilization of resources, including manpower, have been severely condemned.[28]

These themes are certainly familiar to students of developing societies everywhere, but in systems such as Romania improved economic performance is seen as a requirement for the achievement of other even loftier goals. Without a viable economic base "Building of Socialism" will become an impossibility and "Socialist Morality" will forever be faced with competition from selfishness, greed, and careerism found in "bourgeois-landowner mentality." Economic scarcity, based on an uneven distribution of goods and services, will also make the establishment and maintenance of "Socialist Patriotism" a doubtful venture indeed. Political socialization through economic themes, therefore, carries as much urgency as does the quest for "Socialist Man."

Implementation of Political Education

The implementation of political education and socialization is an extremely complicated process, which cannot be described in detail in a work of this scope. As indicated above, political education in Romania tends to run along campaign lines, in which all of the socialization vehicles are mobilized for a major task, be it an "ideological cleansing" of major socioeconomic structures, a struggle for renewed orthodoxy in Party structures, or a fight against recurring "bourgeois-landowner mentality" among youth. It is nevertheless possible to outline some major continuing trends in this field--primarily elite socialization, the socialization of youth, and special efforts devoted to the "cohabiting nationalities," especially the Hungarians and Germans. In addition, continued efforts are expended to reach the masses of industrial proletarians and rural workers.

Socialization of the Elite

Elite socialization is implemented in a variety of ways. First, the Party exercises direct control over political education in the institutes of higher learning that train socioeconomic elites. Such direct control has been a fact of life in Romania since 1947-48, with a partial relaxation in the period 1968-71 and a considerable increase in control since 1971. During the period 1947-68 the Party controlled the basic curriculum in Marxism-Leninism, although the actual teaching of this discipline was carried out by each institution, thus producing considerable differentiation. Each student, regardless of field, had to attend two hours of instruction in Marxism-Leninism per week for at least four semesters.[29]

During the period 1968-71 the compulsory load was reduced to two semesters with two hours of instruction per week. Additional training in Marxism-Leninism could be added by the department heads, but the subject was now primarily confined to the departments of philosophy, political economy, history, and law.[30]

The inauguration of the little cultural revolution in the summer of 1971 marked a massive expansion of Marxism-Leninism in all curriculums and reimposition of direct Party control (through the Central Committee) of all aspects of this subject. Teaching in formal ideology has now increased to more than 10 percent of all semester hours in all fields, while in philosophy, political economy, and history this subject matter accounts for one-third to one-half of all courses taught. Large increases have also been registered in other fields such as economics, philology, and law.[31]

In addition to increased teaching of Marxism-Leninism in the formal school system, the RCP has expanded its Party schools, which train apparatchik cadres in political subjects. Furthermore, the Stefan Gheorghiu Academy, operated under direct RCP control, now offers short-term courses and more long-range programs for "leading cadres" in the economy, culture, and academia, for professional as well as Party elites. In all cases the current version of Marxism-Leninism and the Party's views on social, economic, political, and cultural matters are being presented with great vigor.

A third vehicle for elite socialization is the yearly convention of technical and managerial experts, at which the Party leadership will specify the RCP program of modernization and then elicit discussion on problems connected with implementation. Significantly, such conventions do not encourage discussions of the direction of the program but only deal with the most expeditious way to carry it out at all levels. Thus the "Conference of Leading Cadres in Firms and Industrial Centrals," held in Bucharest in February 1972, wholeheartedly endorsed the RCP program and confined its discussion to questions of implementation.[32]

Variations of the above approaches are also used. During the Ceausescu era it became regular practice to invite leading cadres in important fields to expanded plenums of the RCP Central Committee, in which important questions of implementation in selected fields were discussed. Thus in the fall of 1971, for example, an expanded plenum of the RCP Executive Committee discussed implementation of the ideological offensive with selected ministerial and other governmental personnel.* In the fall of 1972, the same Party body invited personnel from the Ministry of Internal Trade, the Ministry of Agriculture, and the Ministry of Food Production to a discussion of ways to implement the Party's program in light indus-

---

*This was the RCP Central Committee November Plenum, reported in the Party press during the first half of November 1971.

tries and food provisions. An extremely detailed set of directives was established for the ministries to follow. There was apparently only slight discussion of any matters pertaining to the program itself.[33] In each session a major speech by Nicolae Ceausescu emphasized the need for better political education of cadres and fundamentals of the Party's ideological stance were repeated.

The vehicles discussed above naturally represent only a small part of the structures employed by the Party to implement its political education and socialization program. As discussed in Chapter 2, the Party structure and its auxiliary organizations control all major aspects of societal life, and the program is continuously expounded in these structures. As described in Chapter 3, RCP control over the decision-making process and the staffing of important agencies (nomenklatura) further enhances the Party's ability to transmit its major socialization symbols. In all, the RCP has an impressive network of socialization agents at its disposal, and the elites of the country are constantly being confronted by a steady barrage of symbols. Problems in this field are certainly not due to lack of implementation vehicles.

Socialization of the Youth

Another field of major regime effort is socialization of the young. Any political elite that seriously expects to change basic values among its citizenry will naturally concentrate its efforts on those individuals who have not yet been subjected to basic socialization from peer groups, ethnic groups, or other structures that may be considered actual or potential competitors with the political leadership. With such considerations in mind, the RCP has been engaged in massive indoctrination efforts through a multitude of vehicles, among which are the primary and secondary school systems, the Party-dominated youth groups (Pioneers, UTC, and student bodies), conventions and meetings, and social activities such as dances, theater performances, organized vacation tours, and work camps.

Political education starts at a very early stage in the school system. The kindergartens, of which there were approximately 10,000 in 1969-70, have basic political training on the agenda, and this approach is continued throughout the primary and secondary schools up to the university level. At the kindergarten stage the educational effort is of necessity rather simple, emphasizing basic concepts of flag, country, and leadership, almost always personalized, especially during the Ceausescu era. Basic concepts of national allegiance are taught, and some rudimentary knowledge of Lenin and class analysis is transmitted. Basically, the effort is on depicting socialism as a good system, while "imperialism" is decried. National symbols are very important, and the continuity of Romania as "our" country and as a "good" country is a major element in the program.

In the secondary schools the relatively simple socialization program gives way to a full-fledged set of courses that integrate and expand upon much of what has been taught at previous stages. History and social science text books are systematically written within a Marxist-Leninist framework, and the basic ideological tenets find their way into other curriculums as well. This more systematic framework also heavily emphasizes the Romanian interpretation of the ideological classics; it is at this stage that the concepts of "national roads to socialism and communism" and "socialist internationalism" are elaborated. The curriculum relies heavily upon domestic political writing, particularly Party history and documents, and in some courses newspaper reading, particularly of Scinteia, the main Party organ, and Scinteia Tineretului, the organ of the Party youth organization, UTC, is compulsory. Competitions in essay writing are organized around political themes, and debating clubs are formed for further elaboration of major political themes. The regime expects that the basics of Marxist-Leninist thought have been internalized upon completion of secondary education.*

Political training of youth at the university level is conducted under strict Party supervision and control, as indicated above. The content of this training is essentially an elaboration of and systematization upon the base established in the secondary schools. In the social science fields, particularly in political economy and economics, and also in the humanities, the curriculum involves in-depth studies of Party documents, Party history, and the most important documents of the international workers' movement. During the last five to six years there has been an increasing emphasis on the continuity between the present regime and great figures of Romanian

---

*Failure to implement this program was one of the sources of criticism emanating from the Party leadership during the little cultural revolution (see Ceausescu in Scinteia, November 4, 1971).

history such as Michael the Brave and Stephen the Great. This approach is an integral part of a systematic effort to transmit a specifically Romanian version of the ideological classics, to support the RCP's independent stance in the world Communist movement. Thus, the political education at this level represents a highly innovative mix of traditional Romanian nationalism and the contemporary ideological version, strongly influenced by the general secretary. It is a major effort directed toward the important element of youth, the future leaders of the nation.

Socialization through the school system is not only confined to Party control with the curriculum. The RCP has penetrated the ranks of academic personnel and the teaching profession at all levels, and political indoctrination is therefore assured a prominent place everywhere. The various councils and advisory bodies established in the schools are controlled by Party members, and student participation is primarily a privilege of the RCP or UTC activists in this group. The organizational interpenetration and overlapping memberships at all levels of the school system ensure basic political control.

Socialization of youth is also carried out in the Party structures, which normally have special youth sections, and in the UTC. For those young people who leave school after compulsory secondary education and go to work in industry or agriculture, the trade unions and the farm units represent the most important socialization structures. A considerable amount of time is devoted to political education in these economic organizations, which usually have specialized personnel to deal with young workers. (This is especially true of the larger trade unions.)

The various institutional mechanisms used in the socialization of youth are augmented by frequent use of work camps, "socially beneficial labor" during school holidays, organized excursions, sports competitions, and social events such as Saturday night dances. In all of the activities listed political indoctrination plays a vital part. A typical day in a summer work camp for students (which is presumably voluntary and will usually involve such projects as beautification of cities and parks or completion of a road) will be almost equally divided among work, sports, and political study under the guidance of Party activists. At Saturday night dances the band will usually start playing only after the political speeches have been made and the pamphlets have been handed out.[34]

The socialization system described above represents a major ongoing effort to reach the crucial young generation of Romanian society. The efforts in this field have intensified since the start of the little cultural revolution in 1971, and there is no sign that they will abate in the near future.

Socialization of Minorities

The campaign for socialization of societal elites and youth constitutes a major effort of political education, but of equal importance is the quest for socialization of the ethnic minorities in the country to a common "socialist" culture. The political leadership is working against major odds in this field; many of the minorities, especially the Hungarians and Germans, have cultural, political, and economic traditions that are quite separate and different from those of the politically dominant Romanians. For centuries the Hungarians constituted the ruling elite in Transylvania, and the Germans were heavily represented in administration and other important governmental positions. For such groups the establishment of a Communist regime, which has become increasingly associated with Romanian nationalism since 1952, also meant the imposition of a Romanian political and economic elite on previously privileged groups. Hungarians and Germans, therefore, have to assimilate "downwards" to a common socialist culture with strong overtones of Romanian nationalism.

This transition is an extremely difficult one, and the RCP has been engaged in an ongoing socialization effort to accomplish it. The regular socialization agents of Party, UTC, trade unions, other peer groups, and the formal school system have all been used for this purpose, and in addition the political leadership has used certain specialized structures for work among the minorities. One of the most important of these is the so-called nationality council, which is made up of prominent minority members at the local and regional levels. There are also specialized councils, such as the Council of Workers of Hungarian Origin, which have a national structure as well as regional and local outlets. Various literary societies, friendship groups, organizations designed to promote friendly relations among all nationality groups on Romanian soil, youth groups, women's organizations, and numerous other structures are habitually mobilized for the purpose of transmitting the regime-sponsored values to all citizens, regardless of nationality. In addition, the Party branches and local UTC organizations promote a common ideological and political base for all activists and interested citizens. Since the membership distribution in the RCP is roughly proportional to the ethnic distribution of the population, the Party itself serves as both a recruitment vehicle and a source of socialization. Significant minority representation is also found at other levels in the RCP, especially in the counties (judets), thus further enhancing the possibilities of successful socialization of minorities by their own activists.*

The Party's attempt to educate the "cohabiting nationalities" in political matters is carefully executed according to the principle "national in form, socialist in content." Folklore, native language training, and literature in the mother tongue are encouraged, as long as the major cultural themes remain within the parameters established by the political elite. In many cases this has resulted in minority literature providing even less criticism of the sociopolitical system than can be found among Romanian writers. All in all, the political regime has succeeded in producing a considerable uniformity of socialization symbols and vehicles for their transmission across social strata, age groups, and ethnic dividing lines. The success or failure of political education and socialization therefore must depend upon the popular acceptance or rejection of the symbols transmitted rather than a breakdown in the communication of such symbols.

Achievements of the Socialization Effort

Despite the sophisticated apparatus established for the purposes of political education and socialization, there are numerous indications that this massive effort has fallen short of the goal envisioned by the RCP and the general secretary. The shortcomings of the effort are perhaps most dramatically illustrated by the need for frequent campaigns designed to remedy some of the shortcomings and achieve quick and decisive results. If the ongoing socialization effort were successful the need for

---

*In the heavy Hungarian populated judets of Covasna and Mures, for example, Hungarians have always occupied the top Party positions. (See Trond Gilberg, "Regional Political Leadership in Romania: The Case of the Judet Party 1968-1973," East European Quarterly, January 1975.)

dramatic campaigns would disappear or become much less prominent. Instead of such an indication of success, the current campaign, which has been under way for the better part of three years, points to recurring and serious problems.

Because of the lack of survey material, a systematic investigation of this question cannot be undertaken. The researcher is forced to rely on the statements of the political elite itself--a rather dangerous approach. Some advantages nevertheless stem from this reliance on the RCP's own records. The political regime is programmatically committed to achieving success; for political leaders acting on the basis of historical determinism, there can be no admission of regressions, no acceptance of defeat in any fundamental political task. Consequently, a thorough discussion of admitted social and political ills would indicate the existence of a real problem with ramifications possibly going beyond those indicated in the Party press and elsewhere.

Both in published statements and in virtually every major policy speech during his nine years in office the general secretary has referred to major problems of political education, and frequent mention has been made of ways in which to remedy this vexing problem. There has been considerable consistency both in the problems discussed and the solutions proposed, indicating longstanding concerns among the political elite. This very consistency also permits a fairly systematic summary. In many respects Nicolae Ceausescu's speeches at RCP Central Committee plenums in July and November, 1971, when the little cultural revolution was launched, represent the high points of concern in this field and can be taken as representative of more general problems.

According to Ceausescu, the political socialization effort had met with considerable trouble for a long period of time. The most persistent problems were the following:[35]

Formalism and unwillingness to relate political education to real life in Romania. Both in the Party and in other political and social institutions there was a widespread tendency to approach political education, especially the teaching of Marxism-Leninism, with a "formalist" attitude, in which the classics as well as major Party documents would be recited mechanistically, without any attempt to relate them to real life and show how the ideas expressed could become guidelines for action. This "chanting of slogans" was decried as a very serious problem, especially for a society that was in the process of reaching the state of multilateral development, when a firm guide to practical political action was more necessary than ever.

Laxity in political training in the universities and at other levels of the school system. According to Ceausescu, many academic cadres only participated in ideological education because they felt compelled to do so. Instead of a proper balance between political and specialized training, professors only engaged in the former through abstract sloganeering, while the specialized subjects would receive all of the attention and energy. Such a development was seen as extremely dangerous, eventually resulting in the complete erosion of political training and possibly leading to serious problems for the developmental and modernization processes.

Inadequate political commitment in the intelligentsia. Parts of the intelligentsia, particularly in the arts, literature, cinema, and theater, had shown a serious lack of political commitment. Especially dangerous was the tendency among writers to emphasize the problematic aspects of life under socialism rather than focusing on the tremendous achievements of Romania during the last quarter century. Some writers had even argued for a particular form of individualism, in which each person could decide for himself whether to participate in the great nation-building effort under way in the country. This form of "opting out" must be decisively eradicated, and a new commitment to "constructive" literature must be established.

Individuals engaged in widespread corruption in leading positions in society, including Party cadres, who exhibited "bourgeois egotism" and "conduct unbecoming a citizen of a Socialist country" by amassing personal wealth and otherwise taking advantage of their status and power. Corruption and personal enrichment represent aberrations in both values and behavior and must be dealt with decisively and severely.

Low productivity and inadequate use of economic facilities. Both among leading cadres and in the rank and file of the citizenry there is a tendency to work at less than full capacity; "sloughing off" and misuse of equipment are serious problems in the Romanian economy. The general secretary gave numerous examples showing that each wasted minute, each unutilized machine, lost society millions of lei. The Party leader attributed this laxity to inadequate organization and low skill levels, but above all to insufficient moral and political commitment.

Figures were given showing that productivity per worker in industry was very low compared to some other East European countries, not to mention the advanced countries in the West, and Ceausescu made it quite clear that such deficiencies must be remedied in the period of multilateral development. A new campaign to instill increased personal commitment was announced.

Excessive infatuation with bourgeois ideas from the West. Ceausescu complained about the infatuation with Western ideas that had permeated much of the elite, especially in the technical and managerial fields. According to the general secretary, this Western influence had made people less likely to develop Romanian research and technology and promoted the reliance on foreign patents and licenses. This development was heavily criticized, and Ceausescu proclaimed a decisive turning toward domestic talent and equipment. At the same time he denounced the influence of Western life styles and outlooks, particularly among the youth but also in important segments of the intellectual and managerial elites. He decreed much tighter screening of cultural inputs from the West, and during the post-1971 period there has been a marked decline in the number of foreign films and plays admitted to the country.

The points discussed in Ceausescu's speeches reflect serious problems in political education and socialization. Many of the chief socialization symbols discussed above have not been internalized by many of the socioeconomic elites in Romania, and there are serious problems in the political elite as well. The shortcomings exist both in the moral-political and in the "skills" field; some members of the societal elites have either ignored the major moral-political symbols or have acted directly against them by engaging in self-enrichment when the regime is promoting cooperation and commitment to society as a whole. The ideological classics and the major Party documents are widely ignored. Many leading cadres have inadequate skills in the jobs they perform.

The shortcomings openly admitted were dramatically illustrated in elite response to the little cultural revolution. Several prominent writers and artists openly protested the Party's tightening of control in the arts, and many others paid mere lip service to the demands for a new "Socialist realism" that would depict the achievements of the country in positive terms and act as a stimulant to further exertions by the citizenry. Only after extensive purges of the Writers' Union could the Party reassert full control with the literary elite, and dissident voices continue to be heard through books, pamphlets, and plays.[36] The imposition of increased Party control with economic planning and management at all levels resulted in considerable dissent among the managerial elite, both in open criticism and lack of compliance with Party directives.[37] By early 1973 Ceausescu perceived the need to break the back of such recalcitrance through massive reorganizations in the economy, in which economic and managerial elites experienced demotions or transfer to production functions that could more easily be controlled by political organs. This process is still underway, and the repercussions in the economy are beginning to become clear, with loss of production, general insecurity, and lack of initiative. In a relatively short time the political leadership will be forced to choose between a continued campaign of indoctrination, socialization, and control or a relative liberalization, in which economic elites will be given more autonomy in order to increase production. For now, the Party has clearly opted for continued strict control and a massive ideological offensive designed to achieve at least some of the goals of political education and socialization discussed above.

Problems associated with the socialization of youth remain serious as well. The 1971 congress of the UTC was the scene of a massive reevaluation of political work among youth, and much severe criticism was uttered. The young generation appears to be quite apathetic politically. Adherence to the ideas of Marxism-Leninism is primarily formalistic, with little attempt to relate book learning to real life, and there are disturbing tendencies toward a revival of "bourgeois-landowner mentality." The problem is especially severe in rural areas, where organizational coverage is inadequate and political consciousness is at a low level. Even among students and urban youth "careerism" and narrow individualism are rampant.[38]

The same kinds of criticisms were launched at the November 1971 RCP Central Committee Plenum on Ideology. The 1971 UTC Congress had undergone a personnel change in the top leadership of the organization, and purges at other levels of the structure continued throughout 1971 and 1972. There is little evidence to suggest that the Party's problems with youth have abated; exhortations to greater political educational efforts continue, and discouraging reports on ideological lethargy still find their way into the Romanian press.[39] It is true that virtually every article concludes with assurances that most youngsters are politically committed and that mistakes made represent annoying exceptions to the rule. The observer is nevertheless faced with an increasing amount of evidence indicating that political education and socialization of youth, one of the fundamental tasks of the Communist regime, confront very severe difficulties that persist even as society moves toward the target of multilateral development.

Particularly troublesome to the Party in the field of youth work is the persistent laxity among UTC cadres. The most severe criticism meted out at the 1971 ideological plenums was directed against those presumed "activists" whose ideological commitment left much to be desired.[40] The current ideological offensive is therefore a dual attack on the problems of political education and socialization; one must retrain the activist cadres as well as promoting a better ideological consciousness among the masses of the population. If the problems discussed in the Romanian press represent a relatively accurate picture, this task is formidable indeed.

The continuing attempt to socialize the many ethnic minorities on Romanian territory to a common culture that is characterized as socialist is likewise a major problem. Since the dominant political elite is primarily Romanian, socialization efforts in this field can easily be interpreted as "Romanianization." An additional problem is that some of these ethnic groups (particularly the Hungarians and Germans) have undergone social mobilization and development that make them more "modern" than the Romanians (that is, better education, more highly urbanized, proportionally in more advanced positions in the economy).[41] Assimilation to a common culture the parameters of which are basically set by Romanians and containing large doses of Romanian nationalism appears as integration "downwards" into a Romanian culture.

The processes of modernization, which increasingly bring a certain minimum similarity to peoples' lives all over the country, cannot be counted upon to produce assimilation as a matter of course. Available evidence suggests that little assimilation is taking place among Hungarians and that the Germans also by and large remain unassimilated in the sense that they have retained the outward symbols of nationality, particularly the use of the native language as the primary vehicle of expression and communication. Among both Hungarians and Germans the use of the native language increased in the period 1956-66.[42] Literature and plays in these languages have also exhibited considerable vigor. Residential patterns still produce heavy concentrations of these minorities in certain areas.[43]

However, the political regime has retreated from some of its more assimilationist policies of the early 1960s and now exhibits more tolerance of ethnic particularism in nonessential fields such as folk art, national literature, and maintenance of customs and behavior patterns. Concurrently there is considerable political concern that the limited autonomy must be prevented from turning into political separatism, and the regime continues its efforts to inculcate basic political values in the minds of all citizens, regardless of nationality background. The RCP is experiencing considerable problems in political apathy, formalism, and personal careerism among the minorities as well as in the population generally, but the potential for serious trouble among ethnic groups has been reduced. Thus political education and socialization in this field have met with some important successes, primarily of a preventative nature, as well as with the more general failure of creating "new Socialist individuals."

On the basis of evidence presented above, it seems clear that the more ambitious goals of political education and socialization have not been successful in Romania. Parts of the socioeconomic and political elites have exhibited "regressive" views and behavior; the literary and artistic intelligentsia have at times questioned some of the basic political and educational givens of the regime. The younger generation tends toward political apathy, and many ethnic minorities have retained significant elements of separatism, in some cases increasing their commitment to a strong ethnic profile. In short, the quest for the new Socialist Man in moral-political terms has met with severe problems.

Similarly, it has at times been difficult to instill the values of efficiency, regularity, and hard work in a population that has traditionally been rural, economically oppressed, and used to inefficient methods of economic production and management. Multilateral development seems a considerable distance away in this field as well.

Seen in another perspective, however, the RCP can claim considerable success in political socialization. The Party came to power as a result of foreign invasion, not because of widespread popular support. In fact, the RCP could claim only a miniscule membership in 1944, and the bulk of that small band consisted primarily of individuals from ethnic minority groups. Almost from the outset the Party launched far-ranging programs of political and socioeconomic change that involved considerable repression and terror, programs that caused widespread resentment among virtually all social strata. In foreign policy the Stalinist regime subordinated itself to Moscow and became one of the most loyal of satellites. The Romanian regime allowed Soviet economic exploitation of the country through the notorious joint companies, and Soviet military occupation of a traditionally anti-Russian population continued until the late 1950s. With such a combination of political and economic policies the RCP reached a nadir of popular support. During the last 15 years, however, an increasingly independent foreign policy, rapid economic development, revival of traditional Romanian nationalism, and a regime that consciously associates itself with traditional values of patriotism have combined to produce considerable popular support for the current regime. There seems to have been a selective popular response to political education and socialization. While the man in the street has been less than enthusiastic about the creation of new Socialist individuals, he has accepted those political messages that are consistent with his own values of nationalism, sense of progress, pride in development, and occasionally chauvinism. While his work efforts still fall short of the "modern" behavior patterns advocated by the Party, he is immeasurably more efficient and productive than before the Communist takeover. While he might be critical of the restrictiveness of political indoctrination, he most likely supports the paternalism and welfare state elements of the regime's program. In short, the modernizing elite in Romania has achieved at least a minimum of legitimacy in the population and quite possibly a great deal more; while this has failed to produce a new socialist society in terms of moral and political behavior, it has established a secure base of operations for the modernizers. Given the starting point of the RCP in 1944, this must be seen as a major achievement of socioeconomic development and political education.

NOTES

1. Ceausescu in Scinteia, July 20, 1972 and November 4, 1971.

2. For a report on one of the last congresses of the Hungarian party, see Kurt Kwasny, "Ungarns Kommunisten Wagen Mehr Demokratie," Osteuropa, November 1971, pp. 842-50.

3. See, for example, article by Minister of Education Mircea Malita in Scinteia, August 28, 1971.

4. Directia Centrala de Statistica, Anuarul Statistic al Romaniei 1935 (Bucharest, 1935), pp. 46-47 and Anuarul Statistic al Romaniei 1936, pp. 46-47.

5. Republica Populare Romina, Directia Centrala de Statistica, Recensamintul Populatiei 1956--(Rezultate Generale) (Bucharest, 1959), pp. 4, 484-85.

6. Republica Socialista Romania, Directia Centrala de Statistica, Anuarul Statistic al Republicii Socialiste Romania 1970 (Bucharest, 1970), p. 592.

7. For a discussion of Romanian development in the interwar period, see Stephen Fischer-Galati, Twentieth Century Rumania (New York: Columbia University Press, 1965), pp. 29-70.

8. Based on calculations from Table 4.2 and Republica Socialista Romania, Directia Centrala de Statistica, Recensamintul Populatiei si Locuintelor din 15 Martie 1966, vol. 1.

9. See, for example, Viitorul Social, "Management Science and Future Studies in Socialist Romania," September 1972.

10. Anuarul Statistic 1970, pp. 592-93.

11. Ibid., pp. 600-01.

12. Ibid.

13. Ibid., pp. 592-94.

14. For example, Ceausescu, Scinteia, November 4, 1971.

15. Ibid.

16. Congresul al IX-lea al Partidului Comunist Roman (Bucharest: Editura Politica, 1966), pp. 59-60.

17. Congresul al X-lea al Partidului Comunist Roman (Bucharest: Editura Politica, 1969), pp. 44-45.

18. For example, in Scinteia, November 4, 1971.

19. See, for example, speech by Leonte Rautu, RCP Executive Committee member, on the need to strengthen ideological education at all levels, in Lupta de Clasa, no. 4, 1972.

20. Ibid.

21. The extent of Party control over higher education was seen in the Decree on Political Education, published in Buletinul Oficial, December 30, 1971.

22. See his speech at the opening of the school year 1971, in Scinteia, October 2, 1971.

23. See Leonte Rautu in Lupta de Clasa, no. 4, 1972.

24. For a discussion of the concepts "socialization" and "resocialization," see, for example, Richard E. Dawson

and Kenneth Prewitt, Political Socialization (Boston: Little, Brown and Co., 1969).

25. For example, Rautu in Lupta de Clasa, no. 4, 1972, and Ceausescu in Scinteia, November 4, 1971.

26. Such as Hungary (see Kwasny, "Ungarns Kommunisten Wagen Mehr Demokratie").

27. These main symbols are gleaned from major policy statements by Nicolae Ceausescu and other members of the RCP elite on such occasions as the Tenth Congress, the November 1971 Plenum, and the 1972 National Conference.

28. Ibid.

29. The 1948 decree was reviewed and criticized in Monitorul Oficial, August 3, 1968.

30. Scinteia Tineretului, July 21, 1967.

31. This development was discussed by Virgil Cazacu, first deputy minister of education, in ibid., October 29, 1971.

32. Scinteia, February 18 and 19, 1972.

33. Reported in Scinteia, November 18, 1972.

34. Ion Iliescu gave a description of the extent of such activities in his report to the 1971 UTC Congress, see Romania's Youth (1971), pp. 13-17.

35. These points are summaries of the two major speeches mentioned and also the general secretary's speech to the RCP National Conference, July 1972. The two best sources are therefore Scinteia, November 4, 1971, and July 20, 1972.

36. See Le Monde, May 25, 1972, for a discussion of the purges in the Writers' Union.

37. For example, in resistance to the reorganization of the economy, as discussed by G. Gaston-Marin, Chairman of the State Committee on Prices, in Lupta de Clasa, January 1972.

38. Iliescu in Romania's Youth, p. 20.

39. See, for example, Constantin Dascalescu, in Lupta de Clasa, no. 8, 1971.

40. Iliescu in Romania's Youth, pp. 20-22.

41. See my "Ethnic Minorities in Romania Under Socialism," East European Quarterly, January 1974, pp. 435-64.

42. Ibid., p. 463.

43. Figures derived from Recensamintul--1966, pp. 158-62.

CHAPTER

5

INDUSTRIALIZATION

Perhaps no other area of the modernization process in Communist systems has received as much attention as industrialization. All Communist regimes have considered rapid industrialization the most important economic activity, and in every country in Eastern Europe a massive attack was made on the problems associated with inadequate industrial development, which had characterized all of these systems (except for Czechoslovakia) before World War II.

Romania was one of the least developed countries in the area at the time of the Communist takeover in 1944. In 1930 only 7.9 percent of the population was engaged in industry.[1] Most of the industrial enterprises in Romania were located in Bucharest or in the semi-industrial regions of Transylvania. Another manufacturing center was located in the southwest around Craiova, and another in the Ploiesti region with its rich oil wells. This concentration of industrial activity left large areas of the country practically without modern manufacturing enterprises.[2]

Not only was there heavy concentration of industrial activity in a few areas but the capacity of Romanian manufacturing was low and concentrated in a few fields, primarily in light and consumer goods industries, mostly based on agricultural raw materials and oil. Machine building, steel production, and the extraction of minerals and fuels were woefully underdeveloped.[3]

THE RCP CAMPAIGN

Upon ascension to the ruling coalition on August 23, 1944, the RCP started a vigorous campaign for industrial development. This campaign had two major facets; first, the Communist members of the cabinet pushed for expropriation of industrial plants belonging to "collaborators" and for increased state control of the banking system, remaining private enterprises, and credit and fiscal policies, which would allow for sustained and controlled investment in industry; and, second, they promoted centralized planning with compulsory "guidelines" that would, presumably, provide rapid expansion in all industrial fields, but primarily in the heavy and extractive industries.[4]

The gradual destruction of private banking and private manufacturing went hand in hand with the RCP's increasing power in the political realm. By 1947-48 the last remnants of major private enterprise in industry were removed (although small craftsmen and artisans remained, as did private agriculture until 1962). Through a series of five-year plans, the RCP leadership pushed for rapid implementation of its industrialization program, which was designed to develop a Romanian heavy industry very quickly, while making massive advances in the extraction of the vast natural resources of the country, the richest in all of Eastern Europe in minerals and fuels.[5]

As in other fields, the Romanian regime launched a frontal attack on underdevelopment rather than allowing a gradual approach through which sectors of the economy would be developed successively with a smooth transition from stage to stage. The Romanian approach was a clear imitation of the Soviet industrialization drive of the 1930s, and it was carried out with similar elan, disregard for costs, and "frontal storming" of economic problems.[6] Specifically, the program consisted of expansion of existing facilities, development of wholly new industries located near existing "growth poles," and the establishment of industrial cities in areas that had hitherto been rural or even uninhabited.[7]

The vehicles employed for this kind of forced development were many. First of all, the Romanian modernizers drastically reoriented investments and expanded them to a point that the ratio of investment to consumption became one of the highest in the world. Tables 5.1-5.6 illustrate various elements of this investment policy in the period 1949-71, with a comparison with investments in 1938, the last prewar year for which there are accurate figures.

TABLE 5.1

Investment in the Economy, 1938-71
(in millions of lei)

Years	Total Investment	Socialist Sector: Total	Socialist Sector: State Sector	Socialist Sector: Cooperative Sector	Investment by the Population
		1959 Prices			
1938	4,653	--	--	--	--
1949	5,004	4,379	4,379	--	625
1950	6,304	5,663	5,610	53	641
1951	8,628	7,970	7,860	110	658
1952	11,346	10,647	10,526	121	699
1953	14,365	13,567	13,423	144	798
1954	12,992	12,063	11,769	294	929
1955	14,585	13,466	13,061	405	1,119
1956	16,710	15,195	14,813	382	1,515
1957	16,420	14,238	13,734	504	2,182
1958	18,214	15,648	14,947	701	2,566
1959	21,171	18,456	17,498	958	2,715
1960	27,472	24,422	22,788	1,634	3,050
1961	32,402	29,713	27,354	2,359	2,689
1962	36,572	34,088	30,838	3,250	2,484
1963	39,358	37,074	33,042	4,032	2,284
1964	43,290	41,031	37,563	3,468	2,259
1965	46,922	44,602	41,290	3,312	2,320
1951-55	61,916	57,713	56,639	1,074	4,203
1956-60	99,987	87,959	83,780	4,179	12,028
1961-65	198,544	186,508	170,087	16,421	12,036
		1963 Prices			
1965	46,759	44,404	41,222	3,182	2,355
1966	51,312	48,909	45,633	3,276	2,403
1967	59,918	57,458	53,618	3,840	2,460
1968	66,724	64,276	60,109	4,167	2,448
1969	70,752	67,529	63,448	4,081	3,223
1966-69	248,706	238,172	222,808	15,364	10,534
1971	88,424	82,617	76,890	5,727	5,807

Sources: Anuarul Statistic 1970, p. 448; Anuarul Statistic 1972, p. 323.

TABLE 5.2

Investments in the National Economy,
by Field, 1950-1969/70
(millions of lei, percentages in parentheses)

Year	Total Investments	In Material Production	In Nonproductive Fields: Total	In Nonproductive Fields: Social-Cultural
		1959 Prices		
1950	5,663	4,913	750	344
	(100.0)	(86.8)	(13.2)	(6.1)
1955	13,466	11,510	1,956	664
	(100.0)	(85.5)	(14.5)	(4.9)
1960	24,422	20,397	4,025	1,095
	(100.0)	(83.5)	(16.5)	(4.5)
1961	29,713	25,059	4,654	1,325
	(100.0)	(84.3)	(15.7)	(4.5)
1962	34,088	29,121	4,967	1,284
	(100.0)	(85.4)	(14.6)	(3.8)
1963	37,074	31,818	5,256	1,238
	(100.0)	(85.8)	(14.2)	(3.3)
1964	41,031	35,066	5,965	1,468
	(100.0)	(85.5)	(14.5)	(3.6)
1965	44,602	38,447	6,155	1,339
	(100.0)	(86.2)	(13.8)	(3.0)
1951-55	57,713	50,030	7,683	3,031
	(100.0)	(86.7)	(13.3)	(5.3)
1956-60	87,959	73,400	14,559	4,236
	(100.0)	(83.4)	(16.6)	(4.8)
1961-65	186,508	159,511	26,997	6,654
	(100.0)	(85.5)	(14.5)	(3.6)
		1963 Prices		
1965	44,404	38,094	6,310	1,343
	(100.0)	(85.8)	(14.2)	(3.0)
1966	48,909	41,620	7,289	1,830
	(100.0)	(85.1)	(14.9)	(3.7)
1967	57,458	49,682	7,776	1,807
	(100.0)	(86.5)	(13.5)	(3.1)
1968	64,276	56,136	8,140	2,071
	(100.0)	(87.3)	(12.7)	(3.2)
1969	67,529	59,203	8,326	2,160
	(100.0)	(87.7)	(12.3)	(3.2)
1966-69	38,172	206,641	31,531	7,868
	(100.0)	(86.8)	(13.2)	(3.3)

Source: Anuarul Statistic 1970, p. 450.

TABLE 5.3

The Structure of Investments, 1950-1970/71
(millions of lei, percentages in parentheses)

ears	Total Investments	Construction	Equipment and Instruments	Geological Exploration	Miscel- laneous
			1959 Prices		
950	5,663	2,855	2,033	626	149
	(100.0)	(50.4)	(35.9)	(11.1)	(2.6)
955	13,466	7,046	4,309	1,240	871
	(100.0)	(52.3)	(32.0)	(9.2)	(6.5)
960	24,422	11,749	8,844	1,403	2,426
	(100.0)	(48.1)	(36.2)	(5.8)	(9.9)
961	29,713	13,226	11,770	1,666	3,051
	(100.0)	(44.5)	(39.6)	(5.6)	(10.3)
962	34,088	15,239	13,319	1,776	3,754
	(100.0)	(44.7)	(39.1)	(5.2)	(11.0)
963	37,074	16,981	14,073	1,823	4,197
	(100.0)	(45.8)	(38.0)	(4.9)	(11.3)
964	41,031	18,899	15,859	1,998	4,275
	(100.0)	(46.1)	(38.6)	(4.9)	(10.4)
965	44,602	20,304	17,556	2,040	4,702
	(100.0)	(45.5)	(39.4)	(4.6)	(10.5)
951-55	57,713	29,724	18,932	5,635	3,422
	(100.0)	(51.5)	(32.8)	(9.8)	(5.9)
956-60	87,959	43,843	29,242	7,224	7,650
	(100.0)	(49.9)	(33.2)	(8.2)	(8.7)
961-65	186,508	84,649	72,577	9,393	19,979
	(100.0)	(45.4)	(38.9)	(5.0)	(10.7)
			1969 Prices		
965	44,404	20,912	16,315	2,605	4,572
	(100.0)	(47.1)	(36.7)	(5.9)	(10.3)
966	40,909	22,710	18,045	2,679	5,475
	(100.0)	(46.4)	(36.9)	(5.5)	(11.2)
967	57,458	27,455	21,362	2,706	5,935
	(100.0)	(47.8)	(37.2)	(4.7)	(10.3)
968	64,276	30,626	23,924	2,678	7,048
	(100.0)	(47.6)	(37.2)	(4.2)	(11.0)
969	67,529	31,803	26,256	2,722	6,748
	(100.0)	(47.1)	(38.9)	(4.0)	(10.0)
968-69	238,172	112,594	89,587	10,785	25,206
	(100.0)	(47.3)	(37.6)	(4.5)	(10.6)
971	82,617	38,247	33,294	2,876	8,200
	(100.0)	(46.3)	(40.3)	(3.5)	(9.9)

Sources: Anuarul Statistic 1970, p. 452; Anuarul Statistic 1972,). 324-25.

TABLE 5.4

Investments by Industrial Field
(millions of lei, percentages in parentheses)

				1959 Prices				
	1950	1955	1960	1961	1962	1963	1964	1965
Total--industry	2,751 (100.0)	7,685 (100.0)	11,771 (100.0)	14,358 (100.0)	17,062 (100.0)	18,139 (100.0)	20,593 (100.0)	22,22 (100.
Electrical and thermal energy	267 (9.7)	885 (11.5)	1,175 (10.0)	1,271 (8.9)	1,732 (10.2)	2,317 (12.8)	3,031 (14.7)	4,05 (18.
Combustibles	1,342 (48.8)	2,731 (35.5)	3,239 (27.5)	3,711 (25.9)	3,894 (22.8)	3,644 (20.0)	4,011 (19.5)	4,19 (18.
Coal	220 (8.0)	617 (8.0)	528 (4.5)	598 (4.2)	691 (4.0)	750 (4.1)	788 (3.8)	91 (4.
Coke	8 (0.3)	127 (1.6)	71 (0.6)	75 (0.5)	16 (0.1)	25 (0.1)	18 (0.1)	1 (0.
Petroleum	1,062 (38.6)	1,926 (25.1)	2,207 (18.7)	2,524 (17.6)	2,665 (15.6)	2,392 (13.2)	2,653 (12.9)	2,65 (11.
Metan gas	52 (1.9)	61 (0.8)	433 (3.7)	514 (3.6)	522 (3.1)	477 (2.6)	552 (2.7)	62 (2.
Ferrous metallurgy	184 (6.7)	667 (8.7)	812 (6.9)	1,401 (9.7)	1,998 (11.7)	1,841 (10.1)	1,709 (8.3)	2,61 (11.
Nonferrous metallurgy	66 (2.4)	565 (7.4)	474 (4.0)	564 (3.9)	871 (5.1)	1,043 (5.8)	1,779 (8.6)	1,52 (6.
Machine building and metal finishing	203 (7.4)	486 (6.3)	999 (8.5)	1,623 (11.3)	1,935 (11.4)	1,465 (8.1)	1,347 (6.6)	1,46 (6.
Chemicals	91 (3.3)	497 (6.5)	1,521 (12.9)	1,862 (13.0)	2,102 (12.3)	3,204 (17.7)	3,124 (15.2)	2,78 (12.
Extraction of nonmetalliferous minerals	19 (0.7)	34 (0.4)	72 (0.6)	31 (0.2)	32 (0.2)	38 (0.2)	46 (0.2)	5 (0.
Construction materials	104 (3.8)	341 (4.4)	278 (2.4)	434 (3.0)	639 (3.8)	806 (4.4)	947 (4.6)	88 (4.
Exploitation and finishing of wood	110 (4.0)	531 (6.9)	854 (7.3)	1,030 (7.2)	1,310 (7.7)	1,276 (7.0)	1,300 (6.3)	1,36 (6.
Cellulose and paper	36 (1.3)	43 (0.6)	708 (6.0)	687 (4.8)	536 (3.1)	828 (4.6)	1,163 (5.6)	1,24 (5.
Glass and pottery	8 (0.3)	54 (0.7)	70 (0.6)	88 (0.6)	105 (0.6)	83 (0.5)	84 (0.4)	5 (0.
Textiles	107 (3.9)	142 (1.8)	354 (3.0)	408 (2.8)	425 (2.5)	477 (2.6)	672 (3.3)	54 (2.
Ready-made clothing	1 --	8 (0.1)	46 (0.4)	78 (0.5)	74 (0.4)	65 (0.4)	97 (0.5)	9 (0.
Hides, furs, and shoes	17 (0.6)	21 (0.3)	86 (0.7)	74 (0.5)	100 (0.6)	92 (0.5)	110 (0.5)	10 (0.
Foodstuffs	143 (5.2)	573 (7.5)	989 (8.4)	961 (6.7)	1,107 (6.5)	771 (4.3)	926 (4.5)	95 (4.
Soap and cosmetics	3 (0.1)	4 (0.1)	3 --	2 --	2 --	5 --	2 --	--
Polygraphic industries	44 (1.6)	60 (0.8)	24 (0.2)	39 (0.3)	56 (0.3)	33 (0.2)	32 (0.2)	3 (0.
Other fields	6 (0.2)	43 (0.5)	67 (0.6)	94 (0.7)	144 (0.8)	151 (0.8)	213 (1.0)	23 (1.

			1963 Prices			
1965	1966	1967	1968	1969	1966/69	1971
22,887	24,778	30,874	34,626	35,938	126,216	42,850
(100.0)	(100.0)	(100.0)	(100.0)	(100.0)	(100.0)	(100.0)
3,895	4,460	4,513	4,673	4,940	18,586	6,325
(17.0)	(18.0)	(14.6)	(13.5)	(13.7)	(14.7)	(14.8)
4,945	5,411	5,330	5,462	5,343	21,546	5,619
(21.7)	(21.8)	(17.3)	(15.8)	(14.8)	(17.1)	(13.1)
953	1,110	1,222	1,279	1,289	4,900	1,376
(4.2)	(4.5)	(4.0)	(3.7)	(3.6)	(3.9)	(3.2)
12	5	11	16	13	45	366
(0.1)	--	--	(0.1)	--	--	(0.8)
3,137	3,607	3,454	3,592	3,429	14,082	3,117
(13.7)	(14.5)	(11.2)	(10.4)	(9.5)	(11.2)	(7.3)
843	689	643	575	612	2,519	760
(3.7)	(2.8)	(2.1)	(1.6)	(1.7)	(2.0)	(1.8)
2,665	2,670	3,302	3,734	3,632	13,338	3,025
(11.7)	(10.8)	(10.7)	(10.8)	(10.1)	(10.6)	(7.1)
1,558	992	1,339	1,087	1,119	4,537	1,649
(6.8)	(4.0)	(4.4)	(3.1)	(3.1)	(3.6)	(3.8)
1,469	1,978	2,919	4,671	6,025	15,593	8,345
(6.4)	(8.0)	(9.5)	(13.5)	(16.8)	(12.4)	(19.5)
2,820	2,679	5,184	5,808	4,815	18,486	5,801
(12.3)	(10.8)	(16.8)	(16.8)	(13.4)	(14.6)	(13.5)
54	103	132	238	370	843	233
(0.2)	(0.4)	(0.4)	(0.7)	(1.0)	(0.7)	(0.5)
894	1,015	1,182	1,318	1,804	5,319	2,638
(3.9)	(4.1)	(3.8)	(3.8)	(5.0)	(4.2)	(6.2)
1,333	1,315	1,504	1,549	1,762	6,130	1,660
(5.8)	(5.3)	(4.9)	(4.5)	(4.9)	(4.8)	(3.9)
1,244	812	534	234	234	1,814	799
(5.4)	(3.3)	(1.7)	(0.7)	(0.7)	(1.4)	(1.9)
59	124	350	534	847	1,855	386
(0.3)	(0.5)	(1.1)	(1.5)	(2.4)	(1.5)	(0.9)
542	906	1,429	1,488	1,329	5,152	1,882
(2.4)	(3.7)	(4.6)	(4.3)	(3.7)	(4.1)	(4.4)
91	168	181	150	126	625	200
(0.4)	(0.7)	(0.6)	(0.4)	(0.4)	(0.5)	(0.5)
105	236	320	256	224	1,036	187
(0.5)	(0.9)	(1.0)	(0.7)	(0.6)	(0.8)	(0.4)
945	1,459	1,832	2,417	2,607	8,315	2,797
(4.1)	(5.9)	(5.9)	(7.0)	(7.3)	(6.6)	(6.5)
1	4	13	16	9	42	16
--	--	(0.1)	(0.1)	--	--	--
33	100	125	57	73	355	84
(0.1)	(0.4)	(0.4)	(0.1)	(0.2)	(0.3)	(0.2)
234	346	685	934	679	2,644	1,204
(1.0)	(1.4)	(2.2)	(2.7)	(1.9)	(2.1)	(2.8)

Sources: Anuarul Statistic 1970, pp. 462-63; Anuarul Statistic 1972, pp. 332-33.

TABLE 5.5

Investments Put into Operation, by Field, 1960-71
(millions of lei)

			1959 Prices			
	1960	1961	1962	1963	1964	1965
Total--industry	11,194	10,402	14,775	13,770	13,975	18,419
Electrical and thermal energy	2,451	926	1,123	1,349	2,110	2,517
Combustibles	2,440	2,683	3,502	2,644	3,145	2,984
Coal	447	416	458	468	545	601
Coke	157	114	15	14	14	11
Petroleum	1,388	1,841	2,630	1,790	2,166	1,870
Metan gas	448	312	399	372	420	502
Ferrous metallurgy	694	728	1,640	1,115	1,090	1,107
Nonferrous metallurgy	246	374	473	564	414	2,062
Machine building and metal finishing	873	1,227	1,935	1,570	1,314	1,333
Chemicals	1,511	894	1,773	2,437	1,845	3,132
Extraction of nonmetalliferous minerals	101	21	15	27	42	29
Construction materials	213	229	502	730	573	1,124
Exploitation and finishing of wood	728	822	1,241	1,459	1,202	1,397
Cellulose and paper	381	946	679	275	377	986
Glass and porcelain	90	83	147	55	70	91
Textiles	280	458	399	358	574	411
Ready-made clothing	34	62	74	55	98	72
Hides, furs, and shoes	56	125	88	82	112	91
Foodstuffs	974	718	1,049	922	713	897
Soap and cosmetics	10	2	2	5	2	1
Polygraphic industries	22	31	59	41	28	35
Other fields	90	73	74	82	266	150
			1963 Prices			
Total--industry	18,922	23,931	22,902	27,473	31,846	35,946
Electrical and thermal energy	2,417	5,726	3,506	3,096	4,392	4,752
Combustibles	3,533	3,884	3,784	3,051	4,078	3,418
Coal	620	1,100	969	943	1,352	1,329
Coke	11	4	14	17	13	11
Petroleum	2,227	2,294	2,356	1,808	2,369	1,637
Metan gas	675	486	445	283	344	441
Ferrous metallurgy	1,133	2,911	2,016	5,670	2,904	4,215
Nonferrous metallurgy	2,155	1,293	699	1,193	1,084	889
Machine building and metal finishing	1,338	1,718	2,281	2,976	4,332	7,030
Chemicals	3,158	2,815	3,686	3,628	5,294	5,012
Extraction of nonmetalliferous minerals	29	85	73	75	314	476
Construction materials	1,140	759	1,373	1,164	1,730	1,989
Exploitation and finishing of wood	1,365	1,271	1,444	1,224	1,527	1,557
Cellulose and paper	991	1,084	438	579	298	576
Glass and porcelain	92	52	143	272	631	331
Textiles	409	883	1,013	1,519	1,201	1,580
Ready-made clothing	74	93	245	117	105	167
Hides, furs, and shoes	89	132	247	264	318	146
Foodstuffs	883	981	1,263	1,895	2,958	2,731
Soap and cosmetics	1	2	9	7	21	19
Polygraphic industries	35	43	170	49	79	89
Other fields	150	199	512	694	580	969

Sources: Anuarul Statistic 1970, p. 487; Anuarul Statistic 1972, pp. 358-59.

TABLE 5.6

Principal Indicators of Economic Development, 1950, 1955-69 (1950 - 100)

	1955	1958	1960	1963	1965	1969
Population	106.2	110.7	112.8	115.3	116.7	122.7
Population occupied in the economy	112	113	114	115	116	118
Number of wage earners	139	139	153	185	203	234
Volume of investors	238	276	431	655	788	12x
Social product[a]	186	215	263	338	414	582
National income[b]	192	214	268	338	413	561
Total industrial production	202	267	340	502	649	10x
Group A	217	299	397	620	823	13x
Group B	185	229	277	373	457	674
Total agricultural production	162	141	171	170	193	223

[a]National income "plus materials consumed by producing enterprises plus depreciation on the economy's total fixed assets." (See John Michael Montias, Economic Development in Communist Rumania [Cambridge, Mass.: The M.I.T. Press, 1967], p. 267.)

[b]Similar to our concept of "gross national income," but excluding "non-productive" services such as administration, and including turnover taxes. (Ibid., p. 267.)

Source: Anuarul Statistic 1970, pp. 104-05.

The extremely heavy rate of investment in the Romanian economy is well illustrated by Table 5.1. Total investments increased approximately ten times between 1938 and 1965 and roughly 20 times in the period 1938-71. The most important field of expenditure was the state sector, through which most of the industrial projects were financed; by comparison, cooperative investment (primarily in agriculture) and investment by the population (in the form of bonds, "voluntary contributions," and other individual contributions) were relatively insignificant. Table 5.2 sheds further light on the investment policies followed in Romania since World War II.

This table clearly illustrates the tremendous emphasis on material production, which has characterized economic policies in the Communist systems of Eastern Europe since the drive toward heavy industrialization. Investments in "material production" (the bulk of which was industry) have consistently made up more than 80 percent of all funds invested, with a very small proportion allocated for "nonproduction" fields. Of the latter category, "social-cultural" investments have taken an important part, leaving even less to "nonproductive" areas such as services. The result of this policy has been an extremely unevenly developed economy, in which ultramodern industrial plants exist side by side with antiquated service facilities such as shoe repair shops, dry cleaning establishments, and repair facilities for appliances and cars, if such services are obtainable at all.

Much of the Romanian industrialization drive has been centered around the construction and outfitting of new plants. Table 5.3 illustrates this aspect of postwar investment policies. Throughout the 20-year period 1950-71, investments in construction took up almost one-half of all expenditures, and the furnishing of equipment and instruments swallowed more than one-third. The bulk of the equipment bought went into new industrial plants rather than into agricultural machinery, and this policy further enhanced the difference between industrial and agricultural development. Between 5 and 10 percent of all investments went into geological exploration designed to expand the raw materials and fuel bases of the ever-expanding industry. This left a maximum of 10 percent for "miscellaneous" investment, covering all other sectors of economic activity. Surely the Romanian investment policies were among the most heavily geared toward new industrial development in all of Europe, even in the whole world, during this period.

The extreme concentration in industry is graphically illustrated by the fact that in 1950 industry received 48.6 percent of all investment in the country (heavy industry 41.9 percent and light industry 6.7 percent). In 1960, 48.2 percent went into industry with "Group A" (heavy industry) receiving the lion's share of 40.9 percent; by 1965 industry was up to 49.8 percent (Group A--45.1 percent); in 1969, 53.0 percent of all funds went into this field (Group A--44.8 percent). Finally, in 1971 the industrial proportion was 51.9 percent (Group A--43.6 percent). By comparison, the following proportion of total investments went in agriculture: 1950--10.3 percent; 1960--20.0 percent; 1965--18.6 percent; 1969--16.4 percent; and 1971--16.7 percent.[8]

Thus the emphasis on industry has been an ongoing concern, and there is no indication of a major reorientation. The only change in recent years has been a slight upgrading of light and consumer industries, but even this has not constituted a major change.

The trends illustrated above are slated to continue in the period 1971-75. The five-year plan, officially adopted by the Grand National Assembly in the fall of 1971, calls for the following investment policies: According to Premier Ion Gheorghe Maurer, industrial development will receive approximately 60 percent of all funds expended by the state for investment. The rest will be divided among agriculture, transportation and telecommunications, social services, and miscellaneous.[9] The figures released by Maurer have since been revised, first upwards, then somewhat downwards. Planned production, on the other hand, has been revised upwards on numerous occasions, and it is difficult to see how the new targets can be achieved without substantial investments. Thus industry will continue to get an extremely large part of total investments, and the revised production plans aim primarily at an expansion of heavy industry, virtually guaranteeing a continuation of the investment preponderance for Group A.[10]

Table 5.4 shows investment in industrial fields during 1950-71. Once again the trends have remained constant throughout the period; the only major changes have involved increasing emphasis on certain heavy industrial fields, notably chemicals, without any major reorientation toward light industries. A continuation of this trend will aggravate the severe imbalances already present in the Romanian economy to a marked degree.

Despite massive problems of waste and underutilization of investments, the Romanian economy has experienced a vast implementation program every year. Table 5.5 shows the value of investments put into function in the economy in the period 1960-71.

The figures in Table 5.5 are of primary interest as an illustration of the tremendous amount of plants, equipment, and other facilities put into operation every year. In fact, the industrial expansion has been so rapid that it has strained the whole socioeconomic system to the utmost. The transportation and service sectors have not been able to keep up with the output facilities, causing massive bottlenecks and waste. The social sector is underdeveloped and has not been able to provide adequate facilities in such areas as housing and sanitation for the growing urban population. The result of this has been a recent emphasis on housing construction, which is designed to catch up with the backlog in this area. The new drive has been instituted in an economy of real scarcity and has necessitated the rerouting of funds from other sectors, thereby creating shortages in those fields. The "zigzag" performance of an unbalanced growth economy has been a hallmark of Romanian industrialization; and there is every indication that it will continue for the foreseeable future, causing the postponing of the achievement of multilateral, or balanced, growth.

THE RESULTS OF THE INDUSTRIALIZATION DRIVE: PRODUCT GROWTH AND DIVERSIFICATION

The massive investments pumped into the Romanian economy, especially in industry, were bound to yield large production increases. Table 5.6 shows the extent of these increases in the period 1950-69.

Table 5.6 is illustrative of the major trends in production and development during the last 20 years. The volume of investments has gone up tremendously, and total industrial production has gone up at a rate roughly similar to that of investments. Agricultural production, on the other hand, lags considerably throughout the entire period. The number of individuals occupied in the economy has not kept pace with the general population increase, which signifies a relatively high birth rate throughout the entire period together with a considerable expansion in the longevity of life, two processes that have increased the proportion of nonproductive individuals (too old or too young) in the population. At the same time, the number of wage earners has increased much faster than the growth of the population, indicating that many who had previously been in a "nonsalaried profession" (that is, collectivized agriculture) had moved to positions in other fields of the economy, primarily industry.

Table 5.7 is a further illustration of the tremendous importance of industry in the economy after a quarter-century of sustained modernization and development.

TABLE 5.7

Weight of Various Fields of Production in the Total Social Product and National Income, 1938, 1950, 1955, 1960-69

Year	1938	1950	1955	1960	1963	1965	1969
	Percent of Social Product						
Industry	39.0	46.6	44.9	52.4	56.2	57.3	62.7
Construction	5.4	7.4	7.9	9.7	9.9	9.4	9.9
Agriculture and forestry	30.2	25.8	30.5	24.6	21.6	21.7	18.2
Transportation and telecommunications	6.4	4.2	3.9	3.5	3.5	3.3	3.3
Other fields	7.8	8.1	6.1	5.2	3.7	3.7	3.2
	Percent of National Income						
Industry	30.8	44.0	39.8	44.1	46.9	48.9	57.4
Construction	4.4	6.0	5.6	9.0	8.3	8.0	9.0
Agriculture and forestry	38.5	28.0	37.6	33.1	29.8	29.3	24.1
Transportation and telecommunications	6.5	4.3	3.7	3.8	4.2	4.0	3.9
Other fields	4.9	5.9	4.1	3.5	2.9	2.6	2.5

Source: Anuarul Statistic 1970, p. 109.

The trends illustrated in Table 5.7 are classical indicators of an economy in rapid transformation. Agriculture has been replaced as the most important sector in social product and national income. In fact, industry was considerably more important than agriculture in contributions to these indicators as early as 1950--when the bulk of the population in Romania still lived in rural areas and were occupied in agriculture. This phenomenon is explained through productivity studies that have consistently shown that Romanian agriculture was extensive, overpopulated, and underproductive, and that even the beginnings of industrialization in the country provided a massive decrease in the importance of this classical occupation. As industrialization progressed the relative importance of agriculture decreased further, despite some gains in productivity and output in the sector during the last 25 years.

Another interesting aspect of Table 5.7 is the relative lack of importance of fields such as transportation and telecommunications as well as "other fields" (in which "nonproductive" services presumably would be included). This imbalance is becoming a major source of economic problems in Romania (for a more detailed discussion see Chapter 7).

Much of the production increase in Romanian industry during the socialist period is due to a tremendous growth of the urban working class, as illustrated by Table 5.6. Considerable progress has also been made in raising labor productivity and in furnishing skilled manpower for all industrial fields. Table 5.8 illustrates the rise in labor productivity, while Table 5.9 shows the impressive infusion of experts into the main industrial sectors.

The evidence presented above illustrates the massive modernization and industrialization program implemented in Romania since World War II. The country has moved from the ranks of agrarian societies to the level of mixed industrial-agrarian development. An ever-expanding and increasingly sophisticated industry is being fueled by innovation and the infusion of experts and skilled manpower. The high growth rate has been maintained for a considerable period of time, and there is no sign of the political regime's scaling down its development program. All in all, the achievements of Romania in this field are highly impressive. It is precisely this kind of success that is beginning to create serious problems for the Romanian decision makers.

TABLE 5.8

Productivity of Labor in Selected Industries, 1950-71
(per worker, 1950=100)

	1955	1960	1963	1965	1969	1971	Average Annual Increase 1951-69 (in percent)
Industry--total	160	237	291	343	456	510	8.3
Electrical and thermal energy	183	362	443	562	980	12X	12.8
Combustibles	133	178	225	232	295	251	5.9
Coal	91	130	164	166	228	410	4.4
Petroleum	171	216	262	279	371	526	7.1
Ferrous metallurgy (including extraction of ferrous metals)	121	229	283	325	448	517	8.2
Nonferrous metallurgy (including extraction of nonferrous metals)	119	150	158	176	284	289	5.6
Machine construction and metal finishing	219	392	504	615	875	10X	12.1
Chemical industry	170	276	400	502	766	951	11.3
Extraction of nonmetalliferous minerals and production of abrasive substances	240	481	726	824	10X	11X	13.2
Construction materials	179	282	352	455	636	730	10.2
Exploitation and processing of wood products	146	205	254	293	362	386	7.0
Cellulose and paper (including exploitation of reeds)	139	166	198	222	333	385	6.5
Glass, porcelain, and pottery	178	229	285	320	408	485	7.7
Textiles	143	172	202	231	282	314	5.6
Ready-made clothes	160	212	244	276	341	372	6.7
Leather goods, fur, footwear	184	237	283	349	414	434	7.8
Food industries	138	185	202	224	252	264	5.0
Soap and cosmetics	233	228	247	287	364	402	7.0
Polygraphic industries	149	208	285	346	483	499	8.7

Sources: Anuarul Statistic, 1970, p. 228; Anuarul Statistic 1972, p. 174.

TABLE 5.9

Number of Engineers and Technicians in Subsections of Republican Industry, 1960-71

	1960	Percent of Total	1963	Percent of Total	1965	Percent of Total	1969	Percent of Total	1971	Percent of Total
Total	75,675		88,498		102,258		123,648		118,436	
Electrical and thermal energy	2,454	3.2	3,668	4.1	4,479	4.4	5,200	4.2	5,243	4.4
Combustibles	6,040	8.0	6,108	6.0	6,772	6.6	7,516	6.1	7,339	6.2
Coal	2,408	3.2	2,380	2.7	2,736	2.7	3,230	2.6	3,108	2.6
Petroleum	3,235	4.8	3,270	4.2	3,541	3.9	3,760	3.5	3,752	3.2
Ferrous metallurgy (including extraction of ferrous metals)	3,760	5.0	3,940	4.5	4,617	4.5	6,355	5.1	5,959	5.0
Nonferrous metallurgy (including extraction of nonferrous metals)	2,493	3.3	3,277	3.7	4,016	3.9	5,110	4.1	5,060	4.3
Machine construction and metal finishing	27,297	36.1	33,163	37.5	37,189	36.4	47,805	38.7	47,976	40.5
Chemical industry	4,469	5.9	6,141	6.9	7,922	7.7	11,260	9.1	10,780	9.1
Extraction of nonmetalliferous minerals and production of abrasive substances	439	0.6	433	0.5	517	0.5	626	0.5	721	0.6
Construction materials	2,104	2.8	2,478	2.8	3,101	3.0	3,718	3.0	3,680	3.1
Exploitation and processing of wood products	8,992	11.9	9,499	10.7	11,666	11.4	12,073	9.8	10,954	9.2
Cellulose and paper	697	0.9	997	1.1	1,336	1.3	1,807	1.5	1,498	1.3
Glass, porcelain, and pottery	693	0.9	835	0.9	930	0.9	1,140	0.9	1,126	1.0
Textiles	5,011	6.6	5,381	6.1	5,925	5.8	6,981	5.6	6,637	5.6
Ready-made clothing	651	0.9	771	0.9	912	0.9	1,172	0.9	890	0.8
Leather goods, fur, and footwear	1,435	1.9	1,536	1.7	1,728	1.7	1,956	1.6	1,848	1.6
Food industries	7,606	10.1	8,736	9.9	9,484	9.3	8,925	7.2	7,342	6.2
Soap and cosmetics	153	0.2	162	0.2	161	0.2	178	0.1	139	0.1
Polygraphic industries	920	1.2	1,016	1.1	1,275	1.2	1,535	1.2	1,108	0.9

Note: Data apply to engineers and technicians under direct national supervision. Some individuals have been counted more than once, due to "mixed careers"; as a result, the sum total of the 20 subcategories is larger than the total figure for engineers and technicians in 1960, 1963, 1965, 1969, and 1971.

Sources: Anuarul Statistic 1970, pp. 220-21; Anuarul Statistic 1972, p. 163.

THE PROBLEMS OF AN UNEVENLY DEVELOPED ECONOMY

The impressive achievements of the Romanian economy, discussed in detail above, cannot totally obscure the many important problems that have developed throughout a quarter-century of rapid development. The most serious and persistent of these problems are the following:

Serious Imbalances in Overall Growth

As mentioned earlier, the extremely strong emphasis on the heavy and extractive industries has created a series of imbalances that are becoming quite serious at the present stage of development in Romania. At a low level of development it is possible to concentrate on a few basic parameters of performance, such as coal, steel, and metallurgy, but economic experts agree that once the economy has passed through this initial stage and moved on to "take-off," such simple indicators no longer suffice.[11] It now becomes increasingly important to achieve a better and wider mix of products, which can be integrated as the economy becomes more sophisticated. In fact, shortages in less heavily emphasized fields will now have a profound impact on performance in even the high priority sectors. At this point the service sector becomes increasingly important as well; skilled manpower is needed to service the complicated machinery and equipment of an economy that is no longer producing mere fundamentals, and the increasing standard of life requires more amenities. The very success of the industrialization drive has attracted hundreds of thousands, indeed millions, into the older cities and the new industrial centers, creating a major strain on such economic sectors as housing, sanitary facilities, public transportation, repair services, nurseries, old age homes, entertainment, and a host of other activities; yet in many cases such vital sectors of the economy have simply been neglected in the scramble for scarce resources.*

The Romanian press is full of complaints about the imbalances in the economy, especially the service sector. In many cases, new industrial plants will build their own

---

*Nicolae Ceausescu promised more attention to those "side-effects" of rapid economic development in his speech to the RCP National Conference, July 1972 (see Scinteia, July 20, 1972).

apartments, which may fit well with the management's own preferences but may be totally out of line with local zoning regulations. Plants may also establish their own transportation and sewer systems without proper coordination with the existing systems outside of the factory gates. Streets and roads paved by flush factory managers end abruptly or become gravel paths where the less affluent city or town assumes jurisdiction. Masses of workers with children overburden the strained school system and nursery facilities, and lack of facilities results in massive problems in a society in which both parents are needed in economic activity. Requests from local authorities for fund sharing are often sidetracked by factory managers whose jurisdiction is not the local city or municipality but rather the regional economic centrals or the central ministry.*

The picture of local poverty and plant affluence is sometimes reversed; in this scenario the plant is built, workers and dependents flock in, service facilities are required, but funds are not allocated to cover such costs. The result: overcrowding, queuing, especially in the inadequate retail system, poor performance of all public services, and generally lower morale among workers and their dependents. The local authorities may complain; but in most cases the highest priority is production, and local and regional authorities, including the Party bosses, have a vested interest in safeguarding the steady flow of products out of the factory gates, even if this means a continuation of serious imbalances. Thus, harassed local officials find themselves in a most unenviable position of not being able to provide the services that constitute <u>their</u> performance criteria or to successfully appeal to higher authority for redress, at least not until the problems mentioned assume crisis proportions at a national level.†

---

*One of the ways to combat this is to expand the power of local government, as argued by Ion Vintu in "Expanding the Prerogatives of Local Government Bodies," <u>Lupta de Clasa</u>, no. 6, 1972. The problems of housing and commuting are shown to have a direct effect on labor productivity in an article by Petre Nedescu and Adrian Popescu, "'Back and Forth' Migrations and Their Implication for Production," <u>Viata Economica</u>, October 15, 1972.

†This problem did reach national crisis levels and led to Ceausescu's promise that quick remedies would be found (<u>Scinteia</u>, July 20, 1972).

The time-honored practice of disregarding the service sector might be coming to an end in the near future. During the last four to five years the Romanian regime has become increasingly concerned with the so-called "intensive use" of production factors, especially labor. Much of the projected increase in output during this decade is to come from higher labor productivity, not more manpower; yet it is clear that the continuing problems of a low standard of living and poor services have a negative effect on productivity and employee willingness to participate actively in the building of a multilaterally developed society.[12] There has been a modest resurgence of sociology and social psychology in Romania in this period, indicating serious regime concern with this question. In fact, since 1970 there has been a considerable increase in investments in and actual output of housing and municipal authorities have been given more authority to regulate sanitation and other vital sectors. This is certainly a start, albeit a modest one, toward the solution of worker apathy, carelessness, and occasionally rowdyism now so prominently discussed in the Romanian press. Yet the highest economic priority is still increased production of producer goods and an extremely high investment ratio in comparison to consumption, and it is difficult to see how the service field can obtain the vast amounts needed to ensure balance without endangering the rapid production increases mandated by the regime up to the end of this century.

The problems stemming from the underdeveloped service sector are compounded by the inadequate achievements of the light and consumer goods industries. The standard of living in Romania is still among the lowest in Eastern Europe. Even when money is available, the supply of consumer goods is low and quality is often poor; and for the last four to five years unsellable goods have accumulated in the warehouses.* Some recent studies have indicated that the continued problems are of considerable importance in further reducing worker incentive, thus also reducing the likelihood of achieving the kind of socioeconomic and political system envisaged by Nicolae Ceausescu and clearly endorsed by the rest of the elite as well.[13]

---

*The RCP Executive Committee dealt with this problem in a meeting on July 7, 1972 (reports appeared in Scinteia the following day). The Executive Committee agreed to provide higher quality production and stringent control to alleviate the problem.

The unbalanced state of the Romanian economy threatens economic development even more directly than the problems associated with inadequate services, low quality consumer goods, and apathetic workers. Perhaps the most serious deficiency of economic performance in Romania today is the frequent occurrence of bottlenecks created by perennial shortages. Since so much effort has gone into the production of heavy industry, there are constant shortages of a whole range of components and frequent complaints about the underdeveloped stage of services networks even for machinery.[14] Spare parts are also in short supply, causing long waits for repairs of even the most important machines, with constant losses of production.[15] Sophisticated machinery is left idle due to the inadequate training of the operators and mechanics. For example, it was estimated that due to such manpower shortages in 1971 and 1972 equipment valued at millions of lei was not put into operation. Some of the machinery had been in storage for as long as ten years.[16] This is clearly the other side of the investment question; while it is true that an impressive array of facilities and plants is put into operation each year, the perennial bottlenecks of the economy produce much waste and underutilization. In 1972 the industrial plant ran at approximately 75 percent of capacity for long periods of the year--a rather dismal performance, especially in a centralized economy geared to full capacity usage.[17]

Inflexibility in Planning and Implementation

Some of the most serious problems besetting Romania at the present time stem from the continued centralization in both planning and implementation. Centralized planning is appropriate for an economy that is just beginning the long road toward high development, but many economists maintain that such an approach is quite inappropriate for more sophisticated economies. This view is shared by some of the decision makers in Eastern Europe today. Decentralization schemes and even limited "market functions" have been implemented in all of the countries of the area, with the possible exception of Albania; and some states, notably Czechoslovakia in the period 1965-68 and Hungary at present, have at times gone quite far in liberalizing economic planning and production. Romania, on the other hand, was the last country in the area to attempt economic reforms (in 1967), and the Romanian program was very cautious and somewhat contradictory, resulting in mixed performance. By 1970-71 recentralization had become an important trend, and this has continued to the present.

The continued centralization in Romania has created major bottlenecks. Centralized planning assumes accurate information and reliable performance as well as the manpower and equipment necessary to coordinate the output of thousands of industrial plants, producers of raw materials, import trusts, and transportation centrals. Nonfulfillment or underfulfillment in one branch will reverberate throughout the entire system. The Romanian planning system is lacking in most of the crucial elements listed above. There is a constant problem of inaccurate inventories and production estimates. Maxim Berghianu, onetime head of the State Planning Commission, described in detail how inadequate his information was in this area, and he instituted yearly inspections in an attempt to get an accurate picture of this crucial factor.[18] It is openly admitted in the Romanian press that factory managers underreport production facilities, hoard materials and resources, and engage in various other kinds of "deviant" activities in order to ensure that the final production plan, centrally established, will be within their capabilities.[19] The Romanian planning organs are seriously short of computers and other modern equipment needed to produce accurate plans and also lack statisticians and other experts. Forecasting and actual planning are therefore quite inaccurate.[20]

Even with more reliable planning methods and more accurate information the Romanian decision makers would have considerable problems in setting realistic plans and then following through on their implementation. Every year certain sectors of the economy are unable to meet their targets and thus cause dislocations in other fields dependent on them for goods and services. Such shortages often appear in high priority fields such as mining and metallurgy, resulting in major problems in machine building and other subfields within the heavy industrial sector. At the important Central Committee meeting of February 28-March 2, 1973, Ceausescu and others complained about underfulfillment in several important industrial fields and various organizational remedies were proposed.[21]

Nonfulfillment of contracts in many economic sectors leads to "ripple" effects throughout the economy. Many firms underreport capacity, engage in hoarding, and do not fulfill legally binding contracts. The Party leadership has repeatedly denounced such practices, and the main papers have often been used in campaigns against such nefarious activity. Such a campaign was run in Scinteia, Munca (the main trade union paper) and other major publications in 1971, and similar campaigns have followed the recent reorganizations of 1973.[22]

Compounding the serious shortcomings described is the existence on a fairly large scale of outright corruption and various devious pricing methods. There are periodical investigations and purges, but it is likely that hoarding and black marketing will continue as long as severe shortages persist in strategic sectors of the economy. Romania is certainly not alone in this problem, nor is a centralized economy more prone to corruption than other forms of economic management. There is, however, another form of malfunctioning in socialist economies that can be largely attributed to the special conditions existing in such a system--resistance to innovation and a tendency to modernize only as a result of political pressure from the top. This is considered a major problem in Romania, as witnessed by Ceausescu's emphasis on it in his marathon speech to the RCP National Conference, July 1972,[23] and again in important Central Committee plenums in the fall of 1972 and winter of 1973.[24]

Superficially it would seem that a centralized economy is well suited to modernization of equipment and facilities; the central leadership, it is assumed, can simply decree the need for rejuvenation of the physical plant and thus ensure implementation through central control and perhaps coercion. In fact, the overriding concern with production tends to impede innovation. It takes time to install new machinery and train the workers who will manage it; in the meantime production is lost, and this can become a serious problem for a factory struggling to meet yearly or semiannual production quotas. The manager knows what he has and what he can do with it, and he is unwilling to move into uncharted waters by installing equipment that may increase his production in the long run but definitely lower it in the short run. Maxim Berghianu, onetime chief planner, complained in 1972 that many goods are still produced with "twenty year old equipment" that is clearly obsolete, thus reducing output and also creating a supply of outmoded goods, which in many cases end up in warehouses as unsellable.[25] Under such conditions innovation becomes a political task, to be determined at the top of the Party pyramid and implemented through heavy interference by the RCP at the plant level.

Since innovation does not filter through the system from the bottom up, modernization becomes the task of high political officials, who must see to it that new machinery, new processes, and new organizational theories and practices are distributed throughout, even down to the plant level. This creates a whole new set of problems: top cadres must constantly keep abreast of new developments in various fields and be able to establish procedures for the dissemination of such knowledge. The system must also allow for mechanisms that can be used to control the implementation of recommendations and orders from the top.

In the centralized Romanian system there has been considerable difficulty in this field. More than in most East European countries, the political elite, which controls the distribution of innovation from the top, is in the hands of old apparatchiks with relatively meager educational backgrounds (as illustrated by the discussion in Chapter 2). This seems to have become increasingly the case since the beginning of the little cultural revolution of 1971, which has resulted in a considerable reduction of influence for the so-called "technocrats" in Romania. Many of the top political leaders do not have the expertise to properly evaluate the technical and managerial problems associated with innovation dissemination; and many old line apparatchiks at the center and at the regional and local levels have a common, vested interest in maintaining the status quo, especially since more advanced economic and technical methods could tend to increase the power of younger, better-educated cadres. The result of this configuration of forces is often political stalemate and lack of action at the plant level, with further delays in instituting changes and thus growing obsolescence in many fields.

The regime's response to this recurring problem strongly reflects Nicolae Ceausescu's personal style of decision making. The general secretary appears genuinely skeptical of bureaucrats and is therefore loath to turn over more political power to technically trained cadres, who would be competent to supervise modernization of plants and equipment in industry. Yet Ceausescu is a modernizer with a major personal commitment to change and improvement. His dilemma is typically solved by an extraordinarily heavy personal involvement in economic planning, forecasting, and innovation dissemination. The 1967 economic reforms, for example, were planned and drafted under Ceausescu's personal supervision, and the various stages of implementation were only set in motion after a close signal by the Party leader.[26] The reform itself was not a success, and Ceausescu is now increasingly relying on one of his favorite tactics, that of the massive campaign to carry out his program.

One of the most important campaigns for innovation was started in November 1970, when Ceausescu complained about inadequate and misleading data on production facilities. Throughout 1971 and 1972 the State Planning Committee carried out a census of such facilities throughout the country, and a third census was undertaken in record time from early January to early February 1973. The raw material thus gathered was used for an important meeting of the RCP Central Committee Plenum in late February 1973 at which time major decisions were made concerning innovation, modernization, and increased efficiency in the economy. The chief elements of the Central Committee decision were as follows:

- The Ministry of Heavy Machine Building and related ministries were charged with the need to increase production of modern equipment;
- The Ministry of Technical-Material Supply and Control of Fixed Assets was given added power to check on fulfillment of contracts and installation of new machinery at the factory level;
- Party committees at the county and local levels, as well as workers' control bodies, including the Workers' Central Control Council of Socio-Economic Activity, were entrusted with increased control over enterprise planning, pricing, and innovation;
- Ministries, industrial centrals, local enterprises, and Party bodies at all levels were required to find ways to increase efficiency, chiefly through better machinery, higher labor productivity, and more rational use of resources, for an early fulfillment of the five-year plan.[27]

This meeting was the beginning of a concerted drive for the fulfillment of the five-year plan in four and a half years, chiefly through innovative practices. In the spring of 1973 was also begun a massive transfer of personnel from administrative to production posts, ostensibly in the interest of innovation and modernization but probably also in the interest of strengthening Nicolae Ceausescu's personal power. This campaign is still in full swing.

That the RCP is forced to resort to campaigns of this kind to ensure modernization of the existing plant augurs ill for the Party's quest for sustained growth. Presumably, a multilaterally developed society will be able to renew its productive plant as a self-regulatory and more or less automatic process, without heavy central control and massive, often disruptive, campaigns. The built-in conservative tendencies in the heavily centralized Romanian economy seem to militate against such automatic innovation, thus ensuring "innovation by diktat" from the top for many years to come.

Administrative Overlap and Jurisdictional Disputes

Countless studies have pointed to the virtually universal tendency of Communist regimes to establish complicated networks of overlapping jurisdictions, often staffed by the same individuals. These "interlocking directorates" of Party and state, of political decision-making organs and administrative structures, have ensured continued Party control over all major activities in Communist systems, be they political, administrative, social, cultural, or economic. This politicization of administrative activity also ensures a high degree of factionalism and infighting; even minor decisions and procedures can become major political battles, in which personal power and fortune are at stake. Communist systems are therefore fraught with countless jurisdictional disputes that in fact are political controversies.

Romania is no exception to the general rule of jurisdictional disputes. The RCP has maintained a heavy grip over all aspects of socioeconomic decision making in that country, and as a result managers, technical experts, and governmental personnel have been forced to take their views to Party meetings in order to achieve at least a minimum of autonomy. The most important jurisdictional dispute in contemporary Romania is therefore the classical "Expert versus Red" controversy.

It is clearly a simplification to maintain that all Party apparatchiks are more "Red" than "expert" and that all technocrats are primarily interested in their field of speciality rather than "Party spirit." There are nevertheless discernible issues in which it is possible to see a fairly clear split between experts and Reds. The question of control over the economy is one such issue.

The confrontation is a familiar one. While plant managers, economic experts, and much of the state bureaucracy are primarily concerned with production, rational planning, and the autonomy perceived necessary for the completion of economic tasks, the Party apparatchik is preoccupied with political control and penetration of other structures; autonomy becomes anathema to such a person. It is not correct to state that the apparatchik is unconcerned with production; in fact, a substantial part of his career is spent exhorting workers and managers to increase output, and his own advancement or dismissal often hinges upon it. But an apparatchik wants production <u>and</u> Party spirit, effectiveness <u>and</u> ideological orthodoxy. At times he will even sacrifice some output in return for securing or increasing political control with other structures.

During the first few years after Ceausescu's ascension to power in Romania it appeared that the technocratic element was gaining in political power and prestige. The Party leader was busy establishing himself in the RCP apparat, and he was attempting to increase his personal prestige in the population by a concerted drive for industrialization and a higher standard of living. Ceausescu was therefore to some extent dependent upon the technical and managerial intelligentsia. By 1967-68, however, the first secretary (later retitled general secretary) had successfully completed his consolidation, and he was ready for two major moves that to some extent jeopoardized his relationship with technocrats at all levels. The first move was the economic reform of 1967; the second was the territorial reorganization of the country in early 1968.

The economic reform was an imaginative attack on the dual problem of lagging production and jurisdictional overlap. As discussed above, the excessive centralization of the Romanian economy had produced a situation in which production was beginning to lag due to the inflexibility of planning, the artificial price system, and general insensitivity to market demands and conditions. The reform proposals envisioned a cautious decentralization, in which much of the hitherto centralized function of planning, forecasting, and control of economic performance would be transferred to so-called "industrial centrals," which would be units of economic, especially industrial, coordination at the regional level. It was envisioned that the ministries, trade unions, plant managers, technical experts, Party officials, and elected representatives would cooperate to set economic policy and control its implementation within broader "parameter plans" established in Bucharest. It was hoped that this form of decentralization would provide for better coordination and utilization of resources while still maintaining central control with the "commanding heights" of the economy.[28]

The problem of jurisdictional disputes was handled in a way that was highly innovative because of its simplicity. Ceausescu proposed that the functions of Party and state be fused throughout the system, especially at the level of the industrial central. This would ensure improved coordination and accountability. It was also a major increase in the Party's power over the state apparat and as such constituted the beginning of a trend that has continued up to the present (mid-1974).

The economic reform, which was promulgated by the Party and duly established as law by the Grand National Assembly, placed new burdens of planning and innovation on regional and local authorities, while at the same time removing some of the power of the central ministries and planning agencies. Nobody seemed to have been completely happy with it. The regional party bodies, accustomed to specific orders from Bucharest, became uneasy in the new arrangement, which focused attention on their performance. Enterprise managers and other economic elites were given some autonomy but seemingly much more responsibility for plan fulfillment, a development that was as uncomfortable as it was unfamiliar. The central ministries grumbled audibly over their reduced power and Party inroads. Finally, some of the RCP leaders at the center expressed misgivings about the relative transfer of power to the provinces.*

The combined resistance of several such important groups forced a gradual reevaluation and restructuring of the reform. By late 1969 several Central Committee "commissions" were established to "assist" the industrial centrals in their tasks. There was also a partial restoration of state jurisdiction in relation to the centrals; but the program was not clear, and considerable jurisdictional confusion resulted.

Ceausescu, apparently forced to reassess his decentralization schemes by a combination of Party and state interests, had nevertheless ensured a certain amount of decentralization through the territorial reorganization of the country in early 1968, in which old administrative units were dismantled and the so-called judets were reestablished on the basis of the prewar territorial

---

*Gheorghe Gaston-Marin, chairman of the State Price Committee, admitted that there was opposition on the part of some high central officials against the reforms, and implementation was slowed down as a result of this (Lupta de Clasa, January 1972).

organization. The party leader staffed the RCP bodies at this level with his own trusted men as an important counterweight to the central Party hierarchy. Beginning in 1969 and gaining momentum in 1970 and 1971 was also a campaign designed to strengthen the position of the trade unions at the local and regional levels. This move was designed to establish a direct and personal link between Ceausescu and an important mass organization, which could be entrusted with certain control functions over the economic hierarchy at these levels.[29]

Despite Ceausescu's insistence on early implementation of the reform, acknowledged opposition in the Party, in state bodies, and at the enterprise level has forced several postponements of the target date for final implementation. In the meantime jurisdictional disputes continue, there have been several attempts to experiment with other organizational forms, and production has suffered. The general secretary has backed away somewhat from his attempt to fuse Party and state controls in one person and has instead launched a program of "rotation of cadres" whereby prominent Party leaders are transferred to governmental posts. (To some extent the reverse has been allowed to take place; Cornel Burtica, for example, served primarily in governmental positions prior to his appointment as a member of the RCP Secretariat in 1973.) The Party continues to increase its power vis-a-vis the state apparat, and Ceausescu has partly presided over the recentralization of economic decision making by establishing a Supreme Council for Socio-Economic Development, over which he presides, and the functions of which are coordination of Party and state activities in the economic field.

The constant organizational experimentation with the economic hierarchy in Romania and the continued jurisdictional disputes between Party and state and numerous subdivisions thereof illustrate the profound problems facing Romanian economic development at this stage. It is unlikely that major changes will take place in planning, execution, implementation, and control, and it seems quite likely that centralization will remain the primary factor in the economy. This centralization will in turn create massive problems that the political leadership will attempt to solve through piecemeal tinkering and partial reorganizations. In short, the unsettled nature of Romanian economic administration and management will continue.

NOTES

1. John M. Montias, Economic Development in Communist Rumania (Cambridge, Mass.: The M.I.T. Press, 1967), p. 3.

2. A good discussion of Romanian economic development in the interwar period is found in George W. Hoffman, Regional Development Strategy in Southeast Europe (New York: Praeger Publishers, 1972), especially pp. 33-73.

3. Ibid.

4. Academia Republicii Populare Romine, Institutul de Cercetari Economice, Dezvoltarea Economica a Rominiei (Bucharest: Editura Academii Republicii Populare Romine, 1964), pp. 16-81.

5. Ibid.

6. See Kenneth Jowitt, Revolutionary Breakthroughs and National Development: The Case of Romania, 1944-1965 (Berkeley: University of California Press, 1971), pp. 92-131.

7. Dezvoltarea Economica a Rominiei, pp. 81-113.

8. Anuarul Statistic 1972, pp. 328-29.

9. Scinteia, October 21, 1971.

10. See the discussion of the new targets by First Vice Premier Ilie Verdet (now premier) in Era Socialista, June 1973.

11. See, for example, the discussion by Howard J. Sherman in his Soviet Economy (Boston: Little, Brown and Co., 1969), pp. 215-32; 305-20; 351-63.

12. See the plea for better utilization of existing machinery and manpower by Elena Ciucur and Sandu Viurez in "Increasing the Shift Coefficient in Enterprises," Probleme Economice, no. 9, 1972.

13. See, for example, Ceausescu's own words on this to the RCP National Conference (Scinteia, July 20, 1972).

14. For example, Vasile Patilinet, at the RCP Central Committee Plenum, February 28-March 2, 1973 (Scinteia, March 4, 1973).

15. Angelo Miculescu, minister of Agriculture, the Food Industry, and Waters, at the same meeting (ibid.).

16. Ceausescu in ibid., July 20, 1972.

17. The general secretary also revealed wastage of manpower in industry; in 1972 working time was only 94.6 percent utilized (February 28-March 2, 1973, RCP Central Committee Plenum).

18. Berghianu referred to this in his speech at the RCP National Conference (see Scinteia, July 22, 1972).

19. Ibid.

20. Unsigned article in Lupta de Clasa, March 1972, entitled "Fundamental Directions in the Development of the National Economy."

21. The debates at the plenum were published in several issues of Scinteia during the first week of March 1973.

22. See, for example, Scinteia, April 19 and May 11, 1971 and Munca, May 22, 1971.

23. Ibid., July 20, 1972.

24. Reported in ibid., November 22, 1972, and March 3, 1973, respectively.

25. Ibid., July 22, 1972.

26. The decree was published in Agerpres and reproduced by Radio Free Europe Research (December 20, 1967).

27. The decrees were published and discussed in Scinteia, March 3-8, 1973.

28. The Ceausescu speech to the RCP National Conference, December 1967, in Scinteia, December 7, 1967.

29. For an analysis of these policies see my article on domestic politics in Romania, Problems of Communism, July-August 1974, pp. 29ff.

CHAPTER

6

THE DEVELOPMENT OF AGRICULTURE

Romanian industrial development has been strongly emphasized through a massive investment and educational program; but, though agriculture has consistently been utilized as a source of revenue and a provider of essential foodstuffs for the population, relatively little has been done to develop this field along with the rest of the economy. Romanian planners and policy makers tend to look upon agriculture essentially as a "residual" occupation, which constituted the livelihood for most Romanians in the "bourgeois-landowner" period. Under socialism more and more people will leave the countryside, and the farms will become the center of only one of many important economic activities, far outstripped by industry in contributions to the national income.[1] It is true that all program statements consistently emphasize the need for a highly productive and well developed agricultural sector in the stage of multilateral development, but the regime is simply not contributing the wherewithal for this development. Thus, in the 1965-70 five-year plan, which was passed at the Ninth RCP Congress in 1965, agricultural production was scheduled to rise by 20 percent in the five-year period, as compared to a planned increase of 51 percent for industry.[2] Similarly, the 1971-75 plan, passed by the Grand National Assembly in the fall of 1971, called for an increase in agricultural production of 30 percent, while industry was to increase its output an astonishing 60 percent.[3] With policies of this kind Romanian agriculture remains relatively unproductive, with low yields per worker, considerable sowing and harvesting problems, and perennial shortages.

The problem of relative underproduction on the land is an old one in Romania. In the interwar period the countryside was characterized by a considerable concentration of holdings in a few hands, coupled with small and unproductive individual farms. Mechanization was practically nonexistent, and the soil was tilled by means of implements that had not changed much in centuries. The standard of living was abysmally low for the rural masses, and Romania had one of the highest rates of infant mortality as well as one of the lowest life expectancies in all of Europe. Most of the soil was used for extensive grain production, and much of the crop was sold abroad. The constant use of the soil for the same crops produced serious erosion and a gradual exhaustion of fertility. War damage further diminished the yields.[4]

The RCP, after its inclusion in the coalition of 1944, began a campaign to win the rural poor. The Party's platforms during the coalition years emphasized land reform, the extension of social and medical services to the countryside, modernization and mechanization, and easier financial terms for rapid development. Although the ultimate goal was socialization of the land, this element was played down, and redistribution of the large landed estates became the main platform in the RCP's agricultural policy. A series of land reforms in the period 1944-1947/48 did reallocate holdings and established a large number of small family farms,[5] a development that seems to have earned the Communists a modicum of support in the countryside. At the same time, the Party attempted to extend its organizational network into the rural areas in order to capitalize on the political vacuum that had developed there as a result of the increasing persecution of the traditional peasant parties and organizations during the first postwar years.[6] The RCP therefore engaged in a two-pronged attack on the problem of political control of the rural masses, who constituted the vast majority of the population; one was economic, through land reform; the other political, through the gradual destruction of the organizational infrastructure in rural areas. By 1948-49 organized political resistance against the new order in the countryside had been broken, and the RCP could proceed to implement <u>its</u> agricultural development program.

In comparison to the efforts and funds expended on education and industry, the regime treated agriculture, the mainstay of economic activity, as a stepchild. Table 6.1 illustrates the relative stagnation of agriculture in the investment field as compared to other high priority sectors.

TABLE 6.1

Agricultural Investments, 1950-1970/71
(millions of lei, percentages in parentheses)

	1959 Prices							
	1950	1955	1960	1961	1962	1963	1964	1965
Total	5,633	13,466	24,422	29,713	34,088	37,074	41,031	44,602
	(100.0)	(100.0)	(100.0)	(100.0)	(100.0)	(100.0)	(100.0)	(100.0)
Industry	2,751	7,685	11,771	14,358	17,062	18,139	20,593	22,222
	(48.6)	(57.0)	(48.2)	(48.3)	(50.1)	(48.9)	(50.2)	(49.8)
Construction	369	292	530	724	947	1,538	1,599	1,931
	(6.5)	(2.2)	(2.2)	(2.4)	(2.8)	(4.1)	(3.9)	(4.3)
Agriculture	583	1,828	4,984	6,039	6,937	7,410	7,766	8,283
	(10.3)	(13.6)	(20.0)	(20.3)	(20.3)	(20.0)	(18.9)	(18.6)
Forestry	74	159	209	229	248	242	241	263
	(1.3)	(1.2)	(0.9)	(0.8)	(0.7)	(0.7)	(0.6)	(0.6)
Transport	940	1,060	2,032	2,607	2,823	3,044	3,584	4,170
	(16.6)	(7.9)	(8.3)	(8.8)	(8.3)	(8.2)	(8.7)	(9.4)
Telecommunications	39	64	190	246	279	245	241	302
	(0.7)	(0.5)	(0.8)	(0.8)	(0.8)	(0.7)	(0.6)	(0.7)
Trade and commerce	147	364	736	820	770	1,131	988	1,221
	(2.6)	(2.7)	(3.0)	(2.8)	(2.3)	(3.0)	(2.4)	(2.7)
Local economic activity	216	1,051	2,504	2,862	3,126	3,515	4,006	4,337
("nonproductive services")	(3.8)	(7.8)	(10.3)	(9.6)	(9.2)	(9.5)	(9.8)	(9.7)
Education, culture, the arts	193	412	714	836	836	858	966	816
	(3.3)	(3.0)	(2.9)	(2.8)	(2.4)	(2.3)	(2.4)	(1.8)
Science and science-related	106	156	321	315	401	324	306	198
activities	(1.9)	(1.1)	(1.3)	(1.1)	(1.2)	(0.9)	(0.7)	(0.5)
Health, sanitation, and	151	252	381	489	448	380	502	523
sports	(2.7)	(1.9)	(1.6)	(1.6)	(1.3)	(1.0)	(1.2)	(1.2)
Administration	77	43	79	107	108	104	118	147
	(1.4)	(0.3)	(0.3)	(0.4)	(0.3)	(0.3)	(0.3)	(0.3)
Other fields	17	100	61	81	103	144	121	189
	(0.3)	(0.8)	(0.2)	(0.3)	(0.3)	(0.4)	(0.3)	(0.4)

(continued)

TABLE 6.1 (continued)

	1963 Prices						
	1965	1966	1967	1968	1969	1966/69	1971
Total	44,404	48,909	57,458	64,276	67,529	238,172	82,617
	(100.0)	(100.0)	(100.0)	(100.0)	(100.0)	(100.0)	(100.0)
Industry	22,887	24,778	30,874	34,626	35,938	126,216	42,850
	(51.5)	(50.6)	(53.7)	(53.9)	(53.2)	(53.0)	(51.9)
Construction	1,826	2,139	2,366	2,367	2,307	9,179	4,290
	(4.1)	(4.4)	(4.1)	(3.7)	(3.4)	(3.9)	(5.2)
Agriculture	7,450	7,659	8,608	10,238	11,059	37,564	13,796
	(16.8)	(15.7)	(15.0)	(15.9)	(16.4)	(15.9)	(16.7)
Forestry	256	272	277	334	316	1,199	380
	(0.6)	(0.6)	(0.5)	(0.5)	(0.5)	(0.5)	(0.5)
Transport	4,080	5,054	5,501	6,129	6,997	23,681	8,247
	(9.2)	(10.3)	(9.6)	(9.5)	(10.4)	(9.9)	(10.0)
Telecommunications	317	361	399	460	434	1,654	687
	(0.7)	(0.7)	(0.7)	(0.7)	(0.7)	(0.7)	(0.8)
Trade and Commerce	1,226	1,269	1,528	1,850	2,005	6,652	3,454
	(2.8)	(2.6)	(2.7)	(2.9)	(3.0)	(2.8)	(4.2)
Local Economic Activity ("nonproductive services")	4,503	4,890	5,184	5,288	5,498	20,860	5,229
	(10.1)	(10.0)	(9.0)	(8.2)	(8.1)	(8.8)	(6.3)
Education, culture, the arts	825	1,016	1,115	1,336	1,448	4,915	1,517
	(1.9)	(2.1)	(1.9)	(2.1)	(2.1)	(2.1)	(1.8)
Sciences and science-related activities	190	280	376	448	433	1,537	578
	(0.4)	(0.6)	(0.7)	(0.7)	(0.6)	(0.5)	(0.7)
Health, sanitation, and sports	518	814	692	735	712	2,953	777
	(1.2)	(1.6)	(1.2)	(1.1)	(1.1)	(1.2)	(1.0)
Administration	140	195	194	159	99	647	526
	(0.3)	(0.4)	(0.3)	(0.2)	(0.1)	(0.1)	(0.6)
Other fields	186	182	344	306	283	1,115	286
	(0.4)	(0.4)	(0.6)	(0.5)	(0.4)	(0.5)	(0.3)

Sources: Anuarul Statistic 1970, pp. 458-59; Anuarul Statistic 1972, pp. 328-29.

TABLE 6.2

Investments Put into Operation, by Field, 1960-71
(in millions of lei, percentages in parentheses)

	1959 Prices						1963 Prices					
	1960	1961	1962	1963	1964	1965	1965	1966	1967	1968	1969	1971
Total	23,362	25,415	31,084	31,031	32,606	39,473	39,426	45,888	46,983	54,924	61,754	73,680
Industry	11,194	10,402	14,775	13,770	13,975	18,419	18,992	23,931	22,902	27,473	31,846	35,946
	(47.9)	(40.9)	(47.5)	(44.4)	(42.9)	(46.7)	(48.2)	(52.2)	(48.7)	(50.0)	(51.6)	(48.8)
Construction	540	702	966	1,425	1,571	1,897	1,785	2,060	2,355	2,333	2,293	4,218
	(2.3)	(2.8)	(3.1)	(4.5)	(4.8)	(4.8)	(4.5)	(4.5)	(5.0)	(4.2)	(3.7)	(5.7)
Agriculture	4,988	5,987	6,783	6,537	7,061	7,880	7,259	6,536	8,008	9,324	10,054	12,283
	(21.4)	(23.6)	(21.8)	(21.1)	(21.7)	(20.0)	(18.4)	(14.2)	(17.0)	(17.0)	(16.3)	(16.7)
Forestry	206	227	246	234	236	255	254	270	268	335	381	367
	(0.9)	(0.9)	(0.8)	(0.8)	(0.7)	(0.6)	(0.6)	(0.6)	(0.6)	(0.6)	(0.6)	(0.5)
Transport	1,832	2,702	2,554	2,798	3,345	3,874	3,806	4,988	4,902	6,176	6,981	8,198
	(7.8)	(10.6)	(8.2)	(9.0)	(10.3)	(9.8)	(9.7)	(10.9)	(10.4)	(11.2)	(11.3)	(11.1)
Telecommunications	113	184	133	423	205	290	307	340	411	404	459	556
	(0.5)	(0.7)	(0.4)	(1.4)	(0.6)	(0.7)	(0.8)	(0.7)	(0.7)	(0.7)	(0.7)	(0.8)
Trade and commerce	684	743	733	868	1,101	1,086	1,102	1,232	1,428	1,452	1,680	3,491
	(2.4)	(2.9)	(2.4)	(2.8)	(3.4)	(2.8)	(2.8)	(2.7)	(3.0)	(2.6)	(2.7)	(4.7)
Local economic activity ("nonproductive services")	2,271	2,756	3,019	3,308	3,223	4,037	4,199	4,223	4,473	4,970	5,314	4,950
	(9.7)	(10.8)	(9.7)	(10.7)	(9.9)	(10.2)	(10.7)	(9.2)	(9.5)	(9.0)	(8.6)	(6.7)
Education, culture, the arts	649	736	817	856	913	781	789	849	901	1,135	1,323	1,450
	(2.8)	(2.9)	(2.6)	(2.8)	(2.8)	(2.0)	(2.0)	(1.9)	(1.9)	(2.1)	(2.1)	(2.0)
Sciences and science-related activities	296	303	372	279	298	219	209	268	292	325	384	545
	(1.3)	(1.2)	(1.2)	(0.9)	(0.9)	(0.6)	(0.5)	(0.6)	(0.6)	(0.6)	(0.6)	(0.7)
Health, administration, sports	348	458	499	296	421	407	409	835	558	558	637	952
	(1.5)	(1.8)	(1.6)	(1.0)	(1.3)	(1.0)	(1.0)	(1.8)	(1.2)	(1.0)	(1.0)	(1.3)
Administration	82	104	93	106	118	130	128	192	166	157	106	515
	(0.4)	(0.4)	(0.3)	(0.3)	(0.4)	(0.3)	(0.3)	(0.4)	(0.4)	(0.3)	(0.2)	(0.7)
Other fields	159	111	94	131	139	198	187	164	319	282	296	209
	(0.7)	(0.4)	(0.3)	(0.4)	(0.4)	(0.5)	(0.5)	(0.4)	(0.7)	(0.4)	(0.5)	(0.3)

Sources: Anuarul Statistic 1970, p. 486; Anuarul Statistic 1972, p. 358.

According to Table 6.1 agricultural investment has varied from approximately 10 to roughly 20 percent of total investments, while industry has swallowed half or more. The same kind of discrepancy can be found in the amount of funds put into operation each year: agriculture had a much lower performance than industry, as illustrated by Table 6.2. Further information on agriculture is furnished by Tables 6.3-6.6.

TABLE 6.3

Total Agricultural Production, 1948-71
1938 = 100

Year	Total Production	Vegetable Products	Animal Products
1948	62	55	76
1950	74	65	94
1955	120	119	123
1960	126	118	145
1963	126	121	136
1965	143	133	163
1969	165	154	191
1971	186	172	219

Sources: Anuarul Statistic 1970, p. 439; Anuarul Statistic 1972, p. 316.

Several conclusions emerge from a study of Tables 6.1-6.6. First, the investments in agriculture are relatively too small to ensure sustained growth and development. For each year of underinvestment in this field the imbalances in the economy become even more noticeable, with resulting shortages of all kinds in industries that depend upon agricultural raw materials for their plan fulfillment. The population movement into industrial occupations results in a higher monetary standard of living for thousands every year, but the foodstuffs are simply not there to accommodate the rising standard of living and the demands for a better diet. Agriculture constantly loses manpower, and the bulk of the workforce in the countryside now consists of women, old men, and children.[7] Productivity is therefore low; while production per worker in many industrial fields went up 8.3 percent yearly between 1950 and 1971, overall productivity in agriculture gained much less.[8] An example of the low productivity in collective farms is the fact that in 1966, 45 people were required per 100 hectares of land for tilling, sowing, harvesting, and so on; this proportion had been reduced to 37 per 100 hectares in 1970, still a very high figure.[9] Ceausescu has officially claimed that Romania will reach the level of "advanced countries," where two people can handle all agricultural tasks per 100 acres,[10] but the country seems quite far removed from this stage at the present time.

The figures on state and collective farms and the agricultural production enterprises (essentially machine-tractor stations modeled on earlier Soviet methods) clearly show the discrepancy in investments and productivity inside the agricultural sector. The state farms, which are considered a higher form of agricultural organization, have received proportionately a much higher share of investments than did the collective farms. Especially important in this context is the heavy emphasis on agricultural machinery on the state farms; this superior mechanization has enabled these units to outproduce the collective farms in virtually all areas of activity. In fact, the differences are so glaring that they have produced some passive resistance among collective farmers, in the form of go-slow actions and attempts to work private plots "on company time." These efforts have further reduced the productivity of the collectives, with subsequent reduction in the standard of living. Since the overwhelming majority of the agricultural units in Romania are collectives rather than state farms, such actions have a generally depressing tendency for overall performance.

The evidence on the mechanization units at first glance indicates considerable progress, and it is true that Romania has made part of the transition from extensive, labor-oriented production to a more intensive and mechanized performance in this sector. Productivity nevertheless remains relatively low even compared to most of the other socialist states, let alone Western Europe or the United States.[11] Furthermore, there are numerous other problems with the mechanization units that are not indicated by Table 6.4. There is considerable underutilization of equipment, and the lack of skilled operators and mechanics drastically reduces the life of machinery and its performance while in use. A considerable shortage of experts such as veterinarians, botanists, and plant

TABLE 6.4

Main Indicators of Performance: Mechanization Enterprises, 1950-71

	1950	1955	1960	1961	1962
Units	138	222	243	244	250
Total number employees (thousands)	17,508	35,292	44,502	54,161	64,155
Total-fixed fund (millions of lei)	--	2,461	5,522	6,646	7,847
Total investments (millions of lei)	--	--	1,467	1,558	1,782
Agricultural machinery					
Agricultural tractors (physical units)	5,833	13,034	26,598	33,619	39,696
Agricultural tractors (units of 15 hp)	7,486	17,646	39,562	50,404	59,577
Total work performed (measured in millions of hectares ploughed)	2,112.7	4,115.8	14,180.7	20,721.8	27,528.0
ploughing	1,307.9	1,827.5	4,726.0	5,964.2	6,986.4
sowing	105.6	550.7	2,358.2	3,498.4	4,576.1
tilling	--	55.0	852.3	1,176.1	1,726.9
hoeing	25.3	250.1	575.7	977.7	1,259.6
Average work performed (hectares per 15 hp tractor ploughed)	--	233	442	475	506
Average work performed per worker (hectares tilled)	121	117	316	380	427

Sources: Anuarul Statistic 1970, pp. 284-85; Anuarul Statistic 1972, p. 222.

1963	1964	1965	1966	1967	1968	1969	1971
258	260	264	273	289	290	296	772
),189	77,315	85,667	93,533	96,012	93,006	93,471	106,200
3,529	9,153	9,796	10,671	11,178	10,386	11,513	13,615
1,128	1,124	941	1,204	1,331	1,492	1,335	1,934
4,983	50,611	55,439	60,922	63,933	66,743	71,964	80,425
9,563	80,394	90,128	100,281	106,503	113,062	123,099	139,027
),432.4	31,352.9	34,100.2	35,370.2	39,508.4	37,628.7	38,861.0	45,629.0
7,664.1	7,288.7	7,604.3	7,260.5	8,605.7	7,176.3	7,867.2	7,488.2
5,391.2	5,535.9	5,798.5	5,763.0	5,966.2	6,457.7	5,901.4	6,466.0
2,506.3	3,225.9	3,749.0	4,668.0	5,464.6	4,902.7	4,735.9	6,145.9
1,245.9	1,339.9	1,459.9	1,631.3	1,791.3	2,033.3	1,916.3	1,869.7
497	416	401	371	381	338	--	333
434	405	397	377	411	405	416	489

TABLE 6.5

Main Indicators of Performance: Collective Farms, 1950-71

	1950	1955	1960	1961	1962
Units	1,027	2,152	4,887	6,424	5,398
Families (in thousands)	67.7	183.2	1,420.1	2,051.0	3,294.8
Agricultural land (thousands of hectares)	288.9	905.8	4,580.2	5,973.3	9,084.7
Private plots	11.8	35.3	337.3	525.7	928.9
Arable land (thousands of hectares)	262.5	792.8	4,099.6	5,277.9	7,677.7
Private plots	11.2	31.9	276.0	428.1	771.5
Public ownership (millions of lei)	--	791.2	5,323.1	7,561.5	10,973.7
Investments (millions of lei)	21	260	1,462	2,138	2,964
State credits (millions of lei)	8	142	483	939	984
Property fund (millions of lei)	13	118	979	1,199	1,980
Animals (thousands of head):					
Cattle	15.7	64.2	530.8	972.4	1,577.2
Pigs	4.4	80.6	364.5	811.3	1,212.9
Sheep	18.1	592.9	2,224.3	2,955.6	4,233.4
Vegetable production (thousands of tons):					
Cereals	24.3	801.0	3,345.8	4,912.3	6,721.0
Wheat	12.1	360.9	1,314.9	2,040.9	3,010.2
Corn	8.2	299.7	1,721.5	2,491.4	3,277.9
Sunflower	1.1	30.7	226.1	277.2	375.4
Sugar beets	3.6	156.0	2,060.9	2,107.0	2,171.7
Potatoes	6.3	125.7	377.6	485.4	1,177.3
Vegetables	4.4	113.9	407.3	681.6	747.7
Production per hectare (quintals)					
Wheat	9.2	13.7	13.5	14.0	12.2
Corn	8.4	19.3	19.4	19.9	16.0
Sunflower	5.3	9.9	11.8	11.4	10.0
Sugar beets	90.6	146.8	181.9	171.4	140.8
Potatoes	46.8	99.8	104.1	93.3	94.5

Sources: Anuarul Statistic 1970, pp. 292-93; Anuarul Statistic 1972, p. 229.

1963	1964	1965	1966	1967	1968	1969	1971
4,870	4,716	4,680	4,679	4,678	4,673	4,655	4,601
3,345.8	3,380.7	3,409.1	3,427.2	3,441.2	3,452.3	3,455.4	3,455.0
8,999.5	8,959.8	8,993.9	9,000.5	9,004.3	9,076.7	9,069.7	9,041.2
948.6	958.6	967.5	975.0	976.9	982.0	982.2	982.0
7,492.5	7,400.4	7,387.3	7,368.3	7,355.7	7,343.6	7,311.9	7,258.0
783.9	788.8	800.0	801.0	800.4	799.5	796.8	795.9
13,086.7	14,954.6	16,766.9	19,402.9	21,605.5	22,860.0	24,955.5	27,885.6
3,740	3,119	2,811	2,737	3,145	3,249	3,357	4,642
1,170	445	372	539	683	1,037	1,181	2,169
2,570	2,674	2,439	2,198	2,462	2,212	2,176	2,473
1,921.1	1,951.6	1,955.8	2,040.8	2,066.5	2,037.2	2,062.2	2,195.6
1,257.6	1,339.9	1,228.4	1,330.7	1,419.3	1,497.8	1,604.4	1,955.8
4,955.6	5,047.2	4,951.7	5,244.5	5,377.6	5,413.6	5,217.9	5,238.9
7,114.4	7,398.2	8,387.7	9,505.0	9,157.4	8,405.0	8,125.9	9,722.6
2,983.3	2,800.5	4,238.2	3,752.3	4,193.8	3,508.6	3,153.3	4,232.9
3,729.0	4,241.6	3,646.3	5,223.0	4,460.5	4,428.8	4,495.7	4,845.4
417.4	415.5	437.8	518.7	556.5	502.1	520.3	590.8
2,266.0	3,634.7	3,237.6	4,305.9	3,788.6	3,886.8	3,768.3	4,290.8
1,278.7	1,264.5	970.7	1,537.3	1,417.3	1,713.1	845.7	1,636.3
970.9	1,011.4	915.1	1,230.1	1,099.2	1,271.1	1,038.3	1,274.1
12.5	12.0	18.4	16.0	18.7	15.9	14.5	21.4
17.5	20.3	17.6	24.9	21.6	20.9	22.1	24.6
10.2	10.3	11.3	13.5	14.3	12.8	13.2	13.7
128.5	192.4	171.7	224.9	217.1	212.5	200.9	242.6
88.2	91.9	77.2	115.8	104.9	125.1	64.4	135.0

TABLE 6.6

Main Indicators of Performance: State Farms, 1955-71

	1950	1955	1960	1961	1962
Units	363	265	560	587	597
Total employees (in thousands)	161.8	155.2	224.0	240.5	258.7
Workers	140.8	134.4	202.2	216.4	232.9
Agricultural land (thousands of hectares)	753.2	881.6	1,720.1	1,742.9	1,769.6
Arable land (thousands of hectares)	549.8	694.0	1,340.9	1,359.0	1,376.9
Total fixed fund (millions of lei)	--	4,438	8,984	10,172	11,152
Total investments (millions of lei)	217	667	1,516	1,969	1,878
Agricultural machinery					
Agricultural tractors					
Physical units	3,281	6,455	16,093	17,175	16,628
Conventional units of 15 hp	4,156	8,529	23,674	25,382	24,704
Animals (thousands of heads)					
Cattle	60.5	84.7	236.3	342.0	430.1
Pigs	158.7	225.2	801.1	967.3	1,059.1
Sheep	329.4	541.0	1,017.1	1,270.8	1,391.0
Horses	20.2	34.6	36.5	39.3	37.6
Total production of cereals (thousands of tons)	205.9	549.1	1,526.1	1,792.5	1,838.0
Wheat	94.8	251.7	691.3	781.3	906.5
Corn	25.8	160.2	625.4	760.4	728.7
Production per hectare (quintals)					
Wheat	9.6	13.8	17.8	18.2	20.8
Corn	6.6	21.2	18.8	24.4	28.3

Sources: Anuarul Statistic 1970, pp. 274-75; Anuarul Statistic 1972, pp. 214-15.

1963	1964	1965	1966	1967	1968	1969	1971
637	683	721	731	343	352	359	200
276.4	295.4	301.3	310.4	287.2	276.5	290.7	297.8
249.3	265.4	267.5	274.5	257.5	251.6	265.1	275.7
1,925.2	2,020.7	2,077.0	2,077.8	2,092.1	2,114.1	2,112.1	2,067.7
1,510.0	1,585.0	1,626.6	1,630.1	1,645.1	1,671.7	1,670.6	1,659.6
12,108	13,405	15,698	17,017	18,144	19,975	23,609	30,472
2,157	2,691	3,014	3,027	2,923	3,882	4,366	4,487
18,857	23,059	24,716	28,469	27,376	27,960	28,220	31,543
29,000	37,012	40,974	48,501	46,710	49,213	51,377	55,937
449.4	494.0	515.3	513.1	513.9	554.4	595.1	688.6
1,100.3	1,072.7	1,098.0	1,266.2	1,281.5	1,540.6	1,981.6	2,598.1
1,404.4	1,506.5	1,482.0	1,539.4	1,561.9	1,602.3	1,592.4	1,605.6
34.3	34.3	35.8	37.0	36.5	36.4	36.2	28.0
2,143.6	2,432.6	3,009.6	2,716.9	2,830.3	2,821.0	3,028.8	2,890.7
705.4	924.3	1,586.6	1,202.2	1,511.4	1,230.2	1,090.9	1,242.7
1,273.6	1,324.8	1,188.1	1,285.0	1,039.3	1,290.8	1,667.2	1,278.2
19.7	18.6	27.8	20.4	26.6	24.0	22.0	28.4
28.7	30.7	26.7	31.7	27.9	29.2	35.4	33.7

pathologists continues to hamper development, despite concerted regime efforts to improve the flow of manpower into agricultural units.[12] A career in agriculture appears to be the least attractive path for most young people, and enrollment in agricultural fields at the universities remains much too low.[13] In many reported cases, the mechanized brigades have not fulfilled contracts with state and especially collective farms, or such contracts have been filled late, resulting in sowing and harvesting at inappropriate times. Millions of lei are lost annually because of bad scheduling by the mechanization brigades. Finally, these units, which accept agricultural produce as part of their payment, have at times acted as major hoarders of grains, fruits, and vegetables, and part of their stock has been destroyed by rot and other diseases.

The performance figures given above indicate some progress in Romanian agriculture, although this field remains the most underdeveloped area of the economy. In planned output, however, the performance is quite bleak. The 1966-70 five-year plan, for example, called for an increase in total agricultural production of 26-32 percent during the period, but actual output increased only 24 percent. In crucial fields, such as cattle breeding, production increased only 5.5 percent (pig breeding and sheep breeding registered increases of 18.6 percent and 5.2 percent, respectively).[14]

One of the main reasons for these shortcomings in agriculture was the failure to meet planned targets in the production of chemical fertilizers, which was off 32.5 percent; irrigation also fell short by about 17 percent. Finally, tractor production was lower than planned, so that by the end of the period there were 7.5 percent fewer tractors on the land than the projections had originally called for.[15]

In 1971 agricultural production once again fell short of the plan in most fields, especially in corn, vegetables, fruits and grapes, milk and wool. On the other hand, the plan was exceeded in mechanization (numbers of tractors in operation on the land and of sowing machines). The targets were also exceeded in cattle, pig, and sheep raising.[16]

Both in 1972 and 1973 there were important shortcomings, although 1972 registered the biggest wheat harvest in Romanian history. In 1972, for example, total agricultural production was approximately 13 percent below target. Severe supply problems persisted, and there was much wastage caused by delays in deliveries of equipment and fertilizer.[17]

Despite such evidence of fundamental structural problems in Romanian agriculture and its supply system, the planners continue to establish targets that can only be fulfilled if the factors of weather, productivity, and the supply of machinery, fertilizers, and services are all fully coordinated. The 1974 plan, for example, calls for an overall increase in agricultural production of 5.8 percent, but this seemingly modest figure is based on a 91 percentage point improvement in draining and a 30.6 point increase in the supply of fertilizers as well as a 16.2 point jump in the production of tractors.[18] Given the problems of coordinating all these factors, it is unlikely that the overall targets will be met during this year.

STRATEGIES FOR PROBLEM SOLVING

The Romanian regime has adopted several major strategies for problem solving in the field of agriculture. The most important of these approaches are the following:

Frequent Reorganizations

The penchant for organizational solutions to all problems has been dramatically illustrated by the frequent reorganizations in Romanian agriculture. These administrative approaches have included frequent turnover of personnel at the top of the Ministry of Agriculture and occasional revamping of the whole ministerial structure. Thus in the period 1953-62 there were six different ministers of agriculture, and only slightly more stability has been achieved in the last 12 years, during which this important position changed hands three times.[19] There were ministerial reorganizations in 1949, 1962, 1969, and twice in 1971, with further modifications in 1972.[20] In 1965 a "National Union of Agricultural Production Cooperatives" was established in order to organize the members of the collective farms (collectivization had been completed in 1962). Since 1969 there have been frequent changes in the leadership positions of this body as well.[21]

Both the state farms and the mechanization units have been reorganized several times; the last effort in this field was in 1971 (mechanization units) and 1972 (state farms).[22]

While there have been frequent internal changes in agricultural bodies, the RCP has expanded its direct control over planning, production, and management in this field. This trend has been especially noticeable since 1971. During 1973 several joint Party-state bodies were established to direct economic development, including agricultural production, the most important of which is the Supreme Council for Socio-Economic Development, headed by Nicolae Ceausescu. There is currently a major drive for a partial dismantling of the administrative staffs in all state bodies, including those handling agricultural matters. Personnel released from administrative duties are to take up positions in production. Those released will presumably increase the number of skilled personnel working directly in state and collective farms and mechanization units.

Increasing Material Incentives

Since the mid-1960s the traditional regime approach of burdening the peasantry with heavy compulsory deliveries at low prices has been partly abandoned. Instead the regime has raised the purchase price on a number of commodities, especially grains, in order to stimulate production.[23] There have been several reductions in the debts owed by collective farms to the state, and certain kinds of indebtedness have been written off altogether.[24] Increasing social security and medical coverage have been offered to improve the standard of living in the countryside. There are numerous subsidy plans for housing construction in rural areas, and increased scholarships have been offered for rural youth who wish to study zoology, "veterinary sciences," and plant pathology (to mention only a few fields). Special bonuses and other incentives are also offered to economic specialists and teachers wishing to settle in rural areas.[25]

During the last two or three years there have been several campaigns designed to increase production on private plots. The limits on the number of animals kept and the size of arable land for private use have been revised upwards several times. Farmers can now obtain loans for the acquisition of animals, and expanded use of mechanization units for sowing and harvesting has been allowed. All these measures represent a concerted effort by the political and economic leadership to capitalize on the relatively high productivity of private plots in order to increase total agricultural output.

Ideological Incentives

In addition to material incentives, Nicolae Ceausescu (as well as his predecessor) has emphasized the importance of ideological work among the peasantry as a source of expanded production. For this purpose the RCP has attempted to expand its network in rural areas and to enroll more farmers in the Party. The campaign for ideological orthodoxy, which was launched in the summer of 1971, has as an important target substantially expanding political education in all agricultural production units so that a "Socialist outlook" can be firmly established among the rural population. The campaign is also designed to root out "bourgeois-landowner mentality and outlook" in the countryside, where even the most "advanced" farmers tend to be preoccupied with material gain only for themselves and their families, with scant regard for the society as a whole.[26] The ideological offensive has substantially increased the number of hours spent on political education among collective farmers and employees on the state units; and short-term courses in political education, "voluntary citizen participation" in seminars, and youth camps have been drastically expanded. Despite such massive efforts, dramatic increases in total production and individual productivity have not been achieved.

Expanded Use of Campaigns

The emphasis on campaigns, so much a part of economic life in Romania, is perhaps even stronger in agriculture than in industry. Agricultural activity lends itself to the campaign approach; the planting and harvest seasons are periods of frantic activity in all rural areas, no matter what the economic system, while the winter period is much less active. The campaign approach works well in an integrated economic system where storage facilities, transportation, processing plants, and machinery are available in sufficient quantity and variety to handle the added tasks. In Romania there are severe shortages in all these fields, and much waste occurs both at planting time and during harvesting. There is not enough machinery for planting, which means that certain crops get in the ground too late or not at all. Throughout the growing season the lack of equipment and its inefficient use lead to deficiencies in tilling, with subsequent massive weed problems. At harvest time the transport system is unable to handle the added volume of traffic, with the result that produce piles up in inadequate storage facilities or simply rots in the fields. In 1972 alone it was estimated that millions of lei were lost because of inadequate coordination during the harvesting campaign.[27] Industrial workers, soldiers, students, and school children are often mobilized to help bring in the harvest, and rolling stock from industrial plants is commandeered to transport grains, vegetables, and potatoes, thus causing dislocations in the "pirated" fields.

It is assumed that the stage of multilateral development will reduce or totally remove the need for agricultural campaigns, but it is clear that Romania is quite far from this goal. Both in 1972 and 1973 much of the spring and fall work in agriculture took place under the auspices of official campaigns (such as the campaign to get the harvest from the fields prominently publicized in all the major newspapers during the fall of 1972). The results were reasonably good, but much waste was reported, further adding to scarcities. It is doubtful indeed that the campaign approach will be abandoned by 1990 or 2000, the official target years of multilateral development. If such a target is to be reached, a massive reallocation of resources in favor of agriculture will be needed. There is no indication that such a reallocation is contemplated.

NOTES

1. See, for example, Ceausescu's statements to the Ninth RCP Congress, July 1965, in Congresul al IX-lea al Partidului Comunist Roman (Bucharest: Editura Politica, 1966), pp. 45-53.
2. Ibid., pp. 36-53.
3. Approximate figures from Ion Gheorghe Maurer's presentation to the Grand National Assembly, in Scinteia, October 21, 1971.
4. See Hugh Seton-Watson, The East European Revolution (New York, N.Y.: Praeger Publishers, 1968), pp. 1-23.
5. Dezvoltarea Economica a Rominiei, pp. 24-29; 43-52; 70-76.
6. Ghita Ionescu, Communism in Rumania (London: Oxford University Press, 1964), pp. 107-47.

7. This point was made by Ceausescu in his speech to the Congress of the National Union of Agricultural Production Co-operatives, held in February 1972 (Scinteia, February 22, 1972).

8. Derived from Anuarul Statistic 1970, p. 228.

9. Viata Economica, June 30, 1972.

10. For example, Scinteia, July 20, 1972.

11. Viata Economica, June 30, 1972.

12. Angelo Miculescu, minister of Agriculture, proposed several such improvements in Scinteia, August 29, 1972.

13. The low level of expertise in agriculture was discussed in Viata Economica, September 1970.

14. See Radio Free Europe Research Rumania/3, 17 February 1972, "Rumanian Agriculture on the Eve of the Second Congress of the National Union of Agricultural Production Co-operatives."

15. Ibid.

16. Scinteia and Romania Libera, February 2, 1972.

17. Ceausescu severely criticized such economic shortcomings in his speech to the RCP Central Committee, published in Scinteia, March 3, 1972.

18. The draft plan for 1974 was discussed several times during June 1974; the figures above were discussed in a "working session" on June 22. (Scinteia, June 23, 1973.)

19. "Rumanian Agriculture on the Eve of the Second Congress."

20. Ibid.

21. Ibid.

22. Scinteia, January 3, 1971 for the reorganization on mechanization units.

23. One such increase was announced in Buletinul Oficial, January 6, 1973.

24. Scinteia, December 22, 1971.

25. See Miculescu's proposals, ibid., August 29, 1972.

26. Ceausescu's concern over the low ideological level in the countryside was reflected in his so-called "ideological" speech at the November 1971 plenum (ibid., November 4, 1971).

27. Ceausescu at the February-March 1973 plenum (ibid., March 3, 1973).

CHAPTER

7

THE DEVELOPMENT OF COMMUNICATIONS AND SOCIAL SERVICES

TRANSPORTATION

One of the most important areas of economic modernization is the constant development of the transportation system, at sea, on land, and in the air. Many economists maintain that a major reason for American industrial superiority is the highly developed and integrated transportation network in this country, which allows rapid transmission of raw materials to the manufacturing plants and shipment of finished goods to the retail network. Similarly, economic planners in developing countries have generally agreed that an infrastructure of roads, railroads, and perhaps also water transport must be developed before industrialization can make rapid headway.

Communist planners have agreed with this emphasis on transportation development, especially for bulk haulage of raw materials and heavy industrial goods. Soviet economists, who pioneered in this field in Communist systems, attempted to develop major trunk lines that could serve as funnels for manpower and machinery into underdeveloped territories. A major source of military victory in the Russian Civil War was indeed Bolshevik control over the main railroad hubs of Petrograd and Moscow, which permitted the Red command relatively easy access to all major fronts and offered the opportunity of rapid troop transfers from one contested area to another. The Trans-Siberian Railway became a major source of supply for all of Siberia, and to this day most of the economic development of this region is intimately tied to this supply line and sole connector with European Russia. Conversely, the absence of major railroad links between northern and southern Siberia has retarded development of large areas.[1]

The Soviet Model

The Soviet model emphasized rail systems at the expense of truck and automobile transportation, and the result was overburdening of the trunk lines, massive cargo concentrations, and shipping delays. Furthermore, intercity and local traffic became inflexible, and the constant need to load and unload boxcars that had been used for very short hauls caused considerable delays and became increasingly costly. To this day the Soviet transportation system is beset with considerable problems stemming from this imbalance.[2]

Since truck transportation was downplayed the road system remained underdeveloped, and in the spring and early winter seasons many regions were virtually isolated. Service facilities and gasoline stations remained few and far between. Private car ownership was officially discouraged, and this in turn increased the pressure on public mass transit.

While the Soviet Union experienced considerable problems in the development of its transportation system, problems that remain to this day, an infrastructure of communications, especially railroads, was established and helped fuel the rapid advances of Soviet industrialization. Thus, despite delays and waste, tremendous results were achieved.

The Soviet experience has been outlined in some detail because it became the model for all of the less developed countries that fell under Communist rule after World War II, including Romania. The Romanian modernizers took over a transportation system that was badly underdeveloped. Only a few major rail lines existed, running primarily east-west. Part of the Transylvanian network was still oriented toward the earlier economic ties with the Austro-Hungarian empire, primarily Budapest. The rolling stock was outdated, and most of the trains were powered by steam rather than by diesel fuel or electricity. War damages had severely depleted the stock of locomotives, boxcars, and passenger cars. There were almost no cars for specialized haulage.

Road transportation was woefully underdeveloped and in many areas consisted of oxcarts bringing agricultural produce to the nearest village market. Since almost no roads were paved, the familiar problems of impassable mud and snow coverage reduced road traffic to a trickle in the winter and spring seasons. Only some roads between the major cities were kept continually open. Due to the socioeconomic structure of the country private cars were the luxury toys of the privileged few, who used their automobiles on the boulevards of Bucharest, Constanta, and other major cities not for haulage of passengers hurrying to work but for pleasure trips.[3]

Water transportation was also underdeveloped in Romania, although the Danube provided a major waterway from the northwest to the southeast. There was practically no merchant marine, and only a few Romanian coastal steamers plied the waters of the Black Sea. The lack of water transportation reflected the relative underdevelopment of the Romanian economy generally.[4]

The RCP Program

The RCP, upon accession to partial governmental control in 1944 and full power a few years later, started a program of gradual expansion of the transportation network, especially railroads. In this field as elsewhere the Soviet model was followed closely, and the Romanian planners started to expand existing trunklines and building others that could help speed industrialization. Governmental control of the railroads was a tradition in Romania, and nationalization of the transportation system was therefore of lesser consequence than the takeover of industry, banking, and most of the retail trade. By 1947-48 the Romanian Communists were ready to launch an important campaign to upgrade all areas of transportation in the country.

Despite considerable verbal emphasis on expansion in this field, the main modernization campaign has always been conducted in the so-called "productive" fields; most of the investments of money and manpower therefore went into the building of factories and the production of machinery, rather than the transportation network that was to serve the expanding physical plant. This is clearly illustrated by Table 7.1, which shows investments in transportation as compared to funds allocated for industry in the period 1950-1970/71.

According to Table 7.1 investments in transportation were consistently much lower than industry, and after unusually heavy funding in 1950 this category only received one-sixth to one-seventh of the investments into industry. If a comparison is made with investments in agriculture (see Chapter 6), it becomes clear that transportation generally received considerably less than this underdeveloped sector of the economy. The disproportionate emphasis on "productive" industries had the effect of burdening a transportation system that was incapable of handling the increasing amount of goods and the swelling numbers of passengers dependent upon it. Despite the increasing problems of such imbalances no serious rearrangements of funds are envisioned for the near future, as seen by the 1971-75 five-year plan, which was promulgated by the Grand National Assembly in the fall of 1971.

TABLE 7.1

Investments in Transportation and Industry, 1950 1970/71
(in millions of lei, percentages in parentheses)

	Total	Industry	Transportation
	1959 Prices		
1950	5,663	2,751	940
	(100.0)	(48.6)	(16.6)
1955	13,466	7,685	1,060
	(100.0)	(57.0)	(7.9)
1960	24,422	11,771	2,032
	(100.0)	(48.2)	(8.3)
	1963 Prices		
1965	44,602	22,222	4,170
	(100.0)	(49.8)	(9.4)
1969	67,529	35,938	6,997
	(100.0)	(53.2)	(10.4)
1971	82,617	42,050	8,247
	(100.0)	(51.9)	(10.0)

Sources: Anuarul Statistic 1970, pp. 458-59; Anuarul Statistic 1972, pp. 328-29.

Within the field of transportation the early emphasis was heavily on railroads, but by the 1960s a drastic upswing occurred in other fields. Table 7.2 shows the development of Romanian railroads in the 1960s.

Table 7.2 is interesting in that it shows virtual stagnation of the railroads in the 1960s in development of track. The big expansion had come earlier; the length of the network in 1938 was 9,990 kilometers, and in 1950, 10,853 kilometers.[5]

TABLE 7.2

Development of Railroads in the 1960s:
Railroad Lines, 1965-71
(in kilometers)

Year	Total Length	Normal Width Track	Narrow Width Track
1965	10,979	10,302	648
1966	11,007	10,331	647
1967	11,023	10,347	647
1968	11,016	10,349	638
1969	11,006	10,337	633
1970	11,012	10,341	635
1971	11,012	10,359	618

Sources: Anuarul Statistic 1970, p. 498; Anuarul Statistic 1972, p. 372.

During the socialist period a considerable expansion of the road system also took place; while the total road system in 1938 was less than 50,000 kilometers, by 1959 it had reached 76,143 kilometers.[6] In the 1960s, however, relatively little expansion took place, as shown by Table 7.3.

Table 7.3 shows that there has been a virtual standstill in road building as well during the last six or seven years; instead the emphasis has been on improving the quality of the existing system. During the 1960s existing facilities of both roads and railroads were used much more intensively (as was indeed the case with other forms of transportation). Table 7.4 examines this development by illustrating goods transportation by total tonnage and ton-kilometers, in the period 1938-71.

The most important development in Romanian transportation during the socialist period has been the increase in automobile and truck use, as shown by Table 7.4. By the mid-1960s these vehicles were carrying more freight than the railroads in terms of total tonnage, and that gap is widening. The bulk of long distance freight is carried primarily by railroads, however, as indicated by the figures for ton-kilometers. This essentially means that truck transportation is local, primarily deliveries from railheads to retail outlets and vice versa. A great

TABLE 7.3

Expansion of the Road System, 1965-71

Year	Total Kilometers	(Modernized)	National Roads	(Modernized)	Local Roads	(Modernized)
1965	75,898	(8,508)	11,514	(6,788)	64,384	(1,720)
1966	76,557	(9,002)	11,517	(7,111)	65,040	(1,891)
1967	76,815	(9,490)	11,725	(7,452)	65,090	(2,038)
1968	77,019	(10,021)	11,872	(7,884)	65,147	(2,137)
1969	76,566	(10,605)	12,158	(8,322)	64,408	(2,283)
1970	75,879	(11,091)	12,167	(8,688)	63,712	(2,403)
1971	75,717	(11,450)	12,896	(9,082)	62,821	(2,368)

Sources: *Anuarul Statistic 1970*, p. 503; *Anuarul Statistic 1972*, p. 375.

TABLE 7.4

Goods Transported, 1938-71, by Tons and Ton-kilometers

	1938	1950	1955	1960	1965	1969	1970	1971
	(thousands of tons)							
All fields	29,029	38,404	70,132	141,798	256,860	388,379	430,123	466,211
Railroads	26,281	35,069	58,963	77,492	114,354	155,364	171,312	184,787
Automobiles and trucks	14	1,046	7,335	56,608	130,850	215,645	239,776	260,735
River transport	1,326	1,108	1,596	1,914	2,865	3,148	3,396	4,103
Maritime transport	606	181	197	195	1,364	5,043	4,370	4,057
Air transport	--	3	7	3	5	18	18	13
Pipeline (petroleum products)	802	997	2,034	5,586	7,422	9,161	11,251	12,516
	(millions of ton-kilometers)							
All fields	8,950	9,110	16,740	23,708	44,166	90,163	93,913	102,396
Railroads	5,969	7,598	14,675	19,821	30,981	44,031	48,045	50,840
Automobiles and trucks	--	42	272	936	2,533	4,541	5,156	5,496
River transport	606	669	648	865	1,222	1,165	1,346	1,286
Maritime transport	2,213	611	712	1,065	8,368	39,128	37,490	42,579
Air transport	--	1	3	2	5	34	35	24
Pipelines (petroleum products)	162	189	430	1,019	1,057	1,264	1,841	2,171

Sources: Anuarul Statistic 1970, pp. 508-09; Anuarul Statistic 1972, pp. 378-79.

deal of time is thus spent in loading and unloading, especially since the use of containers and piggyback carriers is in its infancy. One of the goals of the current five-year plan is to modernize the freight system in order to reduce time lost in loading and unloading.[7]

Among the other fields of transportation there has been a considerable increase in the use of the many rivers in Romania, after a decline in the 1950s. Maritime transport has registered a massive upswing in the 1960s after a considerable decline in the previous decade. Part of this new emphasis stems from Romania's efforts to expand its foreign trade and a recent move toward establishing new raw materials bases, particularly in Africa.* Such an expansion of trade requires at least a modest merchant marine, and Romania is now in the process of building a medium-sized fleet of modern, specialized ships as well as general freighters.[8]

The increase in pipeline usage reflects the development of the Romanian oil industry, but the figures quoted in the statistical yearbooks may be somewhat inflated, since some of the pipeline shipments are part of the so-called Friendship Line connecting several of the East European countries with the Soviet Union; the Romanian figures therefore probably include oil in transit. Despite such possible inflation the expansion in pipeline usage is rather impressive.

One field in which there has been minimal growth during the last quarter-century is air transport. Very little freight is hauled by this means, and even passenger traffic is minimal. If a diversified and balanced transportation system is to be developed in Romania increased use of the air must become a priority item.

Major Problems

The considerable progress registered in the field of transportation is not without significant problems. The lack of recent railroad building has resulted in overburdened train schedules on existing lines; traffic density on some of the main trunk lines is of such a magnitude that roadbeds and rolling stock alike are becoming

---

*During the spring of 1972 Ceausescu made an extensive tour of Africa, as prominently reported in Scinteia and other papers, March 1972.

dangerously worn. Repair work is difficult to schedule since the traffic is heavy day and night. Most of the roads in Romania are narrow and unpaved and cannot handle excess heavy freight from the railroads, nor is the trucking fleet designed for long distance transport, but rather for local shipments.

As a result of this imbalance frequent bottlenecks do occur, especially since Romanian industry has expanded much faster than the transportation sector and is now overburdening the railroads and other fields with ever-increasing numbers and bulk of products. Bottlenecks have a way of spreading throughout the system, interrupting the flow of essential goods to all branches of the economy, thus causing dislocations throughout the entire economic system. Such dislocations occur in all societies, but they are particularly severe in a tightly controlled economy such as the Romanian, operating at fever pitch in order to fulfill and overfulfill extremely ambitious plans.

Thus even in the transportation field it becomes necessary for the Romanian authorities to engage in frequent campaign-like operations in order to get the freight moving throughout the system. This kind of activity is particularly hectic toward the end of each year, when large backlogs of orders and contracts pile up in most enterprises; but there are quarterly and semiannual crises and campaigns as well. One of the perennial transportation campaigns occurs early in the fall every year, when harvesting is in full swing and produce must be moved from the fields to the markets, to food processing plants, or to ports for exports. In 1972, for example, tremendous problems developed because there were not enough trucks to haul produce to railroad loading docks, and some of the wheat and barley crop rotted in the fields or froze.[9] Military vehicles and the truck fleet of many industrial plants were mobilized for agricultural service, with the result that industrial production suffered for a considerable period in the important last quarter of the year.

Even after the produce had been brought to major railheads the problems persisted. Inadequate storage facilities resulted in further losses, and the rail system simply could not handle the amounts of freight piling up all along the trunk lines. Despite the mobilization of students, school children, soldiers, and some industrial workers for loading and unloading, the delays and bottlenecks persisted until early winter weather brought a halt to the harvesting effort.[10]

The 1971-75 five-year plan is designed to achieve better utilization of existing facilities as well as some expansion of the road and railroad systems. In 1972 about 84 percent of all railroads in the country were operated by diesel or electric locomotives,[11] and it is envisioned that by the mid-1970s almost all lines will operate with this kind of rolling stock. The modernization of existing roads goes on. Despite such efforts Romania seems rather far from developing a balanced transportation system, and this field of the economy will most likely continue to take a back seat to industrial development. Once again it is clear that multilateral and balanced growth will be postponed to some future date.

HOUSING AND SOCIAL SERVICES

It is generally accepted that one of the strongest fields of socioeconomic achievement in socialist states is the establishment of a comprehensive welfare-state system of social services, health care, and pensions, while performance in the housing sector has been distinctly bleak. Romania fits the pattern so common among Communist systems. The combined effects of industrialization, urbanization, and population growth have produced massive housing shortages, especially in industrial centers. However, the Romanian leadership has succeeded in providing the population with a comprehensive system of social and medical benefits, pensions, child and old age care centers, and other features of the welfare state. No one risks the previously common fate of periodic starvation in socialist Romania, and a minimum of material existence has been established. Within the historical context and experience of the Balkans this is a major achievement indeed.

One of the main reasons for the different achievements in the fields of housing and social services is the level of investments in the two sectors. Table 7.5 shows the investments during the last twenty years.

Table 7.5 is a little hard to interpret since official statistics in Romania collapse the categories of health and social services with investments in "physical culture," a category that also includes organized sports. Additional light is shed on investment in the social sector by an examination of the state budget for selected years, in which the "social sector" is broken down into more detailed subcategories. In 1971 expenditures on health constituted 5.3 percent of total state expenditures (total expenditures amounted to some 138,301 million lei); the allocation to physical education was 0.1 percent;

while child allowances, social insurance, and pensions accounted for 3.1 percent, 8.8 percent, and 0.9 percent, respectively.[12] In 1972 health services received 5.0 percent, while physical education remained at 0.1 percent. Child allowances increased to 4.2 percent of a total expenditure of 152,288 million lei, social insurance took 8.6 percent, and pensions 0.9 percent.[13]

TABLE 7.5

Investments in Housing and Social Services, as Compared to Total Investments and Investments in Industry, 1950-71 (millions of lei, percentages in parentheses)

	Total Investments	Industry	Housing	Health, Social Welfare, and Physical Culture
		1959 Prices		
1950	5,663	2,751	150	151
	(100.0)	(48.6)	(2.6)	(2.7)
1955	13,466	7,685	794	252
	(100.0)	(57.0)	(5.9)	(1.9)
1960	24,422	11,771	1,581	381
	(100.0)	(48.2)	(6.5)	(1.6)
		1963 Prices		
1965	44,602	22,222	2,915	523
	(100.0)	(49.8)	(6.5)	(1.2)
1969	67,529	35,938	3,617	712
	(100.0)	(53.2)	(5.4)	(1.1)
1971	82,617	42,850	2,578	777
	(100.0)	(51.9)	(3.1)	(1.0)

Sources: Anuarul Statistic 1970, pp. 458-59; Anuarul Statistic 1972, pp. 328-29.

The figures for expenditures on social and health services in 1971 and 1972 are considerably higher than total investments listed in Table 7.5, for two reasons. First, a concerted effort has been made to improve this sector, and more money is being invested in it than earlier. Second, Table 7.5 shows total investments in the national economy, thus including local and cooperative funds as well as central funds, while the state budget deals strictly with state or central expenditures, not investments. Since health services, pensions, and social insurance are primarily the responsibility of the state, these categories loom larger in the state budget.

In 1973 and 1974 the investments in education, health, culture, and science remained at approximately the same level as earlier (2.8 percent and 3.2 percent of all investment from state funds, respectively),[14] while investments in housing advanced to 3.7 percent and 4.0 percent of total investments.[15] The 1974 state budget calls for the following expenditures in the social sector: health, 5.6 percent of total (total is 154,168.7 million lei); physical education, 0.1 percent; child allowances, 4.5 percent; social insurance, 10.2 percent; pension, 1.0 percent.[16]

The increase in social insurance is particularly impressive, but the plans and budgets for the first four years allocated important new monies for other fields as well. Thus the 1972 plan called for a growth in real income of 8 percent over 1971.[17] The minimum wage was to be raised from 800 lei per month to 1,000 lei, and the average nominal wage was to reach 1,500 lei, up from 1,435 in 1970 and only 305 lei short of the 1975 goal of 1,806 lei.[18] Actually wages rose 6.7 percent in the first half of 1972 alone, and the RCP National Party Conference in July 1972 envisaged a further wage increase that would bring average monthly wages to 1,950 lei by 1974. The Conference also instituted more piece rate remuneration and reinforced the principle of remuneration according to quality and quantity of work performed.[19]

When the final communique of fulfillment of the 1972 economic plan was issued in early 1973, it turned out that real income had increased 6.5 percent during the year, as against a planned increase of 8.0 percent, but income from wages (nominal) exceeded the target (6.2 percent planned, 6.4 percent achieved).[20]

The 1972 Party conference also decreed an increase in 16 percent of average pensions by the end of 1972, with an increase of 30 percent in small pensions, and a 23 percent jump for widows, orphans, and disabled individuals.[21] This was a considerable increase over the planned expansion of 18 percent between 1970 and 1975.

In the field of housing, the 1971-75 plan called for the construction of 522,000 dwellings. The 1972 plan called for 93,600 new dwellings, thus falling below the average annual quota of the longer plan.[22] Actual construction only amounted to 84,500 units in 1972.[23] There were further lags in 1973, and as a result the housing targets were increased substantially in 1974 (investments increased over 1973 by 13.5 percentage points). One must await further economic reports from Bucharest in order to evaluate the 1974 targets in the housing field.

The lags in housing construction have presented Bucharest with an unwelcome dilemma. Industrialization and urbanization are proceeding apace, with increasing numbers of people competing for scarce housing. The regime has no intention of slowing down the rate of industrial expansion, which means that rapid urbanization will continue to plague the system; yet scarce resources prevent a massive offensive to eradicate the housing shortage. In the meantime social psychologists are beginning to point out the harmful effects of overcrowding on worker productivity at a time when the economic planners of the country are banking heavily on increased output per worker and more intensive use of machinery as factors that will ensure the fulfillment of the extremely ambitious economic development plans now in effect. This is yet another painful dilemma of the rapid modernization process now underway in Romania.

MEDICAL CARE

One area in which the Communist regime has made considerable progress is medical care. Before World War II Romania had one of the highest rates of infant mortality in all of Europe, and life expectancy was among the lowest on the Continent.[24] Hospitals and pharmacies existed primarily in the cities, while the peasantry, which constituted the overwhelming majority of the population, was largely without organized medical facilities. A dramatic development in this field has characterized the socialist period. The number of physicians has increased, both in total numbers and relatively. Hospitals have been built in the countryside, while many older facilities in the cities have been expanded and furnished with modern equipment. Births, which earlier took place in the home and often in rather unsanitary conditions, are now usually in hospitals, under the supervision of qualified medical personnel. As a result of such improvements Romania is now among the leaders in Europe in life expectancy, and infant mortality has been reduced to a level similar to that of Western Europe. Tables 7.6 and 7.7 examine some of the most important elements of modernization in the field of health.

TABLE 7.6

Expansion of Medical Personnel, 1938-71

Year	Physicians Total	Physicians Dentists	Inhabitants per Physician
1938	8,234	570	1,895
1950	15,583	923	1,047
1955	21,141	998	819
1960	24,984	1,626	737
1965	27,900	2,025	682
1969	29,471	3,615	679
1971	31,246	4,379	655

Sources: Anuarul Statistic 1970, p. 654; Anuarul Statistic 1972, p. 491.

The expansion of medical facilities and personnel during the last 25 years has had a dramatic effect on the health of the population, especially in preventative treatment of infants. In 1938 only 2.2 percent of all children were born in medical facilities; in 1960 this proportion had increased to 69.8 percent; by 1969 it was 88.3 percent and in 1971 92.3 percent.[25] Infant mortality was drastically reduced. At the same time, the care of the aged improved considerably, with the result that a larger proportion of the population now reaches retirement age (usually 60 years for men and 58 for women). This in turn increased the need for pensions, and the pension fund is absorbing larger sums every year.

Preventive medicine in Romania also made giant strides through the development of pharmacies and the expansion of pharmaceutical personnel. While in 1950 there were 1,289 pharmacies in the country with a total staff of 3,281 pharmacists, by 1969 there were 1,735 such institutions, with 4,537 professionals.[26] In 1971 the figures were 1,763 and 4,637 respectively.[27] During the same period there had been a dramatic increase in the number of so-called "pharmaceutical points" (small first aid

TABLE 7.7

Beds in Medical Facilities, 1938-71

	1938	1950	1955	1960	1965	1969	1971
Total hospital beds:	33,763	69,221	111,503	133,850	144,054	163,983	173,296
Hospitals	30,812	53,889	83,234	104,422	114,338	137,546	148,581
Sanatoriums (tuberculosis)	2,951	8,908	12,728	14,955	15,455	13,480	12,525
Birth clinics	--	4,873	6,483	8,558	8,927	9,336	8,562
Hospital beds per 1,000 inhabitants	2.2	4.2	6.4	7.3	7.6	8.2	8.5
Total beds in "prophylactic" institutions*	1,575	13,140	24,748	37,647	40,581	40,426	44,405
"Prophylactic" beds per 1,000 inhabitants	0.1	0.8	1.4	2.0	2.1	2.0	2.2

*Including policlinics, children's hospitals for short stays, and health spas.

Sources: Anuarul Statistic 1970, pp. 652-53; Anuarul Statistic 1972, pp. 492-94.

stations) from a total of 94 in 1950 to 394 in 1969 and 467 in 1971.[28]

The figures presented above clearly indicate great achievements in the field of health and social services in Romania during the socialist period. While the country was periodically plagued by famine and malnutrition in the interwar period, there were no real famines during the socialist period although occasional food shortages continued to plague the system. Virtually all Romanian citizens now have an adequate diet. The dismal figures on health care, infant mortality, and life expectancy that put Romania at the bottom of European nations before World War II have so drastically improved that this country today is well ahead of many European countries. Pensions have been expanded and increased to a point that every individual residing in Romania has a basic standard of living with considerable security. The socioeconomic and political systems are still very restrictive in that they afford little opportunity to achieve great riches or rapid upward mobility, but all citizens have been provided with a basic level or "floor" of existence. The Romanian regime has done what all Communist systems seem to do best--raising the lower strata to a basic socioeconomic level, while leveling the tops of the social system as compared to pre-socialist periods. In a country of basic underdevelopment such as Romania this is a great achievement indeed. The problem still remains as to how a modern society, with its increasing stratification based on functional specialization, can successfully operate within this social mold provided by the political regime.

NOTES

1. For a discussion of this point see Paul Dibb, Siberia and the Pacific: A Study of Economic Development and Trade Prospects (New York: Praeger Publishers, 1972), especially pp. 21-41.
2. Holland Hunter, Soviet Transportation Policy (Cambridge, Mass.: Harvard University Press, 1957).
3. George W. Hoffman, Regional Development Strategy in Southeast Europe: A Comparative Analysis of Albania, Bulgaria, Greece, Romania, and Yugoslavia (New York: Praeger Publishers, 1972), pp. 33-73.
4. Ibid.
5. Anuarul Statistic 1964, p. 379.
6. Derived from Institutul de cercetari economice, Academia R.P.R., Dezvoltarea Economica a Rominiei

(Bucharest: Editura Academiei R.P.R., 1964), pp. 3-49, and Anuarul Statistic 1964, p. 382.

7. The directives for socioeconomic development in Romania, issued by the Tenth RCP Congress, August 1969, in Congresul al X-lea al Partidului Comunist Roman (Bucharest: Editura Politica, 1969), pp. 692-93.

8. Congresul al X-lea, pp. 692-93.

9. The Romanian press brought daily progress reports on this. See, for example, Scinteia, October 1972.

10. Ibid.

11. Figure derived from Anuarul Statistic 1970, pp. 516-57.

12. Figures derived from the communique on 1971 plan fulfillment, printed in Scinteia, February 2, 1972, pp. 1, 3.

13. This state budget was presented to the Grand National Assembly on December 1971; it was mentioned in Scinteia the following day that such a report had been given by Florea Dumitrescu, Minister of Finance; the details of the budget were listed in Radio Free Europe Research, Rumania/50, 29 December 1971.

14. Ibid., Rumania/43, 1 December 1972, and various sources discussing the 1974-75 economic plan, for example, Scinteia, June 19-26, 1973.

15. Ibid.

16. Ibid.

17. Maxim Berghianu, Romania's chief of planning, reported on the 1972 plan to the Grand National Assembly on December 17, 1971 (details on the plan in Radio Free Europe Research, Rumania/49, 21 December 1971).

18. Ibid.

19. Scinteia, July 20-22, 1972.

20. Ibid., February 15, 1973.

21. Ibid., July 20-22, 1972.

22. Berghianu to Grand National Assembly, ibid., December 17, 1971 (details in Radio Free Europe Research, Rumania/49, 21 December 1971).

23. Scinteia, February 14, 1973.

24. League of Nations, Economic Intelligence Service, Statistical Yearbook of the League of Nations 1938/39 (Geneva, 1939), p. 37.

25. Anuarul Statistic 1970, p. 565.

26. Ibid., p. 657.

27. Anuarul Statistic 1972, p. 496.

28. Ibid., and Anuarul Statistic 1970, p. 606.

CHAPTER

8

THE INTEGRATION OF ETHNIC MINORITIES

THE PROBLEMS OF A MULTINATIONAL SOCIETY

The processes of modernization, as exemplified by education, industrialization, and the development of agriculture, transportation, housing, and social services, are seen as necessary factors in the integration of ethnic minorities into the mainstream of Romanian life. There is agreement that such integration has not yet been achieved. Party leader Nicolae Ceausescu has repeatedly voiced concern over ethnic differentiation in socialist Romania,[1] and academic scholarship in the West has dealt with such issues as the socioeconomic status of various nationalities,[2] the use of ethnic differences as an instrument of foreign policy for some of Romania's fraternal allies in the Warsaw Pact,[3] and the impact of modernization on nationalism and ethnic separatism in the contemporary period.[4]

The 1966 official census figures in Table 8.1 can provide a quick overall view of the magnitude of the problem in numbers alone. Furthermore, most ethnic minorities are heavily concentrated in certain areas, or, in the case of the Jews, primarily in a few major cities, a structural distribution that tends to enhance ethnic consciousness. Thus 75.3 percent of all Hungarians live in the judets

---

This chapter was presented as a paper at the 1973 convention of the American Political Science Association, New Orleans, Louisiana, September 1973. Tables 8.3, 8.7, 8.8, 8.9, 8.10 were published as part of my article "Ethnic Minorities in Romania under Socialism," East European Quarterly, January 1974.

(counties) of Bihor, Cluj, Covasna, Harghita, Mures, Satu Mare, and Timis; 87.8 percent of all Germans in the country live in Arad, Brasov, Caras-Severin, Mures, Sibiu, and Timis judets; of the Gypsies, 52.1 percent are to be found in the judets Bihor, Brasov, Bistrita-Nasaud, Cluj, Mures, Sibiu, and Timis; and 73.7 percent of all Jews are concentrated in Arad, Bihor, Botosani, Cluj, Iasi, Suceava, Timis, and the city of Bucharest, with Bucharest accounting for fully 33.8 percent of the total Jewish population in 1966.[5]

TABLE 8.1

Ethnic Groups in Romania, 1966
(total population 19,103,163)

Ethnic Group	Total Number	Percent of Total Population
Romanians	16,746,510	87.7
Hungarians	1,619,592	8.5
Germans	382,595	2.0
Gypsies	64,197	0.3
Ukrainians, Ruthenians, Hutans	54,705	0.3
Serbs, Croats, Slovenes	44,236	0.2
Russians	39,483	0.2
Jews	42,888	0.2
Tatars	22,151	0.1
Slovaks	22,221	0.1
Turks	18,040	0.09
Bulgarians	11,193	0.05
Czechs	9,978	0.05
Greeks	9,088	0.05
Poles	5,860	0.03
Armenians	3,436	0.01
Others	4,681	0.02
Nondeclared	2,307	0.01

Source: Republica Socialista Romania, Directia Centrala de Statistica, Recensamintul Populatiei si Locuintelor din 15 Martie 1966 (Bucharest, 1969), p. 153.

In four judets, Bihor, Cluj, Mures, and Timis, the concentration of ethnic minorities (Hungarians, Germans, and Jews) is especially strong, as shown by Table 8.2.[6]

TABLE 8.2

Concentration of Ethnic Minorities in Four Judets, 1966

Judet	Ethnic Minorities	Percent of Total	Romanians	Percent of Total
Bihor	200,267	34.7	377,837	64.4
Cluj	172,839	27.4	457,169	62.4
Mures	282,755	50.3	278,386	49.6
Timis	193,044	31.2	378,183	62.2

HISTORICAL ANTECEDENTS

The very distribution of minorities in Romania, coupled with the heavy concentration of the largest groups in certain areas, thus creates one of the important parameters within which Ceausescu's nationality policy must be executed. In addition, each of the major national minorities examined in this chapter (Hungarians, Germans, Gypsies, and Jews) has a long cultural tradition that in many ways differs significantly from that of the Romanians. For centuries the Hungarians were masters in Transylvania, and part of that area was only given to Romania at the end of World War II. Many older and middle-aged Hungarians, now citizens of Romania, remember the "good old days" when they lived within their ethnic homeland. The existence of a large ethnic minority in Transylvania, in areas adjacent to the ethnic home, has created a powerful irredenta that must be reckoned with in the nationality policy of the RCP.

Although the Germans in Romania do not occupy a position of irredentism, the connection between the Saxons and Schwabians of contemporary Romania and Germany has remained strong. During the interwar period the German minority in Romania became one of the objects of Hitler's policy of "Heim ins Reich" for ethnic Germans, no matter where located. The German occupation of Romania during the war further exacerbated animosities between Saxons and

Schwabians on the one hand and Romanians on the other.[7] The stringent measures undertaken by the Groza regime and later by the Communist-dominated People's Democracy regime against ethnic Germans remain as a vivid memory for many citizens of Socialist Romania,[8] and official disavowal of past mistakes in this field probably cannot erase long memories.*

The two remaining ethnic groups under consideration also can boast a tradition quite different from that of the politically dominant Romanians. The Jews were subjected to the discrimination and anti-Semitism so common in Eastern Europe (although the Romanian approach to the "Jewish Question" lacked the ferocity of Russian pogroms or the total isolation of the ghettos in Poland).[9] Traditions furthermore prescribed occupational patterns for Jews that tended to isolate this group from the rest of society: they remained predominantly urban dwellers in a primarily agricultural country, and their occupations were chiefly confined to moneylending, arts and crafts, and petty officialdom, thus in many cases reinforcing already existing stereotypes of "crafty" and "greedy" Jews.[10]

The Gypsies, on the other hand, remained the universally despised nomads, whose ways were incomprehensible to "civilized" men. Steeped in ignorance and poverty, the sizable Gypsy minority experienced the full brunt of discrimination from all quarters.[11] To this day, this nationality group remains a pariah of the cities as well as the countryside, with a social and economic life style that differs rather drastically from that of other groups. (The Gypsies remained largely "nomadic" until the 1950s, and widespread illiteracy among them was not eradicated till the mid-1960s. See Tables 8.9 and 8.10.)

While old nationality problems remain in contemporary Romania, new areas of conflict were created by the policies of the Romanian Communists after the completion of the political revolution in the country. Communist power ushered in a period of leveling, which had a profound effect on nationality status. Among the ethnic minorities examined here, both Germans and Hungarians had enjoyed a higher standard of living than the bulk of the Romanians; their educational level was higher, and in several occupational fields these two groups were of great importance.

---

*Ceausescu has admitted mistakes made in this field by the Gheorghiu-Dej regime but has refused to engage in "de-Stalinization" on a massive scale.

Thus, Germans were plentiful in the professions and in lower officialdom; and Hungarians had become more urbanized than the Romanian population, with a large proportion of the former group in the ranks of industrial labor while the latter remained primarily rural.[12] The rapid industrialization process, inaugurated in 1947-48, has had the effect of transferring large numbers of Romanians from the countryside to the cities, with a concomitant increase of industrial labor as a chief means of occupation for this group.[13] The considerable educational achievements by the RCP regime have massively benefited the Romanians, who were propelled from generally very low literacy levels to universal elementary education and massive enrollment in middle and higher level institutions.[14] The traditional areas of German occupational strength were heavily invaded by Romanians, to a point where officials and members of the professions now are primarily Romanian.[15]

The changes brought about by the Communist-led coup of 1944 and subsequent expansion of RCP power were perhaps most drastically felt by the Jewish minority, at least in the economic field. As pointed out above, the Jews in Romania have been primarily city dwellers, whose main occupations were in banking, arts and crafts, and retail trade. Much of the economic foundation of this group disappeared with the nationalization of the means of production and the subsequent industrialization drive, which downplayed light industry and services.[16] This drastic economic reorientation resulted in considerable hardships for the Jewish nationality and is ultimately one of the reasons for the heavy outmigration that is at least part of the cause of the drastic reduction of this minority. (Romania has been more willing to permit outmigration of Jews than any other country under Communist rule in Eastern Europe.)[17]

Of the four ethnic minorities examined, the Gypsies temporarily benefited most from the establishment of Communist power. This group, which was generally wretchedly poor, uneducated, and despised by all others, had become "domesticated" by 1956, and considerable numbers had found employment as collective farmers or industrial workers.[18] By 1966 all Gypsies had received at least an elementary education; increasing numbers went on to middle level education, and there was even a Gypsy enrolled in a university.[19]

The evidence presented above, then, indicates that the very policies of the Communist elite in the economic field had drastic effects on ethnic minorities. Hitherto privileged groups ("privileged" in the sense that they had occupied certain functional categories in numbers out of proportion to their numerical strength in the population, with a relatively high standard of living and impressive educational achievements) lost in relative standing, whereas Romanians and the underprivileged Gypsies gained considerably in socioeconomic position. On the basis of conclusions reached by Deutsch and others, one would expect that assimilation in the sense of ethnic minority group acceptance of the values, outlooks, and ways of life of the dominant group (Romanians) would be higher among less well developed groups (Gypsies) than among groups that in most instances had reached a higher level of development than the dominant Romanians (Hungarians, Germans, Jews). This major hypothesis will be examined below.

While the socioeconomic policies of the Communist elite generally had a leveling effect on three of the five nationalities examined, other political factors to some extent tended to offset this trend. This was especially true in recruitment to political leadership, primarily at the center. The RCP was dominated by the so-called "Muscovites" around Ana Pauker (a Jewess) until 1952, and this was one of the factors producing a heavy Jewish concentration at the regional and central leadership levels of the Party.[20] Thus, while the masses of the Jewish ethnic group were deprived of traditional sources of livelihood, the Jewish elite could still count on considerable possibilities within the Party apparatus. This privilege did not exist for Germans and Hungarians; on the contrary, the official policy of the RCP was discriminatory against Germans in political recruitment since this nationality was considered "collaborators" with Nazi Germany and the Axis generally,[21] and Hungarians have not been important at the top of the Party. Gypsies remained largely outside of the political mainstream throughout the entire period, primarily due to the traditional patterns of life still prevailing in this group.[22]

After the 1952 leadership changes at the top in the RCP, the Jewish element was considerably reduced in favor of "home Communists," who were primarily ethnic Romanians. With the advent of Gheorghe Gheorghiu-Dej to the top position in the RCP, Romanian nationalism became a major factor. Gheorghiu-Dej produced several major policies designed to force assimilation of ethnic minorities into the "mainstream" of Romanian life. The most important of these measures included the following:

- Restrictions on educational opportunities for ethnic minorities in their native tongue (such as the closing of German and Hungarian language schools at the elementary and intermediate levels and a reduction of lectures in these languages at the university level in areas of heavy minority enrollment);[23]
- Attempts to limit the publication of books, newspapers, and journals in minority languages, as well as restrictions on theatrical performances in non-Romanian tongues;[24]
- Redistribution of apparat positions, both in the Party and the state bureaucracies, which tended to favor the Romanian nationality. This was especially noticeable at the top of the Party pyramid but could be registered at the regional and local levels as well;[25]
- Actual repression of minorities in periods of crisis (for instance, in the aftermath of the Hungarian Revolution in 1956 and demonstrations in Romanian Transylvania);[26]
- A generally anti-Semitic attitude of the top political leadership throughout (although this attitude was rather moderate compared with that in Poland and the Soviet Union).[27]

NATIONALITIES IN THE CEAUSESCU ERA

The nationality policies under Gheorghiu-Dej had the effect of exacerbating minority group tensions. With the advent of the Ceausescu regime there has been a marked decrease in forced assimilation. Ceausescu has instead concentrated on the theme that Romania is the fatherland of all ethnic groups within its borders, where all nationalities can and must live together in fraternal relations in the common quest for socialism and under the common leadership of the RCP.[28] Ceausescu has permitted considerable efforts by ethnic groups to keep their linguistic, literary, and artistic traditions alive.* The number of schools in native languages has been increased, and a recent law specifies that wherever and whenever at

---

*Examples are resurrection of nationality councils for Germans, Hungarians, and Ukrainians; expansion of the number of periodicals and newspapers, especially in Hungarian and German; better educational facilities.

least six children request instruction in their native tongue a teacher will be assigned to provide this service.[29] Folk music, arts and crafts, and theatrical productions in minority languages are permitted, and to some extent encouraged. Ceausescu seems to have opted for the time-honored Soviet slogan "Nationalist in form, socialist in content." Expressions of ethnic particularism must not extend to the fields of politics, where the supremacy of the Communist Party and the inevitability of socialism and eventually communism as the only form of political system are unquestionable givens.[30]

Despite his willingness to permit the expression of nationality traditions in limited fields, Ceausescu is a Romanian nationalist, whose popular support is based primarily on his efforts to propel Romania as a nation, as well as Romanian culture and traditions and Romanian economic and scientific achievements, into the ranks of highly developed and respected members of the international community. Increasingly Ceausescu is equating the role of the RCP with that of other major national liberators in the past. His respect for the ethnic minorities is therefore less a genuine internationalist outlook and more a tactical acceptance of existing facts. The main thrust of this nationality policy seems to be aimed at achieving maximum possible integration of ethnic minorities into the mainstream of Romanian political, socioeconomic, and cultural life through two major procedures: modernization and political socialization. The effect of these two processes will be the achievement of Socialist Modernity, a situation in which all citizens, regardless of nationality background, will have achieved the functional skills required for running a highly technical and complex economy and, furthermore, will have accepted the leadership of the Communist Party to such an extent that they enthusiastically participate fully in socioeconomic life and, within the Party-prescribed limits, in political life.[31] Since the Party is dominated by Romanians, national values of this ethnic group will presumably be important.

Within the parameters of assimilation outlined above, modernization is seen as a crucial factor. The concept modernization has acquired wide usage in the academic world as well as in the vocabulary of Communist elites, including the RCP. According to Deutsch and Huntington, socioeconomic modernization includes urbanization, industrialization, secularization, acceptance of one major language, increased spatial as well as social mobility, improved educational achievements, higher productivity, higher health standards (which include higher life expectancy, lower infant mortality, better medical services), improved transportation and telecommunication services, and increased interaction (in numerous fields) among individuals located in different regions and areas.[32] Political modernization includes increased acceptance of a national center of political life rather than tribal or other local elites, increased citizen participation in and awareness of political life, higher legitimacy of national elites, penetration of national values and decisions even at the local levels, breaking down of old allegiances of a spatial nature and the establishment of new, functionally based attachments, and the reduction of political influence emanating from religious authorities and symbols.[33]

The Ceausescu definition of socioeconomic modernization corresponds quite closely to the Deutsch and Huntington "packages," whereas significant differences exist in the conceptualization regarding political modernization. The most important difference centers around the concept of political participation. As indicated above, political participation in Communist systems is envisioned as a carefully circumscribed activity, in which no person is permitted to question the givens of Party supremacy and the end result of the political process, a Communist society (which will be reached by way of modernity or the multilaterally developed society[34] and socialism). Political participation in Communist systems, as envisioned by Ceausescu and other elites in Eastern Europe, is rather akin to political mobilization of the masses.[35]

SOCIOECONOMIC MODERNIZATION AND ASSIMILATION

The socioeconomic modernization process has clearly had a major impact on the ethnic groups examined. Table 8.3 shows the urbanization process in the decade between the two censa of 1956 and 1966.

Urbanization has clearly affected all nationality groups in Romania, as evidenced by Table 8.3; the most rapid increase in urbanization has been among the traditionally most heavily rural, such as Romanians and Gypsies, but even Hungarians, Germans, and Jews, who were urbanized to a relatively high degree in 1956, experienced further urbanization in the decade 1956-66.

TABLE 8.3

Urbanization in Romania, 1956-66

Ethnic Group	Percent of Nationality Urbanized 1956	1966
Romanians	29.2	36.9
Hungarians	41.1	47.6
Germans	50.1	53.8
Jews	95.2	97.8
Gypsies	17.3	26.5

Source: Trond Gilberg, "Ethnic Minorities in Romania under Socialism," *East European Quarterly*, January 1974. Based on Republica Socialista Romania, Directia Centrala de Statistica, *Recensamintul Populatiei si Locuintelor din 21 Februarie 1956* (Bucharest, 1959), p. 556; and *Recensamintul 1966*, pp. 159-62.

Spatial mobility is one of the important elements of socioeconomic modernization as defined above. Movement from the countryside to the city is one element of spatial mobility. Due to the particular distribution of ethnic groups in Romania, however, a measure of spatial mobility through urbanization is clearly inadequate. It is not enough to know that Hungarians moved from rural to urban residence; we need to know where that urban residence was located, since it is entirely possible that this group simply urbanized internally, that is, Hungarians moved from the Hungarian-populated countryside to the Hungarian-populated cities, a movement that would not bring with it the increased integration and assimilation predicted by Deutsch. A similar problem exists with regard to Germans and Jews, who are also heavily concentrated in certain areas of Romania, while the Gypsies, who were more evenly distributed throughout the country, presumably would move into a large number of cities with mixed populations, thus probably experiencing integration and assimilation tendencies more forcefully.[36]

One way to examine the rural-to-urban population movement would be to compare the number of Hungarians, Germans, Jews, and Gypsies in certain areas at two points in time and to compare this concentration with the concentration of Romanians in the same areas. In order for urbanization to produce increased integration and assimilation, two possible processes would take place, either separately or simultaneously: ethnic minorities would move into predominantly Romanian cities, thereby experiencing forceful integrationist and assimilationist tendencies through daily contact with Romanian cultural patterns; or Romanians in large numbers would move into primarily Hungarian or German cities, or Jewish and Gypsy sections, thus drastically changing the cultural "mix" in those areas in the direction of assimilation to Romanian values.

The census data for 1956 and 1966 provide a wealth of information on population in Romania. According to the 1956 data on the nationality distribution by region, as shown in Table 8.4, the heaviest concentration of Hungarians was in the Magyar Autonomous Region, in Timisoara, Stalin, Oradea, and Baia Mare; Germans were primarily concentrated in Stalin and Timisoara, while Jews and Gypsies are more evenly scattered.

By 1966, when the next census was undertaken, territorial reorganizations had taken place, and a direct comparison of ethnic concentrations in 1956 and 1966 is therefore somewhat difficult. One can nevertheless get an estimate of population movements, since the new counties (judets) were to some extent established by internally dividing the formed regions without too much change of borders. Of primary interest are the Hungarian and German concentrations in the former Magyar Autonomous Region, Timisoara, Stalin, Oradea, and Baia Mare. The Autonomous Region was basically divided into the judets of Mures and Harghita; a slice of it was also incorporated into the judet Covasna. Timisoara became the judet of Timis, and to some extent Caras Severin. Stalin is now essentially Brasov and Sibiu judets; Oradea is Bihor judet; and Baia Mare is essentially Satu Mare and Maramures judets. Table 8.5 shows the concentration of Hungarians and Germans in the judets Mures, Harghita, Covasna, Timis, Caras Severin, Brasov, Sibiu, Bihor, Satu Mare, and Maramures.

The findings presented in Table 8.5 show that the Hungarians and Germans remained heavily concentrated in a few areas in 1966, as had been the case in 1956. Urbanization of these two ethnic groups therefore primarily takes place within ethnically homogenous areas, that is, Hungarians from the countryside move into Hungarian cities, and the same process takes place among Germans. This is further upheld by census figures that show the following concentration of Hungarians and Germans in urban areas: In Mures, 51.8 percent of all urban dwellers are Hungarians, 3.9 percent Germans; in Harghita, 83.7 percent and

TABLE 8.4

Concentration of Romanians, Hungarians, Germans, Jews, and Gypsies in Romania, 1956
(in percentages)

Region	Total Population	Romanians	Hungarians	Germans	Jews	Gypsies
Bacau	100	97.3	1.1	0.06	1.2	0.04
Baia Mare	100	65.9	27.8	0.09	1.1	0.6
Bucuresti	100	99.2	0.03	0.09	0.01	0.4
Cluj	100	76.5	20.5	0.7	0.7	1.5
Constanta	100	88.8	0.2	0.3	0.2	0.2
Craiova	100	99.5	0.04	0.02	0.04	0.2
Galati	100	97.2	0.08	0.1	0.7	0.6
Hunedoara	100	87.7	6.5	3.3	0.4	1.4
Iasi	100	97.9	0.03	0.01	1.8	0.09
Oradea	100	68.1	28.4	1.1	0.6	0.5
Pitesti	100	99.6	0.04	0.03	0.02	0.2
Ploiesti	100	99.3	0.1	0.06	0.1	0.2
Stalin	100	68.3	12.1	16.5	0.4	2.4
Suceava	100	94.3	0.08	0.4	2.0	0.08
Timisoara	100	64.3	12.3	14.5	1.1	0.9
Autonomous Magyar Region	100	20.1	77.3	0.4	0.4	1.5
City of Bucharest	100	93.7	0.9	0.4	3.6	0.07

Note: Based on Recensamintul, 1956, p. 556.

0.2 percent, respectively; Covasna, 79.8 percent and 0.3 percent; Timis, 17.4 percent and 16.4 percent; Caras Severin, 5.1 percent and 11.8 percent; Brasov, 15.9 percent and 7.1 percent; Sibiu, 8.1 percent and 23.9 percent; Bihor, 48.4 percent and 0.4 percent; Satu Mare, 47.4 percent and 0.5 percent; and Maramures, 23.4 percent and 1.8 percent.[37]

TABLE 8.5

Concentration of Hungarians and Germans in Selected Judcts, 1966

Judet	Percent of Total Population in Judet Hungarians	Germans
Mures	44.5	3.7
Harghita	88.1	0.1
Covasna	79.4	0.2
Timis	12.5	18.0
Caras Severin	2.6	6.7
Brasov	14.8	9.2
Sibiu	4.9	23.4
Bihor	32.9	0.2
Satu Mare	41.1	1.2
Maramures	12.5	0.7

Note: Based on Recensamintul 1966, p. 153. My description of the territorial reorganization is only an approximation to the complex rearrangement of territorial borders that took place between 1956 and 1966.

The relative lack of interregional mobility among Hungarians and Germans is further illustrated by a comparison of the percentage of these two groups in heavily Romanian-populated areas. According to Table 8.4, in 1956 the regions of Bucuresti, Craiova, Galati, Iasi, Pitesti, and Suceava had very small numbers of Hungarians; very few Germans were found in the regions of Bacau, Bucuresti, Craiova, Iasi, Pitesti, and Ploiesti. After the reorganizations the following judets essentially comprise these Romanian-populated regions:

Regions	Judets
Bucuresti	Ilfov, Ialomita, Teleorman
Craiova	Dolj, Mehedinti, Gorj
Galati	Galati, Vrancea, Braila
Iasi	Iasi, Vaslui
Pitesti	Arges; partly Dimbovita, Olt, and Vilcea
Suceava	Botosani, Suceava
Bacau	Bacau, Neamt
Ploiesti	Prahova, Buzau; partly Dimbovita

According to the 1966 census figures, the percentage of Hungarians and Germans was negligible in Ilfov, Ialomita, Teleorman, Dolj, Vrancea, Vaslui, Dimbovita, Olt, Vilcea, Botosani, and Buzau; furthermore, very few Germans lived in Gorj, Galati, Braila, Iasi, Arges, Bacau, and Neamt. Hungarians constituted 0.2 percent of the population in Mehedinti (Germans also 0.2 percent), 0.1 percent in Gorj, Galati, Braila, Iasi, Arges, Suceava, Neamt, and Prahova; Germans registered 0.6 percent in Suceava and 0.1 percent in Prahova.[38] Thus there was no important move of Hungarians and Germans into Romanian-populated areas of the country. Even in the city of Bucharest, the political and administrative center of the country, Hungarians constituted only 0.6 percent of the population in 1966 (down from 0.9 percent in 1956) and Germans 0.3 percent in 1966 (down from 0.4 percent in 1956).[39]

While the masses of Hungarians and Germans remained concentrated in the period 1956-66, there was a certain movement of Romanians into areas of minority concentration. Table 8.6 shows the increase in the Romanian population in areas of heavy Hungarian and German concentrations, 1956-66.

Table 8.6 indicates that despite some movement of Romanians into traditionally Hungarian and German areas the nationality distribution was not drastically altered during the decade 1956-66. The stationary nature of Hungarian and German settlement has therefore not contributed to the massive ethnic interaction with the dominant nationality that is required for assimilation. This fact also tends to cast doubt on some of the other modernization processes that presumably would contribute to interaction and assimilation. If Hungarians and Germans simply move from a homogeneous ethnic setting in the countryside to a homogeneous urban environment, ethnic particularism will not diminish and may indeed be heightened. Furthermore, educational improvement in this situation is likely to lead to increased awareness of national background and traditions rather than acceptance of an essentially "foreign" culture such as the Romanian.

TABLE 8.6

Romanians in Hungarian and German Populated Areas, 1956, 1966

		Percent Romanians
Region:	Autonomous Region (1956)	20.1
Judets:	Mures (1966)	49.6
	Harghita (1966)	11.1
	Covasna (1966)	19.3
Region:	Timisoara (1956)	64.3
Judets:	Timis (1966)	62.2
	Caras Severin (1966)	82.5
Region:	Stalin (1956)	68.3
Judets:	Brasov (1966)	74.8
	Sibiu (1966)	70.7
Region:	Oradea (1956)	68.1
Judets:	Bihor (1966)	64.4
Region:	Baia Mare (1956)	65.9
Judets:	Satu Mare (1966)	56.7
	Maramures (1966)	79.5

Note: Based on Recensamintul 1956, p. 556, and Recensamintul 1966, p. 153.

On the other hand, ethnic groups such as Gypsies who are widely scattered throughout the country would probably experience a certain amount of assimilation through the modernization process; urbanization would propel them into cities dominated by another nationality, and the tendency toward acceptance of the dominant culture would be stronger. The Jews have been basically urban for decades and would not experience the same effect; but Jews have historically been assimilationist, at least in terms of using a language other than Yiddish, and may therefore "integrate" better despite their concentration. It should be pointed out that Jews in some areas are concentrated in heavily Hungarian- or German-settled districts (such as Sibiu and Cluj), and thus this group might find itself in a culture dominated by another minority, not the Romanians. The

Gypsies, on the other hand, tend to be located in areas of heavy Romanian population; their assimilation, if any, would presumably be toward Romanian culture.

Unfortunately, there is inadequate data for a thorough examination of the relationship between settlement and integration. We do not know, for example, how the Jews and the Gypsies settle in each city: do they mix with the other population groups, or do they live in ethnic ghettos? Conclusions to this question must of necessity be tentative. It nevertheless seems reasonable to assume that, on the basis of population figures showing density of settlement by region or judet, Hungarians and Germans are less assimilative to a national culture with Romanian overtones than the Jews and the Gypsies.

Without surveys, this hypothesis can be tested only inadequately. One measure of assimilation frequently employed by students in the field is the use by ethnic groups of the dominant language as a means of expression (as opposed to continued use of the mother tongue). Table 8.7 examines the extent of mother tongue use among Romanians, Hungarians, Germans, Jews, and Gypsies in 1956 and 1966.[40]

Table 8.7 upholds the hypothesis outlined above. Among Romanians, Hungarians, and Germans the use of native language increased during the decade 1956-66, although all three nationalities were experiencing such aspects of modernization as urbanization, improved social conditions, better education, and changing employment patterns (in the direction of industrialization and upward social mobility). The explanation for this phenomenon is, in all probability, primarily that the three major nationality groups in Romania continue to live in rather concentrated and homogenous ethnic settlements, in which modernization elements simply reinforce already existing allegiances to ethnic traditions within each nationality group.

While it is clear that the overwhelming majority of Hungarians and Germans continue to use their native tongue as the chief means of expression, a certain amount of bilingualism exists, due to mixed language instruction at the intermediate and higher education levels. Thus, as educational levels increase the knowledge and use of Romanian as a necessary vehicle of communication also increases. In the long run, such frequent use of Romanian for "business purposes" may lead to increased use of this language as the primary one by some Hungarians and Germans. This form of linguistic integration would be primarily an elite phenomenon, chiefly experienced by those whose upward

TABLE 8.7

Use of Mother Tongue as Chief Means of Expression, 1956, 1966
(percentages in parentheses)

	Total Population	Native Language				
		Romanian	Hungarian	German	Yiddish	Gypsy
1956						
Romanians	14,996,114	14,898,638 (99.35)	45,966 (0.31)	8,916 (0.06)	2,067 (0.01)	17,901 (0.12)
Hungarians	1,587,675	18,937 (1.20)	1,564,959 (98.55)	2,669 (0.19)	8 --	879 --
Germans	384,708	8,322 (2.08)	6,131 (1.56)	370,041 (96.10)	3 --	36 --
Jews	146,264	83,866 (57.53)	22,910 (15.75)	6,518 (4.79)	32,246 (21.92)	-- --
Gypsies	104,216	47,207 (45.19)	8,625 (8.65)	14 --	-- --	47,962 (46.15)
1966						
Romanians	16,740,310	16,686,074 (99.63)	28,152 (0.17)	6,660 (0.04)	407 --	10,606 (0.07)
Hungarians	1,619,592	14,668 (0.93)	1,602,259 (98.89)	1,739 (0.12)	4 --	652 --
Germans	382,595	5,831 (1.57)	3,959 (1.04)	372,644 (97.39)	-- --	8 --
Jews	42,888	27,867 (64.93)	7,790 (18.16)	2,137 (4.98)	4,727 (11.02)	-- --
Gypsies	64,197	19,795 (30.83)	6,526 (10.17)	9 --	-- --	37,754 (58.81)

Source: Trond Gilberg, "Ethnic Minorities in Romania under Socialism," East European Quarterly, January 1974. Based on Recensamintul, 1956, p. 562; Recensamintul, 1966, p. 113.

social mobility would lift them out of their ethnic "base." It is doubtful that such a trend would assume massive proportions in the foreseeable future.

While Hungarians and Germans have remained relatively immune to linguistic inroads from the dominant tongue, Jews and Gypsies have been much less resistant. Among Jews, a linguistic assimilation trend has been in existence for decades, and it continued unabated in the period 1956-66. This trend is undoubtedly also connected with the high educational and occupational standards of the Jews; increased use of the Romanian language has become a necessity for maintaining such upward mobility. Among Gypsies, the underdeveloped state of the group, its relative residential dispersion, and cultural traditions that are relatively weak compared to Hungarians and Germans are all factors that contribute to linguistic assimilation. For Gypsies modernization has meant spatial mobility, chiefly into Romanian-populated areas. The fact that a higher proportion of Gypsies spoke their native tongue in 1966 than was the case ten years earlier is probably attributable to a tendency among many in this ethnic group to simply abandon the "Gypsy" label altogether and instead declare themselves Romanian. (This would also explain the drastic reduction in the total number of Gypsies during the decade.) Thus only those who remained self-identified as Gypsies would retain use of the native language, but this use would probably be high among those who remained in the group.

While urbanization and spatial mobility have failed to provide for substantially increased interaction among ethnically concentrated nationalities, such as Hungarians and Germans, on the one hand, and Romanians, on the other, other elements of modernization, specifically industrialization and improved education, can be expected to provide equalization of the socioeconomic conditions of ethnic groups, thereby providing common assimilation to a similar level of modernity. Table 8.8 shows the impact of the modernization process on the major ethnic groups studied, in occupational shifts during 1956 and 1966, while Tables 8.9 and 8.10 examine educational achievements of the same groups.*

---

*Due to some reorganization of the school system comparisons cannot be made directly, but the figures presented nevertheless illustrate major trends.

TABLE 8.8

Occupational Distribution within Nationalities
(percent of total nationality engaged in selected occupations, numbers in parentheses)

1956	Workers		Functionaries[a]		Collective Farmers		Individual Farmers		"Liber Profesionisti"[b]	
Romanians	21.59	(3,237,850)	13.14	(1,969,580)	2.86	(428,713)	54.31	(8,145,068)	0.26	(38,596)
Hungarians	32.62	(517,718)	12.66	(201,214)	5.67	(90,129)	40.11	(636,925)	1.25	(3,890)
Jews	25.34	(37,478)	53.42	(77,713)	0.00	(37)	0.68	(973)	1.37	(2,238)
Gypsies	40.38	(41,738)	0.58	(574)	6.73	(7,037)	16.35	(17,278)	2.88	(3,017)
Germans	57.14	(219,907)	13.77	(53,110)	10.91	(41,782)	10.39	(40,098)	0.16	(640)

1966	Workers		Intellectuals-Functionaries[c]		Collective Farmers		Individual Farmers	
Romanians	38.86	(6,507,669)	12.33	(2,065,083)	39.69	(6,646,623)	5.54	(926,911)
Hungarians	45.86	(742,623)	11.60	(189,215)	34.20	(553,724)	1.98	(32,063)
Jews	29.01	(12,440)	59.45	(25,496)	0.33	(142)	0.00	(71)
Gypsies	47.30	(30,362)	0.50	(324)	30.38	(19,501)	2.60	(1,670)
Germans	58.49	(224,264)	13.58	(52,028)	19.58	(75,478)	1.04	(3,772)

[a]Includes "engineers, technicians and specialized personnel."

[b]Includes "lawyers (members of the bar association), physicians and sanitary personnel, artists (painters, sculptors), actors and instrumental performers, as well as others not employed in an institution or enterprise for pay."

[c]No official explanation of this category is yet available in this country, but I shall venture to assume that it includes those groups in the "functionaries" category, plus artists, writers, and others making a living through writing or artistic expression.

Note: The 1956 census had several categories for farmers: "collective farmers," "individual farmers," "members of agricultural associations." I have used only the figures for "collective farmers" in this table; it should thus be noted that this category does not exhaust the total number of farmers but only the category most relevant for comparative purposes in this chapter.

Source: Trond Gilberg, "Ethnic Minorities in Romania under Socialism," East European Quarterly, January 1974. Based on Recensamintul, 1956, p. 563; Recensamintul, 1966, p. 157.

TABLE 8.9

Nationalities in Various Educational Categories, 1956

	Total	Romanians	Hungarians	Germans	Gypsies	Jews
Total population 8 years and over	14,566,957	12,426,484	1,358,256	345,015	76,485	131,172
Percent	100.00	85.30	9.32	2.37	0.52	0.90
Total population in schools of 4 years (not finished) and miscellaneous schools	1,624,669	1,414,641	137,584	12,297	14,306	11,587
Percent	100.00	87.08	8.49	0.74	0.86	0.74
Total population in 4-year schools	9,488,801	8,053,413	955,479	252,143	32,837	60,998
Percent	100.00	84.87	10.06	2.66	0.35	0.64
Total population in 7-year schools	1,139,299	884,488	156,048	57,663	484	24,884
Percent	100.00	77.61	13.70	5.09	0.04	2.19
Total population in middle level schools	628,383	532,101	53,271	15,327	9	19,153
Percent	100.00	84.71	8.44	2.39	--	3.03
Total population in higher schools	213,723	183,299	13,391	3,629	1	10,454
Percent	100.00	85.51	6.07	1.87	--	4.67

Source: Trond Gilberg, "Ethnic Minorities in Romania under Socialism," East European Quarterly, January 1974. Based on Recensamintul, 1956, pp. 576-77.

TABLE 8.10

Nationalities in Various Educational Categories, 1966

	Total	Romanians	Hungarians	Germans	Gypsies	Jews
Total population 12 years or over	15,191,248	13,253,588	1,339,716	315,345	42,581	40,258
Percent	100.00	87.25	8.82	2.07	0.28	0.26
Total population in primary schools	11,441,062	10,047,710	961,202	215,681	41,139	16,270
Percent	100.00	87.82	8.40	1.89	0.36	0.14
Total population in general (7-8 years) schools	1,680,443	1,413,357	195,067	46,531	1,236	5,124
Percent	100.00	84.11	11.61	2.80	0.06	0.30
Total population in professional schools	729,477	624,074	72,467	23,997	179	2,252
Percent	100.00	85.60	9.88	3.29	0.03	0.27
Total population in middle technical and special schools	452,645	393,090	40,985	11,399	11	2,910
Percent	100.00	86.75	9.05	2.43	--	0.66
Total population in middle schools (lycees)	559,380	484,251	49,806	12,044	15	6,621
Percent	100.00	86.58	8.94	2.15	--	1.25
Total population in institutions of higher education	328,241	291,106	20,189	5,693	1	7,081
Percent	100.00	88.72	6.10	1.83	--	2.13

Source: Trond Gilberg, 'Ethnic Minorities in Romania under Socialism," East European Quarterly, January 1974. Based on Recensamintul, 1966, p. 115.

Table 8.8 shows that while industrialization has had a marked impact on all nationalities to the extent that all groups examined now comprise more industrial workers than in the 1950s, the impact has been decidedly uneven. The largest relative gain has been among the Romanians, although most members of this group remain in nonindustrial occupations. The Gypsies remain considerably underdeveloped in this area, while Jews continue to be primarily occupied in the professions and in white-collar fields. Hungarians and Germans, traditionally strongly represented in the industrial occupations, remain entrenched in them; they have lost some of their importance in the professions and in officialdom, probably due to the movement of Romanians into these areas.

The impact of industrialization and social diversification, then, is so unevenly felt by the five ethnic groups studied that it is hard to speak of major assimilationist tendencies resulting at this point. It is clear that with continued industrialization more and more members of each nationality group will move into industrial occupations. This process will surely take at least a generation more before drastic equalization of occupational status will have taken place, especially among groups now so far apart as Germans and Gypsies. And even if most Gypsies by the end of this century have become industrial workers, is it not likely that many of the other, more highly modernized groups will have proceeded to take decisive control over managerial, white-collar, and supervisory and service occupations, thus further deepening the occupational diversification? This question, which only time can answer, reflects a major dilemma for Communist modernizers everywhere: While the ideology is egalitarian, the demands of the modernization process may supersede equality. Thus, if the increasingly sophisticated Romanian economy demands expertise, it is likely that such skills will be furnished by groups with a tradition of relative "modernity" (such as Hungarians, Germans, Jews) as well as the politically dominant nationality, while groups such as Gypsies will be left with menial, unskilled work. Modernization will thus breed differentiation, not equalization; and it is unlikely that unassimilated Gypsies, for example, can manage to bridge the chasm separating them as a group from the more developed nationalities.

While the Gypsies may tend to continue in their relatively inferior status, industrialization and occupational specialization may lead to equalization among Romanians, Hungarians, Germans, and Jews. This equalization will, however, be primarily unidirectional; that is, it will consist of Romanians catching up with the other nationalities more highly developed in terms of occupational and educational achievements. As long as it is the politically dominant nationality that is catching up, the modernization process itself is likely to be perceived as a form of "Romanianization" by Hungarians, Germans, and Jews, and this outlook is not conducive to minority assimilation. Basic socioeconomic equality among these four groups may, on the contrary, be perceived by the three minorities as intentional Romanian interference in the opportunity for free development, with possible subsequent isolation and animosity.

Tables 8.9 and 8.10 on educational achievements by nationality lend themselves to interpretations very similar to those listed above. The greatest educational achievement in the period 1956-66 was posted by the Romanians, who are now invading higher educational institutions in increasing numbers. The proportion of Romanians with university education is now roughly comparable to the proportion of Hungarians and Germans with similar education. This massive improvement in the educational achievements of Romanians, compared to the much more modest upward trend for the two largest minorities, may indeed be perceived by the latter as "leveling," a charge that is not conducive to increased friendship among ethnic groups. In this context, educational achievements may act as a deterrent to assimilation, at least until such a high stage of educational achievement is reached by the entire population that this indicator ceases to be salient as a factor of comparison. This stage is undoubtedly far off and may indeed never be reached, since perceptions of educational needs are not static but will continue to change with developments in the socioeconomic environment.

The Jews remain far ahead of the other groups in educational achievement; in fact, a higher proportion of Jews had university training in 1966 than any other group, despite rumors about discrimination against Jews in higher education, including formal quota systems in enrollment.* One of the reasons for this high educational level among Jews may be outmigration, which accounted for a considerable drop in the total Jewish population during the decade

*The extent of this system is not well known. It is likely that the Ceausescu regime has eased restrictions in this field in recent years.

1956-66. It seems probable that the Romanian authorities in permitting outmigrations of Jews would attempt to let the less well educated leave, while retaining the highly skilled manpower reserves within this ethnic group as a necessity in an increasingly complex economic and social system.* Despite this factor, the importance of which cannot be readily and accurately assessed, it seems fair to conclude that Jews have retained considerable opportunities in the educational field and that it will take a long time for other groups, including the Romanians, to reach such a level.

While the Jewish educational achievement is highly impressive, the Gypsies remain woefully underrepresented, especially in intermediate and higher education. In 1966 only one Gypsy was to be found at the university level, and relatively very few members of this nationality went to middle-level schools. The main achievement of the Romanian regime affecting the Gypsies in the 1956-66 period was to do away with illiteracy in this group, which had been quite high as late as 1956. But even as late as the mid-1960s most Gypsies had only the most elementary of educations, and it will take a very long time before this group catches up with any of the other nationalities, even if the others remained at the 1966 levels (which, of course, they will not). Once again, educational improvements for the population as a whole may tend to increase the differentiation among nationality groups--certainly it will increase the distance between the Gypsies and the others at least temporarily. Assimilation via education will therefore be primarily an elite phenomenon (that is, limited to individual Gypsies who leave their area of residence and cultural background and subsequently accept Romanian culture and language).

Unfortunately, there are no official statistics on such social indicators of modernization as improved health care, lower infant mortality, higher life expectancy, improved living conditions (in housing and sanitation facilities), and so on among nationality groups per se.† However,

---

*More than 300,000 Jews have been permitted to emigrate from Romania since the establishment of the Communist regime, but there are no reliable figures on the educational background of emigrants.

†The 1966 census, for example, only listed territorial distribution of nationalities, use of native language, and social categories among ethnic groups.

informal information continues to indicate strong variations in these areas, especially between Gypsies and the rest, but also between Romanians (still burdened by underdevelopment among the rural masses) and the three more highly developed groups. Massive improvements will tend to equalize conditions among all ethnic groups, but since the overwhelming majority of the population is Romanian the impact will certainly be largest on this group, thus possibly fostering feelings of leveling among hitherto privileged nationalities.

To sum up: The modernization process has only been operating in Romania for a quarter of a century, and this relatively short historical period has not erased centuries-old differences among ethnic groups in the country. On the contrary, the process has in some cases exacerbated old differences (Gypsies versus the rest) or has resulted in a certain leveling tendency, which primarily has benefited the Romanians at the relative expense of Hungarians, Germans, and Jews. Assimilation may be achieved at some distant point, when modernization permeates all ethnic groups equally. (Social stratification would then be based on function, not on ethnicity, which now to some extent predetermines function.) This stage is indeed quite distant from the present, and until it is realized societal forces and developments will remain inadequate to the task of accomplishing assimilation.

ASSIMILATION THROUGH POLITICAL SOCIALIZATION

The Ceausescu approach to nationality questions relies heavily on political socialization for the perceived necessary assimilation of all ethnic groups in Romania to a common culture. This common culture is termed the multilaterally developed society,[41] which is to evolve into socialism and then communism.[42] The multilaterally developed society is primarily a functional definition, not an ethnic one; and it is theoretically possible to be assimilated to modernity as defined without being integrated into a Romanian-dominated modernity. However, as pointed out above, Ceausescu has made it clear that the multilaterally developed society is the crowning achievement of Romanian national culture, the coming of age for a nation that has been subjugated for centuries.[43] Since the political leadership, which determines the content of the values espoused in the quest for multilateral development, is primarily made up of ethnic Romanians, it is inevitable that ethnic Romanian values become mixed with others, lending a strong flavor to the total package. For many ethnic minorities the political socialization process in contemporary Romania must appear as "Romanianization" in the garb of "modernization."

The Ceausescu regime has pressed for the acceptance of a large number of concepts, seen as crucial to the multilaterally developed society and socialism. The most important concepts include:

- "Socialist Ethics and Morality." This concept denotes important values seen as necessary in the building of a new consciousness among the citizenry. It includes such character traits as honesty, trustworthiness, commitment to society and the community rather than to individual well-being, and commitment to hard work. An individual's crowning self-fulfillment, then, comes through service to the community and its political leadership, the Communist Party.[44]

- "Building of Socialism" and the creation of "Socialist Man." Building of socialism is only possible through the creation of a New Socialist Man, an individual imbued with socialist ethics and morality, whose commitment to society is threefold: contributing his occupational skills to the further development of the material base; contributing to the moral and ethical education of others and the eradication of undesirable or dangerous traits of the past, such as "bourgeois nationalism"; and, finally, acceptance of the Party's claim that its policies are by definition in the best interest of all citizens, thereby stimulating supportive political behavior among the masses.[45]

- "Patriotism." Patriotism in the Ceausescu regime is an interesting mix of old Romanian nationalist values and socialist concepts. Basically, it denotes a commitment to the building of socialism in Romania, with due consideration for the national context.[46] At the same time, Patriotism is sharply distinguished from old-fashioned "bourgeois nationalism," which is seen as a dangerous attitude that helped separate the various nationality groups in Romania. Patriotism, or commitment to the common Fatherland, which is now the Socialist Fatherland, is perceived as a uniting force, a banner around which all ethnic groups can rally.[47]

Concomitantly with the emphasis on positive slogans, the Romanian Communist leadership has singled out a number of values as negative traits, which have no place in the "multilaterally developed society" on its way to socialism. Chief among these negative themes is "bourgeois individualism," which indicates commitment to individual profit, selfishness, greed, and career-mongering; this trait is also at times connected with "bourgeois nationalism," possibly to indicate that some nationality groups pay insufficient heed to the interests of society as a whole,[48] a fairly clearcut, if esoteric, signal that ethnic minorities have not wholeheartedly accepted the nation-building process under way, essentially with Romanian supervision.

There are numerous indications that political socialization in Romania has failed to achieve its goal of establishing Socialist Men with a clearcut commitment to the social, political, and economic leadership of the RCP. Ceausescu has repeatedly charged corruption in high places,[49] severe mistakes in academic institutions, in which the teaching of Marxism-Leninism has become an empty formula,[50] and wasteful management in industry and agriculture, which is costing the country millions of lei per week.[51] The Party leader has been unwilling to attribute such failures to human error and has persisted in maintaining that they are due to remaining "bourgeois" and even "antisocialist" values, which must be eradicated before the "multilaterally developed society" can come to full fruition.[52] In the summer of 1971, severe economic problems combined with internal Party dissatisfaction and an increasingly outspoken and critical intelligentsia to force Ceausescu into the so-called Little Cultural Revolution. The Central Committee of the Party, in plenary sessions in June and again in November, 1971, issued a tough new set of directions, which essentially envisioned increased Party control over all walks of life, but especially in the areas of industrial and agricultural management, higher education, and the arts and literature.[53] A few months earlier, at the congress of the youth organization, UTC (Uniunea Tineretului Comunist), a change in the top leadership was brought about by failures in the "Party-education" activities among youth in all nationality groups.[54] Both in Ceausescu's speeches at the June and November plena and in the speech by Martian Dan, head of the UTC, bourgeois nationalism was mentioned as one of the major causes of recurring troubles in the economy and in ideological-educational work, indicating that political apathy among ethnic minorities continues to pose a major problem for the regime.[55] Both Ceausescu and Dan were also conspicuous in their references to the need for all citizens to work together to overcome the serious problems discussed.[56]

It is not possible to establish the extent of minority indifference or hostility to RCP policies. The remarks by Ceausescu, Dan, and others in 1971 and subsequent concessions made to the minorities, especially the Hungarians and Germans, in such fields as improved educational opportunities in the native tongue, more Hungarian and German language books and periodicals published, and more frequent scheduling of plays by groups performing in non-Romanian languages, indicate both serious Party concern with the minorities and, apparently, significant concessions made to continued national feelings.

Ceausescu has also attempted to gain greater support from the minorities by establishing "nationality councils," especially among Hungarians and Germans.* These councils carry out their work in a predictable manner, expressing strong support for the RCP and Ceausescu's domestic and foreign policy. Since 1971, when the meetings of these councils became relatively frequent, the Romanian press has also given added emphasis to their work, once again stressing the need for all citizens, no matter what ethnic background, to work for the common goal of socialism.[57] The regime apparently feels that by mobilizing ethnic Hungarian and German activists for regime policy, minority concern over possible Romanianization can be reduced and greater positive activism and support for the regime can be engendered. The same concern by the top Party leadership can also be seen in recent efforts to increase the representation of minorities in the Party and state apparats, especially at the regional and local levels.[58]

Despite such efforts of mobilization, it is quite clear that the ethnic minorities in Romania, particularly the Hungarians and the Germans, are far from being assimilated into a Romanian-dominated "socialist" culture. The self-admitted failure to achieve significant value reorientation among large sectors of youth, the intelligentsia, and even in parts of the Party rank and file, through political socialization also means that the RCP has been unable to eradicate older values such as "bourgeois nationalism." Thus the regime is faced with a dual problem that will remain high on the agenda for some time to come: on the one hand, political autocracy, thought control, and excessive economic centralization have succeeded in rendering large sectors of the population, no matter what the

---

*The nationality councils have been especially active since 1968.

ethnic background, indifferent to the regime's ambitious efforts at nation-building with a socialist content. On the other hand, this indifference has negated regime efforts to erase old values such as ethnic particularism.

Thus both modernization and political socialization have failed to produce significant assimilation of ethnic minorities in Romania, and both processes may have exaggerated already existing differences, at least temporarily. The Communist regime in Romania must attempt to live with this situation, and the main policy thrust in the near future will probably be directed toward limitation of ethnic particularism to the area of "form," while continued efforts will be made to ensure that nationalism remains "socialist in content."

NOTES

1. For example, speech by Ceausescu to the Council of Working People of German Nationality, printed in *Scinteia*, February 21, 1971; also some remarks to the RCP CC meeting, November 1971, in ibid., November 4, 1971.

2. See, for example, Trond Gilberg, "Ethnic Minorities in Romania under Socialism," *East European Quarterly*, January 1974, pp. 435-64.

3. For example, Robert R. King, "Rumanian Concern for the National Minorities," *Radio Free Europe Research*, Rumania/19, 23 July 1971.

4. Ibid.

5. Figures derived from Republica Socialista Romania, Directia Centrala de Statistica, *Recensamintul Populatiei si Locuintelor din 15 Martie 1966* (Bucharest: 1969), pp. 158-62.

6. Ibid.

7. For a discussion of such relations, see Germany (Federal Republic, 1949) Bundesministerium fur Vertriebene, Fluchtlinge and Kriegsgeschadigte, *Dokumentation der Vertreibung der Deutschen aus Ost-Mitteleuropa*, vol. 3, *Das Schicksal der Deutschen in Rumanien* (Bonn: Bundesministerium fur Vertriebene, 1953-61).

8. Some of these measures have been discussed in ibid.

9. For a discussion of Soviet policies toward the Jews in that country, see Lionel Kochan, ed., *The Jews in Soviet Russia Since 1917* (London: Oxford University Press, 1970).

10. For an excellent historical introduction to Romanian politics, see Stephen Fischer-Galati, *Twentieth Century Rumania* (New York: Columbia University Press, 1970), especially pp. 29-70.

11. No academic study has been completed on the position of Gypsies in Romania, but disdain for this group is a common theme in literature, the arts, and in day-to-day conversations.

12. Those trends are revealed in the 1956 census; see Republica Populara Romina, Directia Centrala de Statistica, Recensamintul Populatiei din 21 Februarie 1956, p. 563.

13. Ibid.

14. Ibid., pp. 576-77.

15. Ibid., p. 563.

16. For a discussion of the industrialization drive in a comparative perspective, see Zbigniew K. Brzezinski, The Soviet Bloc (Cambridge: Harvard University Press, 1971), especially pp. 67-155.

17. See Jewish Chronicle, 28 April 1972, for a discussion of outmigration of Jews from Romania.

18. Recensamintul . . . 1956, p. 563.

19. Ibid., pp. 576-77.

20. The 1952 leadership change has been discussed in Fischer-Galati, op. cit., pp. 107-28.

21. For a discussion of the treatment of Germans, see Dokumentation der Vertreibung, vol. 3.

22. See Robert R. King, "Rumania's National Minorities: Isolation or Assimilation?" (Paper given at the Fifth National Convention of the American Association for the Advancement of Slavic Studies, Dallas, Texas, March 15-18, 1972), p. 148.

23. See ibid. This policy was also reflected in reduced use of the Hungarian language in some universities.

24. See, for example, Ghita Ionescu, Communism in Rumania, 1944-1962 (Oxford: Oxford University Press, 1964), especially pp. 197-219.

25. Ibid., pp. 255-88.

26. Ibid.

27. A discussion of anti-Semitism in Romania can be found in Peter Meyer, et al., The Jews in the Soviet Satellites (Syracuse, N.Y.: Syracuse University Press, 1953).

28. This is a recurrent Ceausescu theme; see, for example, speeches by the Party leader, printed in Scinteia, February 21, 1971, and his speech to the UTC (youth organization of the RCP) Congress, in Romania's Youth, 1971, pp. 5-9.

29. Interview with Mircea Malita, Radio Bucharest, March 26, 1971, mentioned in Radio Free Europe Research, Rumania/19, July 23, 1971.

30. See Ceausescu's major speech to the Tenth RCP Congress, in Congresul al X-lea al Partidului Comunist Roman (Bucharest: Editura Politica, 1969), pp. 20-24, 64-69.

31. Ibid., pp. 79-89.

32. See Karl W. Deutsch, "Social Mobilization and Political Development," American Political Science Review, September 1961, 493-575; and Samuel P. Huntington, Political Order in Changing Societies (New Haven: Yale University Press, 1968).

33. Ibid.

34. A favorite Ceausescu concept, extensively used by the Party leader. For a definition see his speech to the 1969 Party Congress, in Congresul al X-lea, pp. 19-89.

35. For a thorough discussion of Ceausescu's views on this, see his speech to the 1971 RCP CC Plenum, printed in Scinteia, November 4, 1971.

36. Based on Recensamintul 1956, p. 556, and Recensamintul 1966, pp. 159-62.

37. Recensamintul 1966.

38. Ibid.

39. Based on Recensamintul 1956, p. 556, and Recensamintul 1966, p. 153, respectively.

40. For an excellent discussion of assimilation through socioeconomic and cultural processes, see Vernon V. Aspaturian, "The Non-Russian Nationalities," in Allen Kassof, ed., Prospects for Soviet Society (New York: Frederick A. Praeger, 1968), pp. 143-202.

41. See his speech to the Tenth RCP Congress, in Congresul al X-lea, pp. 19-89.

42. Ibid.

43. See, for example, his speech to the RCP National Conference, July 19-21, 1972, printed in Scinteia, July 20, 1972.

44. For example, Ceausescu in his speech to the RCP CC, November 1971, in ibid., November 4, 1971.

45. The Party leader in National Conference of the Romanian Communist Party, July 19-21, 1972, Report Presented by Comrade Nicolae Ceausescu, General Secretary of the Romanian Communist Party (supplement to Romania Today, no. 8/213, 1972), 28-40.

46. As indicated by Ceausescu in Congresul al X-lea, pp. 57-74.

47. Ibid.

48. See Ceausescu's speech in Scinteia, November 4, 1971.

49. Ibid.

50. Ibid.

51. Ibid. A press campaign was started to save money in this field; see, for example, a scathing attack on wasteful use of night shifts, Scinteia, October 19, 1971; the same topic was covered in Probleme Economice, no. 9 (September, 1972).

52. At November 1971 Party meeting, in Scinteia, November 4, 1971.

53. Ibid.

54. See the 1971 issue of Romania's Youth (organ of the UTC Central Committee).

55. Ceausescu in Scinteia, November 4, 1971; Dan in ibid., November 7, 1971.

56. Ibid.

57. See Scinteia, February 21, 1971; Lupta de Clasa, March 1971; Scinteia Tineretului, May 4, 1971.

58. See, for example, Ceausescu's report to the RCP National Conference, July 1972, in National Conference of the Romanian Communist Party, pp. 36-40.

PART III

THE FEEDBACK PROCESS

CHAPTER

9

THE FEEDBACK PROCESS AND THE RELATIONSHIP BETWEEN MODERNITY AND POLITICAL POWER

The process of educational expansion, industrialization, the development of agriculture, communications, and social services, and the integration of ethnic minorities have created a Romanian society vastly different from the one in which the RCP emerged as the sole official political force in the 1940s. In this chapter we shall examine the influence of a semimodern society on the political system and the relationship between modernization and political power.

The Romanian Communist regime has achieved great successes in its modernization policies during the last 25 years. The RCP has successfully destroyed all meaningful political opposition and has managed to extend its unquestioned superiority into the most remote mountain village, rural hamlet, or isolated trading center; in a real sense it has made politics a relevant factor for every citizen of the country. Through its enormous network of Party organizations, youth groups, women's clubs, and assorted mass organizations it has brought politics to the grassroots. Through this kind of structure it has been possible to transmit the most important political symbols to every individual. The innumerable organizations in the cities, and to some extent the countryside, provide opportunities for political activity, albeit within carefully proscribed limits, whereas earlier regimes never managed to penetrate beneath the surface of isolation of the peasant masses.

True, there is ample evidence to indicate that the Party has not been successful in instilling the values of Socialist Man into every heart and soul, and ethnic minority groups remain somewhat separate from the Romanian mainstream; but it appears that at least a minimum of regime legitimacy has been established. The RCP may not engender glowing enthusiasm among the masses of the population, but it certainly has no meaningful competitor in the political realm. Everybody knows about the major political goals of the regime; a fair amount of effort is being expended in order to achieve these goals, and the steady, if slow, rise in the standard of living has apparently produced the kind of basic, minimal support that is indispensable for any political regime. The Communist leadership has succeeded in making politics a national affair, an activity that has some saliency for almost all citizens. This is a far cry from the parochialism and isolation that characterized large sectors of the Romanian population in earlier times.

The Communist regime has achieved great things in the cultural field as well. Slowly but steadily, the norms of conduct, the behavioral patterns, and the outlooks of the capital spread over the country and penetrated into the masses of rural Romania. These new norms and values clashed mightily with prevailing outlooks in the traditionally oriented peasant masses, and important conflicts did occur. This process is still underway, and will be for some time to come. The process described is certainly one of modernization; ascriptive values in the traditional setting are giving way to achievement criteria of a modernizing elite, and the Communist Party is clearly willing to furnish the direction, even the coercion, necessary to ensure the final victory of modernization values over traditional norms.

Together with the spread of a modernized culture has also gone a general cultural penetration; education has opened the doors for literature, the arts, and a widening of horizons that were so sorely lacking in rural Romania during pre-Communist regimes. This is not to say that one should uncritically subscribe to Marx's definition of rural life as "idiocy"; there were many important cultural traditions and achievements emanating from the villages of Romania, and the present regime is clearly attempting to incorporate such achievements into the concept of a modern Romanian culture. It is nevertheless true that whatever cultural achievements were brought forth from the villages reflected isolation and relative parochialism. The breaking down of spatial and cultural barriers has resulted in a cultural penetration from the national center that is threatening to engulf the old patterns. One may question whether this is progress; but from the regime's point of view the answer is a resounding "yes," and there is little likelihood that current policies will change in this field.

Cultural penetration cannot take place in a vacuum. It is usually associated with significant socioeconomic changes that drastically alter peoples' lifestyles. The massive drive for economic modernization, which was analyzed in Part II of this book, has fundamentally altered the lives of millions in Romania. Industrial occupations have superseded agricultural tasks as the economic mainstay of the country; urban residence is increasingly the fate of Romanian citizens; there is increasing diversification of tasks; and education has penetrated to all levels of society, even the recently nomadic Gypsies. The younger generation no longer remains in the countryside, but migrates to the cities, where it is uniquely available for modernizing trends, culture, and behavior.

The massive economic development in Romania is of such a magnitude that it constitutes a social as well as an economic revolution. The fundamental changes wrought in the country as a result of these trends are such that no individual has been left untouched by it. The political revolution of August 1944 was therefore only the prelude, albeit a necessary prelude, to the tremendous changes that were to follow. At the present time the modernization and development process described has produced a society that is in rapid transition from the preindustrial to the industrial stage. Such a society poses a fundamental challenge to the modernizing elite, as will be discussed below. It may sound dramatic, but it is hardly an exaggeration to say that Romania and the RCP are at a crossroads in the mid-1970s. The societal effects of modernization are now profoundly influencing policy and will become increasingly important in years to come. The main societal effects are as follows:

SOCIAL STRATIFICATION AND FUNCTIONAL SPECIALIZATION VERSUS IDEOLOGICAL PRECEPTS

The rapid development of industry and related service activities has produced increased social stratification and functional specialization in Romania. Given the RCP modernization goals and the requirements of the economy, this development appears inevitable. Only skilled personnel can handle complicated machinery, and the Romanian regime is pushing heavily for more and more sophisticated machinery to do the jobs of production and planning.

With such social differentiation comes status differentiation. Romania is one of the least developed countries in Eastern Europe in the field of sociology, and we therefore have little systematic information on such status differentiation. According to Nicolae Ceausescu, however, there is a marked tendency among elites as well as masses to elevate certain technical and scientific occupations to a high status position, whereas manual work or even skilled industrial occupations appear much further down on the list. The general secretary is also very unhappy about the relatively low prestige of professional politicians. All this sounds strikingly similar to the findings in Poland and Czechoslovakia, where systematic sociological investigations have been carried on for years. Romania is apparently no exception to the general rule that despite regime efforts to produce high status for certain occupations that are ideologically preferred the population tends to use other criteria for their assessment.

The economic modernization drive in Romania is spearheaded by education, and it is clear that higher educational achievements are necessary for increased and diversified output. But this emphasis on education is in itself a major promoter of social stratification; Romania, like many Western countries, will reach a stage in which a new "nobility of the brain" will be fundamentally separated from the rest whose intellectual endowments are more modest. This may be an inevitable concomitant of socioeconomic modernization; but it augurs ill for political stability, and it runs counter to the major ideological commitment to equality so often stressed by the political leadership.

The discrepancy between avowed regime goals and the requirements of a modernizing economy is a painful problem for the current leadership in Romania. As shown in Chapter 2, much of the top leadership, including the general secretary, consists of old apparatchiks whose commitment to ideology is presumably of some importance. A major element in that ideology is egalitarianism. One may also assume that this commitment is rather attractive to elements of the population, primarily low achievers. The masses of the population are also committed to improved conditions of life, and this commitment is increasingly a fundamental one, which will test the legitimacy of the regime to the utmost. How can a steady and increasing supply of goods and services for the population be ensured without increased functional specialization and social stratification? The present solution to this problem is to allow increased functional specialization while keeping incomes relatively equal, and providing for upward social mobility and some political mobility for achievers. Increasingly, however, those measures have proven inadequate; production cannot be sufficiently raised without material incentives, and upward political mobility for economic specialists is a dangerous concept for the present leadership of old apparatchiks. Nicolae Ceausescu has rather grudgingly accepted the idea of increased differentiation in remuneration based on skills, specialization, and education, while significantly reducing the political power of such social elites. In the end, even this approach will prove insufficient for the regime, and a gradual loosening up of political careers will most likely take place. This may be another ten or fifteen years in the making, however; in the meantime social stratification and functional specialization will continue, without adequate means of political expression for new groups in society. This is potentially a very dangerous situation indeed.

THE EMERGENCE OF INDISPENSABLE ELITES

As the modernization process continues social stratification will give rise to indispensable socioeconomic and cultural elites with nonpolitical skills. This stage has indeed been reached already in Romania; and, as indicated in previous chapters, the current emphasis on ideological orthodoxy can be interpreted as a Party effort to limit the political ambitions of specialized elites. There is indeed a fundamental contradiction between the tight political control exercised by a centralized regime that sets unquestionable goals for all sectors of society, on the one hand, and the interests of the many social and economic elites that can now be identified in Romania, on the other hand. It would be highly unusual if such nonpolitical elites abstained completely from political activity or demands; group interests have a way of asserting themselves in spite of political limitations. The Romanian regime therefore needs to decide whether the socioeconomic elites should be granted political access as groups or whether individuals from such groups should be coopted into the top political leadership.

Nicolae Ceausescu and his close associates must also determine whether or not functional autonomy will be granted in the economy, in education, and in cultural life, so that ambitious individuals can act out their energy in such settings, leaving the politicians to political activity. A relative "functionalization of tasks" has taken place in Hungary and in post-Gomulka Poland; Kadar and Gierek are apparently willing to grant some autonomy for nonpolitical elites as long as these groups do not become politically active in a way that runs counter to primary regime goals, or threaten undisputed Party control in the polity. Perhaps this is a necessity in more highly developed societies. If that is the case, Romania will end up in the same category within the next fifteen to twenty years.

Despite the indications of relative "autonomization" in socialist states elsewhere, it is not likely that Romania will follow the same path in the near future. The entire style of a Nicolae Ceausescu and the mode of operation of the RCP militate against such a reduced role for the professional politician. Nicolae Ceausescu is concentrating power in his hands rather than delegating it, and the RCP leadership seems firmly committed to training people not only in required tasks but in "civics" as well, thus invalidating the idea that there can be autonomy even in nonpolitical spheres. The emphasis on the creation of a new Socialist Man politicizes everything, and there is no way that one can opt out as long as the Party attempts to use its formidable power and organizational network to achieve such a goal. Without such autonomy, however, it seems certain that nonpolitical, functional elites will become increasingly political. It is only through growing influence within the political elite that they can ensure relative functional autonomy and increased recognition as well as remuneration. The current political regime in Romania is caught in this fundamental dilemma, and there is no easy way out.

THE ANOMIE OF MODERN SOCIETY

Romanian society is exhibiting strong symptoms of what can be called the "anomie" of modernity. It is possible to build a new society with popular enthusiasm; the magnitude of the task and the noble goals can ignite public response of considerable proportions. There were certainly strong elements of this in the early industrialization drive in the Soviet Union, especially among young ideologues; and the same kind of commitment was also exhibited during the rapid build-up stage of the Romanian economy in the 1950s and part of the 1960s. The goals are so fantastic compared to contemporary resources, and the target dates for fulfillment are so far off, that the man in the street does not expect to achieve them in his lifetime; he remains content to build for a glorious future, for his "children and grandchildren."

As the achievements of the economy and society increase, however, so do the expectations of the citizenry. One is close to the goal--perhaps it is even possible to enjoy some of the fruits in one's lifetime. At this stage concrete achievements, such as better services and a marked increase in the material standard of living, are necessary tonics the presence of which will spur the population on to even higher achievements, but the absence of which may have a dangerous effect on public morale. At this stage it is no longer possible to promise a brighter tomorrow, and reported postponements of the target date for fulfillment of the great society can only produce fatigue and cynicism. A collective relaxation appears, and some will start talking about opting out of the race for achievement, since no personal benefit can be expected. The opting out process is likely to become even stronger in regimes in which the political leadership incessantly campaigns for target achievements, overfulfillment of plans, and continued frantic activity. It becomes much stronger still whenever politicos refuse to let go in areas such as arts, literature, and private life of its citizenry. In such a system actual depoliticization takes place, and the home and the family become areas where the citizen sheds his enforced political and economic straightjacket and becomes an island unto himself, an atomized individual whose best efforts go into insulation of those he loves from the cruel, rat-race world "out there."

Similar problems arise even in modern systems without a command economy oriented toward a distant future and a mobilization regime in the political field. There is much evidence to show that the frantic pace of social and economic activity, the impersonal, bureaucratized lifestyle, and the rapid changes in man's environment that cut individuals loose from their past and stability tend to produce a fundamental need for a base, something to hang on to, in the whirlwind of change. Hence the nostalgia for a simpler past; hence the quest for fundamental religions, which can unequivocally establish right and wrong, thus reducing or obliterating the painful choices of cross-pressured individuals. Hence, therefore, the insulation of modern man from his society, despite the spatial shrinkage of the world through jet planes and the modern mass media.

Romania is already experiencing problems of opting out. The rapid transformation of society through socioeconomic development has created the kind of anomie described above. The incessant efforts of the regime to mobilize its citizens has further aggravated the tendency toward insulation and atomization. Old differences among groups in the population, particularly ethnic groups, are not being eradicated by the modernization process but seem rather to be exacerbated by it. (See Chapter 8.) This tendency is especially strong among youth, as indicated in many speeches and articles debating the youth organizations and their failure to make headway with political education in this population stratum. Elites opt out as well. During the last decade there have been many works published by well-known writers and poets, whose message is one of fundamental challenge to any mobilization regime: the individual has the right to decide whether or not he will be actively involved in the building process established by the political leadership and carried out under RCP guidance and control.

The anomie of modernity will most likely increase in Romania as the achievements of the economy propel the country ever closer to the multilaterally developed society. Once again, the regime will be confronted with the need to cope with this phenomenon, either through accommodation to the society it has created, which essentially means a lower political profile in areas that can meaningfully be separated out as "nonpolitical," or through confrontation, whereby the Party continues to penetrate an increasingly complex society in order to control it in all its aspects.

THE COMPLEX SOCIETY AND THE NEED FOR DECENTRALIZATION

The very success of the modernization drive has clearly produced a highly complex society that will be increasingly difficult to control and develop further through centralization and strict political control. Centralization may be a prerequisite for rapid transformation of an underdeveloped society into an industrializing one, but most students of this topic agree that once a high level of socioeconomic development is reached decentralization of function and to some extent of political power becomes a necessity.

Romania must be considered one of the most highly centralized systems in all of Eastern Europe, both in concentration of political power and in economic decision making and control. There have been attempts at cautious decentralization, most recently through the 1967 economic reform; but the reform proposals were somewhat confusing, with contradictory elements abounding, and practice has been toward recentralization in the 1970s. There is some indication that Ceausescu's massive transfer of top Party and governmental personnel, some of it to the provinces, is the beginning of a partial drive for decentralization; but this tendency is more than outweighed by the general secretary's increasing personal power and the establishment of new, central bodies that combine the functions of Party and state.

For the foreseeable future it seems likely that centralization will prevail, both in the economy and in the polity. It is also fairly clear that the complexity of Romanian society will soon make such centralization a major problem. Once a certain level of development is reached, central decision making will increasingly result in massive delays and mistakes, both in the upward flow of information and the downward flow of decisions. So far, the relatively uncomplicated nature of Romanian society and its economy has allowed for rapid return on investment and extremely high growth rates. This can no longer be expected to hold true, certainly not by the end of this decade. Thus society itself will impose certain fundamental needs on the polity, and it will be up to the latter to devise a meaningful response to it, which must include both increasing flexibility and subsystem autonomy and continued political monopoly by the Communist Party. As it now stands, the Romanian political system, so admirably suited to the task of propelling the country from underdevelopment to industrialization, is increasingly archaic in the face of its own creation, a developing, semimodern society. As Samuel P. Huntington has pointed out on numerous occasions, the dichotomy between a modern society and an archaic polity is potentially a major factor for instability.

THE SCENARIOS OF POLITICAL CHANGE

Several options remain open to the Romanian political regime for dealing with the societal feedback effects of social stratification, functional specialization, elite assertiveness, cultural anomie, and societal complexity. The political leadership may accept the fruits of its own policies, thereby allowing increasing group autonomy, relative decentralization of the economy, increased socioeconomic elite participation in political decision making, and more privacy for the individual citizen. In short, the regime may assume a lower political profile, which will also involve abandonment or a substantial scaling down of political indoctrination and the quest for the New Socialist Man. Conversely, the political leadership, frightened by the untamed monster of modernity that it has created in the societal field, may decide to attempt to tighten its grip on society, through more orthodox ideological policies, increased control over all groups, particularly the socioeconomic and functional elites. There may be an increase in the use of force and generalized coercion as the traditional apparatchik elite takes a last-ditch stand against pluralization, for its continued all-embracing control. Such a stance may be taken even at the expense of production and social services.

Neither accommodation to society nor confrontation with it will be likely scenarios for Romanian political development in the 1970s. Nicolae Ceausescu (assuming that his position is relatively secure at the top of the Romanian Party) is too much of a charismatic leader, too much of an ideologue, and too much concerned with his own position as a great national leader to accept a relative dismantling of the enormous power concentrated in the Party apparatus and in his own hands. However, he is too intelligent and too concerned with "Socialist legality" and basic regime legitimacy to launch a full-scale confrontation with the complex society he has helped create. The Party's response to the problems arising from a modern society relating to an autocratic, centralized polity will be one of compromise between accommodation and confrontation. The most likely scenario will be as follows:

After a period of increasing Party control, manifested as it now is through recentralization of decision making, political domination by one individual or a small group of Party leaders, expanded RCP interference in the planning and production process, and frequent ideological campaigns, the needs of the economy and society will reassert themselves and force greater, though still limited, subsystem autonomy, increased representation for economic, technical, and managerial experts and other functional elites, and a relative decrease in ideological campaigns. "Rational," production oriented criteria will become more important in decision making, and pragmatic compromise will become increasingly palatable. There may be more emphasis on material payoffs rather than symbolic remuneration (such as medals, honors, and titles). Such a period of relative accommodation between polity and society will be followed by another period of increasing Party power, more centralization, low subsystem autonomy, and so on; such a development will most likely again be superseded by an upswing in accommodative tendencies.

Because of the inexorable march of Romanian society toward modernity, it seems likely that each peak of orthodox, centralized Party control, and ideological activity will be a bit lower than the preceding, and each period of polity-society accommodation will be a bit longer. In the end, relative accommodation will have become the norm, and a future leader of Romania may declare (as Kadar has done in Hungary) that there is room for discussion about the ideological blueprint, the methods of achieving socialism and communism, and the approaches to sociopolitical problems. Individuals and groups may be accorded relative autonomy on the assumption that as long as they are not directly against the regime they will be perceived as being for it. The socioeconomic complexities of Romania will have forced relative decentralization in day-to-day execution of policy (although the main parameters will still be set centrally) and considerable local initiative, in the form of both input into the decision making structure and pressure group activity, may become important features of the political system. The technical and managerial elites will have become at least equal to the general apparatchik in political power; in fact, it is the expert group that may furnish the bulk of the membership in top political organs. This, then, is most likely the multilaterally developed society.

Although the scenario of the future portrays Romania functioning rather like contemporary Hungary or Poland, the immediate future still belongs to the centralizers and the charismatic leader. The developmental path sketched above may also be changed by external factors such as a drastic worsening in the relation between Bucharest and Moscow. Given the present wizardry of Nicolae Ceausescu in foreign policy matters, it is likely that the general secretary will prevent a drastic deterioration in relations with the Soviet Union, thus preserving control with domestic developments as well. Given the political genius of that same general secretary, it is also entirely possible that Nicolae Ceausescu, the present centralizer and ideologue, will preside over the gradual accommodation between the mobilization regime and the modern society it created in Romania.

BIBLIOGRAPHY

WORKS ON MODERNIZATION AND DEVELOPMENT

Apter, David. The Politics of Modernization. Chicago: University of Chicago Press, 1956.

Azrael, Jeremy. Managerial Power and Soviet Politics. Cambridge, Mass.: Harvard University Press, 1966.

Banfield, Edward C. The Unheavenly City: The Nature and Future of Our Urban Crisis. Boston: Little, Brown, 1966.

Banfield, Edward C., and James Q. Wilson. City Politics. New York: Random House (Vintage Books), 1966.

Beer, Samuel H., et al. Patterns of Government. New York: Random House, 1973.

Birnbaum, Norman. The Crisis of Industrial Society. New York: Oxford University Press, 1969.

Black, C. E. The Dynamics of Modernization. New York: Harper and Row, 1966.

Brzezinski, Zbigniew. Between Two Ages: America's Role in the Technotronic Era. New York: Viking Press, 1970.

Brzezinski, Zbigniew K., and Samuel P. Huntington. Political Power: USA/USSR. New York: Viking Press, 1963.

Cattell, David T. Leningrad: A Case Study of Soviet Urban Government. New York: Frederick A. Praeger, 1968.

Crozier, Michel. The Bureaucratic Phenomenon. Chicago: University of Chicago Press, 1964.

Downs, Anthony. Inside Bureaucracy. Boston: Little, Brown, 1967.

Durkheim, Emile. The Division of Labor in Society. Translated by George Simpson. New York: Free Press, 1933.

Etzioni, Amitai. The Active Society. New York: The Free Press, 1968.

Fisher, Jack C., ed. City and Regional Planning in Poland. Ithaca, N.Y.: Cornell University Press, 1966.

Greer, Scott. The Emerging City: Myth and Reality. Glencoe, Ill.: Free Press, 1962.

Hough, Jerry F. The Soviet Prefects. Cambridge, Mass.: Harvard University Press, 1969.

Huntington, Samuel P. Political Order in Changing Societies. New Haven and London: Yale University Press, 1968.

Huntington, Samuel P., and Clement H. Moore, eds. Authoritarian Politics in Modern Society. New York: Basic Books, 1970.

LaPalombara, Joseph, ed. Bureaucracy and Political Development. Princeton: Princeton University Press, 1963.

Lerner, Daniel, et al. The Passing of Traditional Society: Modernizing the Middle East. Glencoe, Ill.: Free Press, 1958.

Lowi, Theodore J. The End of Liberalism: Ideology, Policy and the Crisis of Public Authority. New York: W. W. Norton, 1969.

Mannheim, Karl. Man and Society in an Age of Reconstruction. New York: Harcourt, Brace, 1940.

March, James G., and Herbert A. Simon. Organizations. New York: John Wiley, 1958.

Moore, Barrington. Social Origins of Dictatorship and Democracy. Boston: Beacon Press, 1969.

Organski, F. K. The Stages of Political Development. New York: Knopf, 1965.

Rostow, W. W. Politics and the Stages of Growth. Cambridge: Cambridge University Press, 1971.

Rustow, Dankwart. A World of Nations: The Problems of Political Modernization. Washington, D.C.: Brookings Institution, 1967.

Taubman, William. Governing Soviet Cities. New York, Washington, and London: Praeger Publishers, 1973.

WORKS ON ROMANIA

Balcescu, Nicolae. Istoria romanilor sub Michaiu Voda Vitezul. Bucharest: 1878.

Dezvoltarea economiei R.P.R. pe drumul socialismului 1948-1957 (The development of the economy of the Rumanian People's Republic on the path to Socialism 1948-1957). Bucharest: Editura Academiei R.P.R., 1964.

Economia Rominiei intre anii 1944-1959 (The economy of Rumania between the years 1944-1959). Bucharest: Editura Academiei R.P.R., 1964.

Fischer-Galati, Stephen. The New Rumania: From People's Democracy to Socialist Republic. Cambridge, Mass.: The M.I.T. Press, 1967.

______, ed. Romania. New York: Frederick A. Praeger, 1957.

______. The Socialist Republic of Rumania. Baltimore: The Johns Hopkins University Press, 1969.

______. 20th Century Rumania. New York: Columbia University Press, 1965.

Floyd, David. Rumania: Russia's Dissident Ally. New York: Frederick A. Praeger, 1965.

Gheorghiu-Dej, Gheorghe. Articles and Speeches. Bucharest: 1963.

______. Articole si Cuvintari. Bucharest: 1962.

Institutul de cercetari economice, Academia R.P.R. Dezvoltarea economica a Rominiei 1944-1964 (The economic development of Romania 1944-1964). Bucharest: Editura Academiei R.P.R., 1964.

Ionescu, Ghita. Communism in Rumania 1944-1962. London, New York, and Toronto: Oxford University Press, 1964.

Jowitt, Kenneth. Revolutionary Breakthroughs and National Development: The Case of Romania, 1944-1965. Berkeley and Los Angeles: University of California Press, 1971.

Mitrany, David. The Land and the Peasant in Romania: The War and Agrarian Reform, 1917-1921. London: Oxford University Press, 1930.

Montias, John Michael. Economic Development in Communist Rumania. Cambridge, Mass. and London, England: The M.I.T. Press, 1967.

Oleinik, I. P. Dezvoltarea industriei Rominiei in anii Regimului Democrat-Popular (The development of Rumania's industry in the years of the Democratic-Popular Regime). Translation from the Russian. Bucharest: Editura Politica, 1960.

Seton-Watson, R. W. A History of the Roumanians: From Roman Times to the Completion of Unity. Cambridge: Cambridge University Press, 1934.

______. Eastern Europe Between the Wars, 1918-1941. Hamden, Conn.: Archon Books, 1962.

Spulber, Nicolas. The Economics of Communist Eastern Europe. New York: Published jointly by The Technology Press of M.I.T. and John Wiley and Sons, 1957.

CONGRESSES OF THE RCP

Congresul al IX-lea al Partidului Comunist Roman, 19-24 July 1965. Bucharest: Editura Politica, 1966.

Congresul al X-lea al Partidului Comunist Roman, 6-12 August 1969. Bucharest: Editura Politica, 1969.

WORKS BY NICOLAE CEAUSESCU

Romania on the Way of Completing Socialist Construction: Reports, Speeches, Articles, July 1965-September 1966. Bucharest: Meridiane Publishing House, 1969.

Romania on the Way of Completing Socialist Construction: Reports, Speeches, Articles, September 1966-December 1967. Bucharest: Meridiane Publishing House, 1969.

Romania on the Way of Completing Socialist Construction: Reports, Speeches, Articles, January 1968-March 1969. Bucharest: Meridiane Publishing House, 1969.

Romania on the Way of Completing Socialist Construction: Reports, Speeches, Articles, May 1971-February 1972. Bucharest: Meridiane Publishing House, 1972.

Romania, Achievements and Prospects: Reports, Speeches, Articles, July 1965-February 1969. Bucharest: Meridiane Publishing House, 1969.

STATISTICAL YEARBOOKS

Republica Socialista Romania: Directia Centrala de Statistica, *Anuarul Statistic al Republicii Socialiste Romania, 1965-1972*. Bucharest: 1965-72.

HANDBOOKS

Yearbook on International Communist Affairs, 1968-1973. Stanford, California: Hoover Institution Press, 1968-1973.

PERIODICALS AND NEWSPAPERS

Era Socialista

Lupta de Clasa

Probleme Economice

Scinteia

Scinteia Tineretului

Romania Libera

Viata Economica

OFFICIAL PUBLICATIONS

Buletinul Oficial

Agerpres

RESEARCH PUBLICATION

Radio Free Europe Research

INDEX

ABOUT THE AUTHOR

TROND GILBERG is Associate Professor of Political Science and Assistant Director of the Slavic and Soviet Language and Area Center at Pennsylvania State University. He is the author of a book on Scandinavian Communism and has contributed chapters to two other Praeger Special Studies books, Political Socialization in Eastern Europe and Testing the Soviet Model: The Impact of Modernization on Political Development in Eastern Europe. He has contributed articles to Problems of Communism, East European Quarterly, Osteuropa, and Current History and has been a frequent participant in professional conferences in his field.

Dr. Gilberg earned his Ph.D. at the University of Wisconsin, Madison, and has been the recipient of grants for research abroad.

RELATED TITLES
Published by
Praeger Special Studies

BULGARIAN ECONOMIC DEVELOPMENT SINCE WORLD WAR II
Bogoslav Dobrin

ECONOMIC CONSUMPTION IN EASTERN EUROPE: Social and Economic Dimensions in Poland, Czechoslovakia, Hungary, and East Germany
Bogdan Mieczkowski

THE PATTERN OF REFORM IN HUNGARY: A Political, Economic, and Cultural Analysis
William F. Robinson

POLITICAL SOCIALIZATION IN EASTERN EUROPE: A Comparative Framework
edited by
Ivan Volgyes

THE POLITICS OF MODERNIZATION IN EASTERN EUROPE: Testing the Soviet Model
edited by
Charles Gati

SOCIAL CHANGE AND STRATIFICATION IN EASTERN EUROPE: An Interpretative Analysis of Poland and Her Neighbors
Alexander Matejko